PRAISE FOR *WHO DO YOU THINK YOU ARE?*

"The key to understanding your true identity is shaped by your relationship with Jesus Christ. 'In Christ' you are completely acceptable, extremely valuable, eternally loved, totally forgiven, and fully capable. Pick up a copy of *Who Do You Think You Are?* and learn the truth about *who you really are*."

—RICK WARREN, Pastor of Saddleback Church, Author of *The Purpose Driven Life*

"'Who do you think you are?' is a far-reaching, belief-revealing, life-shaping, and identity-forming question. My friend Mark Driscoll is an exciting new voice speaking to a newly minted generation of men and women who are hungry for spiritual truth today. *Who Do You Think You Are?* brings us insights from ancient history that speak to us powerfully today. Mark unpacks truth that every believer, young and old, needs to know. I highly recommend this book to you."

—GREG LAURIE, Pastor of Harvest Christian Fellowship,
Evangelist for the Harvest Crusades

"There are a few things that stir affections, intensify worship, and change the way we interact with God and others like understanding our identity in Christ. Almost all that robs us of vitality in life and faith is a fundamental misunderstanding about who we are in Christ. Mark Driscoll continues to write books that are not only extremely well written but are also needed in our day and age."

—MATT CHANDLER, Pastor of The Village Church, President of Acts 29 Church
Planting Network, Author of *The Explicit Gospel*

"So many people stumble through life desperately trying to fit in, never knowing who they are or what God wants them to do. Mark Driscoll's book will empower you to stop living for people's approval and start living from God's truth. This book will give you an unshakeable, biblical understanding of who you are in Christ. When you know who you are, you'll know what to do."

—CRAIG GROESCHEL, Senior Pastor of LifeChurch.tv, Author of *Soul Detox:
Clean Living in a Contaminated World*

"This book hits very close to home for me. I spent years in ministry for Christ without understanding my identity in Christ. I know now that I was not alone. When we place our identity in anything but our relationship with Jesus, we have built our future on a platform that could crumble at any moment. When, by the grace of God, we understand who _____ crumble and we will still be standing. I hig_____

—SHEILA W_____ *People*

"Mark has an uncanny gift of communicating very complex truths in an extremely accessible way. In a world filled with authentic identity replacements; Mark seeks to show how being transformed by Jesus is true transformation. However, it also will help you to know the one who gives new identity. Transformation without a relationship is to be an orphan. Yet transformation with relationship creates the deepest sense of meaning possible. That is why *Who Do You Think You Are?* is a helpful tool to bring clarity to the point of identity."

—ERIC MASON, Pastor of Epiphany Fellowship, Philadelphia, PA

"Finally someone has given the foundational and transformational subject of gospel identity the thorough treatment it needs. Jesus didn't just forgive your sins, he also gave you a brand new, life-altering identity. Sadly, many believers in Jesus Christ continue to frantically look horizontally for what they have already been given vertically in Jesus. In this very helpful book, Mark powerfully addresses both our identity idolatry and our identity amnesia. I am very thankful for this book, and soon you will be too."

—PAUL TRIPP, Author and Executive Director of Center for Pastoral Life and Care

"Mark Driscoll is a gifted teacher able to make complicated spiritual truths easy to understand and applicable in our lives. In *Who Do You Think You Are?*, you will be transformed by the truth that we are made in the image of God, and made new in Christ. This isn't just an abstract theory to think about—it's a practical reality to live by."

—STEVEN FURTICK, Pastor of Elevation Church,
New York Times Best-Selling Author of *Greater*

"Mark Driscoll makes a compelling case that properly understanding who we are in Christ is the key to living out our calling in Christ. When our self-talk and self-image are based primarily on what we've done and what others think of us, we inevitably end up with a skewed and bogus image. This book will help you realign your self-talk and self-image with the truth of God's Word, so that the next time you look in the mirror you'll see the same person Jesus sees."

—LARRY OSBORNE, Author and Pastor of North Coast Church, Vista, CA

"I am very pleased with Mark Driscoll's latest book, *Who Do You Think You Are?* Normally that question makes me start guiltily, but in this case Driscoll is simply unpacking the ground of every believer's identity from the book of Ephesians. Many people will be enormously helped by this book."

—DOUGLAS WILSON, Author and Pastor of Christ Church, Moscow, ID

"For those who feel the acute pressure of thinking you have to be the best in order to be somebody, you have to win in order to count, you have to succeed in order to matter, you have to be liked in order to be valuable . . . this book is for you. My friend Mark Driscoll shows that our identity is not the sum of our achievements, and that our worth is not measured by our performance. In fresh and captivating ways, he shows how the gospel frees us from this obsessive pressure to perform, this slavish demand to 'become,' and how the gospel declares that in Christ 'we already are.'"

—TULLIAN TCHIVIDJIAN, Pastor of Coral Ridge Presbyterian
Church, Author of *Jesus + Nothing = Everything*

"People are suffering from an identity crisis. It seems everywhere we turn we see people striving to become someone or something that they perceive will bring them some sort of contentment when in reality the opposite is true. In this unbelievable book, Pastor Mark Driscoll uncovers the reality that before we can discover what we are supposed to do or become in life, we must first discover who we belong to. A life wrapped up in Jesus has way more passion for things that matter and the potential to make a difference!"

—PERRY NOBLE, Pastor of NewSpring Church

"This book was written by a father and dedicated to his teenage daughter. I believe it is a book any dad would be delighted to have his daughter or son read, comprehend, believe, and walk in. Built around Ephesians and the believer's 'identity in Christ,' this work is filled with biblical and theological wisdom. It deals with a significant number of subjects and lays a superb foundation for a life that can know Christ and enjoy all his benefits. I like this book a lot. It has my glad and heartfelt endorsement."

—DANIEL L. AKIN, President of Southeastern Baptist Theological Seminary, Wake Forest, NC

"The best professionals in the world and of the world give their very best to shape our identity so that we will be and buy what they want. Mark Driscoll's *Who Do You Think You Are?* is an outstanding voice helping us hear Jesus, as he tells us who we are. From that identity we can live a life that is fulfilling to us, contributing to our community, and glorifying to our Lord."

—GERRY BRESHEARS, PhD, Professor of Theology, Western Seminary, Portland, OR

"Who we are—our identity—shapes everything we do. The choices we make, the relationships we nurture, and the work we pursue all are guided by how we answer Mark's question: 'Who do you think you are?' I pray this book drives you to the authority of God's Word in order to answer that question along the way."

—ED STETZER, President of LifeWay Research, Author of *Subversive Kingdom*

"This is not a self-help book. It reminds you that your life is not about you; it's all about Jesus. Driscoll's latest teaches Christians that true freedom can only be found in rejoicing in who you are in Jesus. Did you know that you are a saint? What an antidote to low self esteem! Forgiven? Watch that guilt flee away! And if that's not enough, you've been adopted into the best family the world has ever known! Driscoll's pithy meditations will help these wonderful truths make the all important jump from head to heart. It might just help you more than you expected!"

—ADRIAN WARNOCK, Blogger at adrianwarnock.com, Author of
Raised With Christ—How the Resurrection Changes Everything

"With his characteristic pastoral wisdom, Mark Driscoll offers us theologically deep and emotionally satisfying insights into our true identity in Christ. *Who Do You Think You Are?* exposes our false views of God and of ourselves. It opens up powerful encouragements that can change your biography into a timeless testimony about who you really are in Christ."

—JANI ORTLUND, Renewal Ministries

"My wife and I became Christians at about the same time early in our marriage. We needed what every Christian needs: a clear understanding of who we are so that we would know how we are to live in Christ. Pastor Mark Driscoll leads readers through Ephesians to provide words to describe that identity. It's a helpful guide for new believers as well as a useful tool for believers who need to be renewed. *Who Do You Think You Are?* is not only a book I will commend to my church, it's also a book I'm giving to my kids."

—STEVE MCCOY, Pastor of Doxa Fellowship in Woodstock, IL, Blogger at
Reformissionary (www.stevekmccoy.com)

"When it comes to defining my identity, I often 'hand the pen' to my culture, to my peers, to my competitors, to my family, to my accomplishments, to my profession, even to the good things I do. Mark Driscoll pulls us back to the Garden, to creation, and then to Jesus in a clarion call to anchor ourselves in the ageless, changeless, and liberating reality of who we are. In doing so, the spotlight shifts off of me and onto the God who knows, loves, redeems, and restores."

—DAN WOLGEMUTH, President/CEO of Youth for Christ/USA

WHO
DO YOU
THINK
YOU ARE?

Finding Your True Identity in Christ

MARK DRISCOLL

THOMAS NELSON
Since 1798

NASHVILLE   DALLAS   MEXICO CITY   RIO DE JANEIRO

To Ashley Driscoll. It's a continual honor and joy to be your "Papa
Daddy." Now that you're a teenage young woman, I think the
big idea in this book is very timely as the Holy Spirit prepares
you for the future Jesus has for you. I rejoice that you know
who you are in Christ and pray that you always remember it.
Your Dad in heaven and your dad on earth absolutely *adore* you!
Mommy and I are so blessed to have you. Thank you for being a
means of God's grace in our family. Daughters are delightful!

Published in Nashville, Tennessee, by Thomas Nelson. Thomas Nelson is a registered trademark of
Thomas Nelson, Inc.

Published in association with Yates & Yates, LLP, www.yates2.com.

Thomas Nelson, Inc., titles may be purchased in bulk for educational, business, fund-raising, or sales
promotional use. For information, please e-mail SpecialMarkets@ThomasNelson.com.

Unless otherwise noted, Scripture quotations are taken from the NEW KING JAMES VERSION. © 1982
by Thomas Nelson, Inc. Used by permission. All rights reserved. Scripture quotations marked ESV are
from THE ENGLISH STANDARD VERSION. © 2001 by Crossway Bibles, a division of Good News Publishers.
Scripture quotations marked NASB are from the NEW AMERICAN STANDARD BIBLE®, © The
Lockman Foundation 1960, 1962, 1963, 1968, 1971, 1972, 1973, 1975, 1977, 1995. Used by permission.
Scripture quotations marked NIV are taken from the Holy Bible, New International Version®, NIV®.
Copyright © 1973, 1978, 1984 by Biblica, Inc.™ Used by permission of Zondervan. All rights reserved
worldwide. www.zondervan.com. Scripture quotations marked UPDATED NIV are taken from the Holy
Bible, New International Version®, NIV®. Copyright © 1973, 1978, 1984, 2011 by Biblica, Inc.™ Used by
permission of Zondervan. All rights reserved worldwide. www.zondervan.com.

ISBN: 978-1-4002-7596-0 (IE)

Library of Congress Cataloging-in-Publication Data

Driscoll, Mark, 1970–
  Who do you think you are? : finding your true identity in Christ / Mark Driscoll.
    p. cm.
  Includes index.
  ISBN 978-1-4002-0385-7
  1. Identity (Psychology)—Religious aspects—Christianity. 2. Self-perception—Religious aspects—
Christianity. I. Title.
  BV4509.5.D75 2013
  248.4—dc23   2012029280

Printed in the United States of America

13 14 15 16 QG 6 5 4 3 2 1

CONTENTS

1

I AM _____?

You see, I have this condition.

—LEONARD SHELBY IN THE MOVIE *MEMENTO*

I n the movie *Memento*, Leonard Shelby tries to track down his wife's killer. Complicating the search is the fact that as a result of a blow to the head by the murderer, Leonard suffers from anterograde amnesia, a condition that makes it impossible for him to remember anything new for more than a few minutes.

To cope with his amnesia, Leonard creates a complicated system of notes, Polaroid photos, and tattoos to remember facts and string together evidence to find his wife's killer and exact revenge. Unfortunately, several shady characters try to manipulate Leonard's condition for their own gain. Using his amnesia against him, they tell him lies about his past, who he is, and their intentions for him.

Memento toys with the concepts of identity and truth. As the movie progresses, doubt is cast on Leonard's version of the story, and you begin to wonder if the Leonard the movie portrays is really the true Leonard.

In one important scene, Teddy, Leonard's crooked "friend," says to him, "You don't know who you are anymore."

"Of course I do," Leonard responds. "I'm Leonard Shelby. I'm from San Francisco."

"No, that's who you *were*," Teddy says. "Maybe it's time you started investigating yourself."

What follows is a series of revelations about Leonard that cause him to question the identity he's built for himself. He then suffers a severe identity crisis that leads to the movie's shocking ending—all because he can't remember who he is.

IDENTITY CRISIS

As Christians, we're a lot like Leonard. We have a condition. We're continually forgetting who we are in Christ and filling that void by placing our identity in pretty much anything else. This leads us to often ask, as Leonard did, "Who am I?" The question is far-reaching, belief-revealing, life-shaping, and identity-forming. How you answer determines your identity and your testimony. Tragically, few people—even few Bible-believing, Jesus-loving Christians—rightly answer that question.

How we see ourselves is our identity. Our culture talks about identity as self-image or self-esteem. As a parent and pastor, I believe that correctly knowing one's true identity is the one thing that changes everything.

For years, I pastored and counseled people struggling with issues such as alcoholism, sexual perversion, pride, depression, anger, bitterness, and more. Often I felt as though I were talking to a wall because, though I gave biblical counsel, many people seemed to either not hear or not care and instead continued down a path of destruction. It was frustrating and heartbreaking. I felt there had to be a way to help people find freedom.

Then, thanks in large part to the wise words of older and more seasoned counselors, it dawned on me that underlying our struggles in life is the issue of our identity.[1]

This world's fundamental problem is that we don't understand who we truly are—children of God made in his image—and instead define ourselves by any number of things other than Jesus. Only by knowing our false identity apart from Christ in relation to our *true* identity in him can we rightly deal with and overcome the issues in our lives.

My hope is that, by the grace of God, truth of Scripture, and power of the Holy Spirit, this book will help you know your identity in Christ so you can live as you should.

You aren't what's been done to you but what Jesus has done for you. You aren't what you do but what Jesus has done. What you do doesn't determine who you are. Rather, who you are in Christ determines what you do. These are fundamental truths that we'll explore in depth throughout this book.

I'M A CREATED IMAGE BEARER

Who do you think you are? Where do we even start to answer that enormous question? Let's start at the beginning. You are an image bearer of God.

Genesis 1:26–27 says, "Then God said, 'Let Us make man in Our image, according to Our likeness; let them have dominion over the fish of the sea, over the birds of the air, and over the cattle, over all the earth and over every creeping thing that creeps on the earth.' So God created man in His own image; in the image of God He created him; male and female He created them."

The trinitarian God who lives in eternal friendship and community created us to image him. God uniquely honors humanity in this way. He's made nothing else in his image. Practically, this means that God made us to image, or reflect, him, as a mirror does. And in a world where we're encouraged to spend much time gazing at ourselves in a mirror, it's helpful every time we look in the mirror to be reminded that we're to mirror God to others. He created us to reflect his goodness and glory in the world around us, like Moses, who radiated the glory of God after being in God's presence.[a]

All the Wrong Places

The question of identity is one with which humans have struggled since the very beginning of creation. Only by seeing ourselves rightly and

---

a. Ex. 34:30.

biblically *between* God and the animals can we have both humility and dignity. There alone are we as God intended us to be. By understanding our position *under* God as created beings, we should remain humble toward and dependent upon God. By understanding our position of dominion *over* creation, we embrace our dignity as morally superior to animals and expect more from others and ourselves as God's image bearers.

You were created by God, are on the earth to image and glorify God, and when you die, if you are in Christ, you will be with God forever, imaging and glorifying him perfectly in a sinless state.

Ways We Image God

Imaging God involves thinking with our heads, feeling with our hearts, and doing with our hands. We're to think God's thoughts and agree with his truth as revealed in Scripture. We're to feel God's feelings, such as hating injustice and oppression, loving people, grieving sin's devastating effects, and rejoicing in redemption. We're to join God's work using our hands to serve others—Christian and non—with acts of compassion and generosity. When we reflect something of God with our heads, hearts, and hands out of love for him and others, we do what we were created for. This is joyful for us, helpful for others, and worshipful toward God.

As image bearers of a trinitarian God, we're also made for friendship, community, and conversation. Much of what God designed us to do must be accomplished in and through community. This is why in Genesis 2:18, God said it was "not good" for us to be alone even though sin had not yet entered the world, and why he made another human so our first father, Adam, would have our first mother, Eve, with whom to image God.

When God created Adam and Eve, he spoke to them, explaining that they were free to enjoy all of his creation with only one exception—the Tree of the Knowledge of Good and Evil. God spoke to them not because they were sinners—the Fall had not yet happened—but rather because they were human. As humans, and even more so now as sinful humans, we need to hear from God so we can know who we are and subsequently what we should do and not do.

God's enemy and our adversary tempted our first parents to sin by creating an *identity crisis*. The father of lies implied that their eyes were closed to their true identity and that their "eyes [would] be opened, and [they would] be like God." Tragically, the Bible then records the dark, devastating, damning, destructive day when sin entered the world.[b]

Here is the truth: God made us with our eyes open in his "likeness," which is our true identity. But Satan and people like him, with the same sinful motives (much like Leonard's friends in *Memento*), lie to us about who we are in order to serve their *own* plans. And here is the lie: we will be "like" God if we'll base our identity upon someone or something else other than God and the grace God bestows upon us.[2] Adam and Eve fell for it. Rather than simply believing that they were already "like God" because God made them in his "likeness," our first parents disbelieved their God-given identity and instead sought to create their own apart from him. The result was the first sin and the Fall. We humans have had an identity crisis ever since, seeking to construct an identity ourselves while forgetting about the one God has already given us.

I'm a Worshipper

God created us as worshippers, and worship, rightly understood, begins with the doctrine of the Trinity and the doctrine of Image. In his magnificent book on worship, Harold Best describes the Trinity as the uniquely Continuous Outpourer who continually pours himself out between the persons of the Godhead in unceasing communication, love, friendship, and joy.[3] We, then, created in God's image, are also unceasing worshippers and continuous outpourers. Best says:

> We were created continuously outpouring. Note that I did not say we were created *to be* continuous outpourers. Nor can I dare imply that we were created *to* worship. This would suggest that God is an incomplete person whose need for something outside himself (worship) completes his sense of himself. It might not even be safe to say that we were

b. Gen. 3.

created *for* worship, because the inference can be drawn that worship is a capacity that can be separated out and eventually relegated to one of several categories of being. I believe it is strategically important, therefore, to say that we were created continuously outpouring—we were created in that condition, at that instant, *imago Dei* [image of God].[4]

Worship is not merely an aspect of our being but the essence of our being. Best synthesizes his thoughts on worship by saying, "I have worked out a definition for worship that I believe covers every possible human condition. It is this: *Worship is the continuous outpouring of all that I am, all that I do and all that I can ever become in light of a chosen or choosing god.*"[5]

Our worship never starts and stops. It's not limited to a building in which we attend sacred meetings and sing worship songs. Rather, our entire life is devoted to pouring ourselves into someone or something. Saying it another way, we're "unceasing worshippers."[6] We aren't created *to worship*, but rather we're created *worshipping*.

Everything in life is sacred, and nothing is secular. It's a lie from Satan that life can be compartmentalized in such a way. Everyone—from atheists to Christians—worships unceasingly. In the eyes of God, our choices, values, expenditures, words, actions, and thoughts are all acts of worship. They make up our identity. The only question is, what is your object of worship?

All of humanity can be divided into two categories: those who worship the Creator and those who worship created things. Because of sin, we're prone to worship anyone and anything other than the God who made everyone and everything. That is idolatry.

Idolatry is when we make a created thing a god thing, which is a bad thing. Idolatry is so destructive and pervasive that biblical counselor David Powlison has rightly said, "Idolatry is by far the most frequently discussed problem in the Scriptures."[7]

Whatever we base our identity and value on becomes "deified." Our deified object of worship then determines what we glorify and live for. If our object of worship is anything other than God, we're idolaters worshipping created things, including the fallen angels whom God created.

This is precisely what Paul was getting at in Romans 1:25, which speaks of idolaters "who exchanged the truth of God for the lie, and worshiped and served the creature rather than the Creator, who is blessed forever. Amen." To put it simply, underlying our sinful false worship is the fact that our identity has become rooted in our idolatry. Therefore, it's vital that we learn to know our *identity idolatry*.

IDENTITY IDOLATRY

To help you understand idols, think of them in terms of Items, Duties, Others, Longings, and Sufferings.

I – Items

What we own is our public way of projecting our desired image. The examples are endless and include such things as our vehicles, wardrobes, technologies, homes, jewelry, furniture, and more. Consumerism is now essentially the American religion. Consumer culture is so pervasive that we take it for granted, and almost no aspect of life is untouched by it. Everywhere we turn, we run into advertising telling us to buy things we don't need, with money we don't have, to impress people we don't know.

There are three main characteristics of the phenomenon of consumerism in America today. First, consumerism isn't just a *behavior* but is, in Christian terms, a worldview that tells us who we are. If possessions define your identity, then the brand name on your clothes and the maker of your car are vital.

Second, consumerism is often driven by the desire to gain status and prestige with one's peers. Sociologist Thorstein Veblen, who coined the phrase "conspicuous consumption," articulated this idea at the turn of the last century. Veblen argued that the chief way we obtain social prestige and power is through conspicuous displays of leisure and consumption.[8] Social prestige is connected to wealth, and we demonstrate our wealth by flaunting it.

Today, with television tours of the world's wealthiest people's homes, we no longer compare our possessions to those of the generations before us or our neighbors but rather to the elite's. The results are coveting, overspending, and debt fueled by advertising. Some sociologists call this "competitive consumption," which forces average people and families to work harder, spend less time with those they love, and live more miserably enslaved to debt in an ongoing effort to prop up some false sense of identity and personal value.

Third, products are not simply valued for their usefulness but rather play a central role in the cultivation and maintenance of our identity. This is a powerful explanation for why consumer goods are so much more than objects we use; they are things for which we will fight and sometimes even kill.

The point is that in today's consumer culture, our goods are carriers of meaning. They define us, send social signals to others, and construct our identities. Subsequently, wearing non-designer clothes, driving an old car, and using anything but the latest technology somehow devalues us as human beings. Put bluntly, when consumerism is your religion and stuff the object of your worship, "the things you own end up owning you," to quote Tyler Durden from the movie *Fight Club*(1999).

The problem is not in the mall but rather in us. It's not a sin to purchase items or even to appreciate and enjoy them. But when those things become the source of our identity, we become guilty of idolatry.

D – Duties

Life is filled with duties, starting with chores when we are young, then homework in school, job requirements in the workforce, ministry obligations in the church, relational duties in marriage, and parental and grandparental duties in our families. Our duties can rightly be a way we worship God or wrongly be a god we worship.

If you find your identity in the achievement of your duties, you'll have many troubles. First, you'll always search for something to excel at in an effort to outperform others and demonstrate your superiority. Once you believe you've found that "thing," you'll become overly committed and possibly even obsessed with mastering it. Other people and things (like your health) will no longer matter much to you and will instead be placed on the altar of success to the god of achievement. Soon you'll become so competitive that winning is all that matters. The more you win, the less compassion you have for others. In time, this will turn into disdain for those who are hurting, struggling, or failing. As you succeed, you will become proud and unpleasant to be around, with all your boasting about your accomplishments—even if it's only by subtly moving conversations toward you and your achievements while fishing for compliments. When you fail or lose, you become depressed, panicked, and devastated, which makes you both miserable and miserable to be around.

The truth is that you're not what you do. You have God-given natural talents, Holy Spirit–endowed gifts, and unique abilities. You also have duties, but these duties do not define you, because your identity is not determined by what you do. Rather, who you are in Christ helps you faithfully pursue your duties and use your abilities without them becoming the essence of your dignity and identity.

O – Others

God made us for friendship and community. It's good to have others in our lives. But like all things, this good thing can become a god thing if others become the source of our identity. This happens broadly in our identification with a collective *tribe* of people, and narrowly in our *individual* relationships with others.

Your tribe is the greater community with which you most closely identify. Its members can include not only your family, but also people from your city, school, class, and sports team. Your tribe can also include those having the same nationality, race, gender, ethnicity, culture, income level, hobby, political party, theological affinity, sexual orientation, and more. While it is good to have community, we often turn this good thing into a bad thing by basing our identity on and idolizing our tribes.

If you idolize your tribe, you will also demonize other tribes. This explains why there is often unnecessary and unholy hostility between nations, cities, genders, races, schools, classes, cultures, sports fans, churches, political parties, educational systems (e.g., private, public, homeschool), and even Christian denominations.

More narrowly speaking, if others form our identity, then our personal relationships become unhealthy. This propensity to find our identity in others is commonly referred to as giving in to peer pressure, people pleasing, codependency, and having a fear of man. Practically, this explains why we'll often change our appearance and behavior depending on whom we're with and whom we seek to impress.

Obtaining an identity from our relationships can manifest itself in the idols of independence or dependence. With the idol of independence, we rightly fear allowing our identity to be determined by others. Unfortunately, in the midst of our right fear, we wrongly avoid close relationships because we don't want to risk being emotionally hurt—which means others still control our identity.

Conversely, those of us who serve the idol of dependence simply cannot be alone. We have to be in some sort of deep friendship if single, or place unrealistic expectations on our partners if married or dating. We cannot bear the thought of being alone. While this may look loving, when we struggle with an idol of dependence, we're in fact not loving people as much as we're using them to fulfill our need to belong, be liked, and be desired.

This explains why some friends and family members can be so demanding, smothering, and needy. It also explains why we're so easily inflated by praise and deflated by criticism. It's as if others have the ability to determine our identity for that day based on a word or even a glance. In giving this power over our lives to others, we give them a godlike position to rule over us and define who we are. And in the age of technology, when folks can wield this power publicly for others to witness online, a low-level, constant anxiety slowly robs us of peace and joy.

L – Longings

Longings give us hope that tomorrow might be better so we can persevere today. We all have longings, but when they become the source of our identity, our life becomes inordinately governed by our feelings and our future rather than our present, and God's past, present, and future work on our behalf.

Our longings can cause our identity to shift like an airborne balloon, pushed by every breeze. On days when we're healthy, receive good news, or achieve something, we feel powerful and hopeful. On days when we're sick, hear bad news, or fail, we feel powerless and hopeless. This causes some people to live emotionally volatile lives with towering highs as their identity soars, and defeating lows as their identity crashes.

Living for the future causes one's identity to always be out there, tomorrow, just around the corner, rather than a present reality secured by Jesus and his work on the cross. We live for the future, hanging all our hopes on grabbing the proverbial carrot dangling in front of us.

Often, identity idolatry rooted in longing is mistaken for good and necessary biblical hope. The Bible talks a lot about hope because it's the result of faith in God. If we truly believe that God is alive, good, and at work in our lives, that changes our attitudes and actions. Hope helps us get out of bed in the morning, seek the Lord in prayer, and face whatever the day may bring. But sometimes we use hope in a sinful way, convinced that our desired identity will come in the future rather than living in the identity that is already a present reality.

People who base their identity in the future are often religiously devout, sincere, optimistic, and like to talk about faith and trusting the Lord. They are often also prone to sounding pious and quoting out-of-context Bible verses about Christians being victorious, complete with pithy statements such as, "When God closes a door, he always opens a window," or, "God must have something even better in store." Their identity is found in such things as getting physical healing, getting married, having children, fulfilling vocational ministry, achieving financial security, reaching the next season of life, and so forth.

While it's not a sin to plan and strive for a better tomorrow, it is a sin to set one's joy and identity on who we will be, what we will do, or what we will have tomorrow in our own efforts rather than on Christ today and who he will make us, what he will have us do, and what he will give to us tomorrow.

S – Sufferings

As long as we're alive, we'll suffer. We suffer physically. We suffer emotionally as we hurt others and they hurt us. We suffer financially, each of us struggling to get by and to find or keep a good job. We suffer mentally with everything from the overwhelming responsibilities of life to the name-calling bullying and criticism that are dished out in large portions every day. We suffer relationally as friends betray us, children ignore us, and spouses leave us. We suffer spiritually as, in the midst of our distress, it sometimes seems as if God is busy, far away, and uninterested.

When we suffer, we can easily allow our hurt to become our identity. Our pain can become all-consuming and overwhelming. Admittedly, it's hard to tell a cancer patient, divorcee, or rape victim that his or her pain isn't the defining aspect of who that individual is. But if we truly love those who suffer, we must humbly, graciously, and patiently explain that to be a Christian is not to live a life free from suffering, but rather, suffering should lead us to identify with Jesus, who suffered more than anyone in history on our behalf.

Tina knows this only too well. She was diagnosed some years ago with brain cancer. Two weeks later, she had surgery to have the tumor removed. She thought it would be a quick recovery and she'd be back to normal. But she soon realized that life would be very different for her from that point on.

The tumor had eaten away at her skull, pushing through it and causing a bump on her head (the primary symptom that led to diagnosis). As a result, the neurosurgeon had to remove that portion of her skull and cover the hole with titanium plates and screws. Since then, she's dealt with constant headaches, and the daily, chronic pain is a continual reminder of her brain tumor. She also suffered from other side effects that continue to the present day, including changes in how she responds to people, how she processes certain kinds of information, and more.

Making matters worse, six months after her surgery, in hopes of recovering and "getting back to normal," she quit her job and moved in with her parents. Instead of finding a loving and healthy environment in which to heal, she ended up dealing with significant problems her parents were facing on top of her own problems—putting her recovery on hold. As she puts it, "My life became about day-to-day survival, as I was trapped in that whole situation because I had no money and wasn't able to work to get any so I could leave. The turmoil and darkness continued for years."

By God's grace, Tina finally won a disability claim, someone stepped in to take care of her parents, and she was free to move out on her own again. She relates, "It took about a year and a half of being in a safe and normal environment, where there's steady week-in, week-out preaching, teaching, and singing about Jesus, not to mention interaction with other Christians (I had been isolated for a very long time) and quiet seed-planting by the Holy Spirit, before I was able to recognize that I had based my primary identity on being a brain-tumor survivor. I wasn't a Christian who'd had a brain tumor. I was a brain-tumor survivor who was also a Christian."

This realization helped Tina move from defining her identity as a brain-cancer survivor to seeing herself as a beloved daughter of God with a big brother in Jesus, who suffered for her so she wouldn't have to be defined by her suffering. She realized that while being a brain-tumor survivor, with the limitations and scars that resulted, is an important part of her life, it's not her identity. "They may help explain me," she says, "but they don't define me."

This is not to say life is easy. "Where I'm at right now is trying to take what I know, which is that my identity is in/through/because of Jesus, and applying it to my life. That old identity was entrenched in me for so long, I know it will take a while for old ways to be gone and new ways to come," she says. "I know that, for the first time since it all happened, this year I was able to acknowledge my anniversary of my diagnosis and surgery with celebration that I'm alive instead of the mourning of years past. I know that the name of Jesus has proceeded from my mouth (in conversation) and my hands (in my writing) more than it ever has before. I know that, even though there are still days of struggle and falling back into that mentality, I finally have hope that I just might have a future after all, not just any future, but one worth having. And I know that I want to know more about grace."

How about you? How has your worst day, greatest suffering, or deepest loss so marked your life that it has become your identity? How can you, like Tina, move from your pain and suffering defining you to Jesus defining you? It won't be easy, but it is necessary.

IDENTITY CRISIS

Most of us live unaware of the source of our identity until change occurs, often in the form of hardships and pain. When an individual faces adversity, it leads to a crisis as his marriage, children, appearance, wealth, success, career, religious performance, political party, favorite cause, loving relationship, treasured possession, or something else crumbles under the weight of being a god. Suddenly he realizes that the source of his identity was the idolatry of that treasured thing.

Once he senses this identity crisis emotionally, even if he lacks the words for it theologically, a pattern of crisis management sets in. First, he lives in anxiety and fear that the source of his identity may fail him or be taken from him. Then, as his identity begins to totter, he becomes panicked and seeks to salvage his identity idol. Finally, when his identity fails him, he looks for someone to blame.

Blame takes many forms. Some people blame God for taking their idol away and become bitter toward him. Some blame other people and become resentful, angry, and even violent against those whom they blame. Still others blame themselves and feel like failures, hating themselves for it.

Tragically, many who lose their individual identity idol simply choose another one, rather than turning to Jesus Christ. Consequently, they repeat the entire painful process over and over in their lives. Such people go from one addiction and compulsion to another, one religious commitment to another, and one relationship to another, continually seeking the answer to the question, "Who am I?" Meanwhile, they never find the only true answer to their identity crisis—Jesus.

The rest of this book is dedicated to helping you discover the power and joy that is found only in an identity founded and sustained in and by Jesus. My prayer is that you'll find the answer to "Who am I?" in Christ, who is the I AM.

2

I AM IN CHRIST

For as in Adam all die, even so in Christ all shall be made alive.

—1 CORINTHIANS 15:22

We love a good biography, don't we? We crave hope and examples of courage, dedication, sacrifice, and triumph. If you go to a bookstore, you'll see an entire section dedicated to biographies. If you turn on your television, you'll be inundated with one biography after another. But God offers us something even greater than a biography. He offers us a testimony.

A biography is about a person—his or her life, accomplishments, and determination. In a biography, the person is the hero who rescued his or her own self from some terrible fate. In a biography, we overlook sin and make someone into a mythical savior. This explains why most people don't know that Abraham gave his wife away twice to another man,[a] Noah passed out drunk and naked in his tent,[b] and the great King David suggested a political assassination from his deathbed.[c] It also explains why the majority of readers are unaware that Gandhi was a bisexual who left his wife to live with a male bodybuilder and also enjoyed having underage, nude girls share his bed;[1] that famous Christian leaders John Wesley,

---

a. Gen. 12, 20.
b. Gen. 9:20–21.
c. 1 Kings 2:8–9.

A. W. Tozer, David Livingston, and Hudson Taylor were all horrific husbands and fathers with grossly neglected families,[2] and that William Wilberforce, who fought for the abolition of slavery, also struggled with an opium addiction.[3]

A testimony, on the other hand, is about Jesus—his life, his accomplishments, and his determination. In a testimony, Jesus is the hero who rescues me from the terrible fate of sin, death, hell, and the just wrath of God. In a testimony, sinners should be honest so that it's clear who the real Savior is.

THE FIRST AND LAST ADAM

In the Bible, Paul called Jesus the "last Adam"[d] because he is the remedy for idolatry and the redeemer of humanity, whereas the first Adam was the source of idolatry and the downfall of humanity. The first Adam turned *from* the Father in a garden; the last Adam turned *to* the Father in a garden. The first Adam was naked and unashamed; the last Adam was naked and bore our shame. The first Adam's sin brought us thorns; the last Adam wore a crown of thorns. The first Adam substituted himself for God; the last Adam was God substituting himself for sinners. The first Adam sinned at a tree; the last Adam bore our sin on a tree. The first Adam died *as a* sinner; the last Adam died *for* sinners.

According to the Bible, we die in Adam but are born again in Christ: "For as *in Adam* all die, even so *in Christ* all shall be made alive" (emphasis added).[e] In Adam there is condemnation, but in Christ there is salvation. In Adam we receive a sin nature, but in Christ we receive a new nature. In Adam we're cursed, but in Christ we're blessed. In Adam there is wrath and death, but in Christ there is love and life.

There are two teams in life; each of us takes the field with one of them, and the decisions made by the team captains affect the whole team, for better or worse. Not only does the captain win or lose; his whole team wins or loses along with him. One team has Adam as its captain. The

---

d. 1 Cor. 15:45.
e. 1 Cor. 15:22.

other has Jesus as its captain. While there are many ways to categorize people in our society, the Bible has these two categories—those whose identity is in Adam and share in his defeat, and those whose identity is in Christ and share in his victory.

In Jesus Christ, God became a man and shows us what it looks like to live a life of perfect, unceasing worship out of an identity as God's image bearer. Many New Testament scriptures, and even Jesus himself, declare this, saying:

- "Christ, who is the image of God . . ."[f]
- "He is the image of the invisible God. . ."[g]
- "[He] being the brightness of His glory and the express image of His person . . ."[h]
- "And he who sees Me [Jesus] sees Him who sent Me."[i]
- "He who has seen Me [Jesus] has seen the Father."[j]

We're incapable of knowing how to image God until we look to the Trinity in general and Jesus in particular.

The absolute worst place to begin constructing an identity is you, which is precisely where most counseling begins. The absolute best place to begin constructing an identity is Jesus Christ, which is precisely where Scripture begins. Knowing Jesus and being saved by him in faith is the key to your identity and the defeat of your idolatry. It's not about you. It's all about Jesus.

IDENTITY IN EPHESIANS

This book is about constructing your identity in Jesus through the Scriptures. For that to happen, I want to help you study a book of the

---

f. 2 Cor. 4:4.
g. Col. 1:15.
h. Heb. 1:3.
i. John 12:45.
j. John 14:9.

Bible called Ephesians. Don't worry; this won't be a complicated, academic commentary on everything in Ephesians. Rather, this book is a practical journey through one thing in Ephesians—who you are in Christ.

My goal is to take one massive need in your life, your need for identity, and connect it to one book of the Bible, Ephesians. Thankfully, the Holy Spirit penned Ephesians through Paul for just this purpose. Clinton Arnold, a leading scholar on Ephesians, says, "Paul wrote this letter . . . to affirm [the Ephesians] in their new identity in Christ as a means of strengthening them."[4] New Testament scholar Klyne Snodgrass says the main purpose of Paul's letter is "identity formation."[5] And a leading Catholic theologian commenting on Ephesians says, "Union with Christ gives human beings a radically new identity. We have put off the old self, the old humanity, and have put on the new (4:20–24)."[6]

Across the theological spectrum, there is an understanding that the book of Ephesians is about our identity in Christ. Sadly, "from the middle of the seventeenth century on . . . this great jewel in the crown of God's grace [being in Christ] has gone into eclipse. Today not much is said about union with Christ from the pulpit, and until recently, little was written about it."[7] For some reason, the subject, though prominent in Scripture, has become largely overlooked in everyday application. But by returning to Scripture in general and Ephesians in particular, you can recover a biblical identity and live a new life in Christ.

Ephesians is an amazing book. Church fathers Origen, Chrysostom, and Jerome were so drawn to the richness of Ephesians that each wrote a commentary on it. It was the favorite book of the Bible for Protestant Reformer John Calvin, who preached 48 sermons from the book, wrote a 172-page commentary on it, and quoted it some 275 times in his magnum opus, *The Institutes*.[8] Scottish Reformed John Knox kept transcripts of Calvin's sermons on Ephesians at his bedside and had his wife read them to him as he was dying. Others who have preached multiple sermons on Ephesians include Augustine, Martin Luther, John Owen, Jonathan Edwards, John Wesley, Charles Hodge, and Charles Haddon Spurgeon.

Church father John Chrysostom (c. 347–407) called Ephesians "sublime."[9] More recent Protestant theologians have called it "one of the most significant documents ever written,"[10] "doctrine set to music,"[11] "the crown of St. Paul's writings,"[12] "the divinest composition of man,"[13] "theological gold,"[14] and "the greatest piece of writing in all history."[15]

As a pastor, I've spent years seeking to help people meet Jesus and experience the life transformation he alone can accomplish. I consistently see people who wrongly but earnestly seek to change their behavior rather than first understand their identity.

But God knows that what you do flows from who you are. As Christians, we live *from* our identity, not *for* our identity. We are defined by who we are *in* Christ, not what we do or fail to do *for* Christ. Christ defines who we are by who he is and what he's done for us, in us, and through us. Understanding this information is the key to your transformation.

GETTING TO KNOW APOSTLE PAUL

Today, it's common when we're struggling with issues such as identity and idolatry to talk with a friend or family member, counselor, or church leader. While that can be helpful, what if we could actually meet with someone like the apostle Paul? How incredible would it be to sit down with the person responsible directly or indirectly for most of the New Testament, learn from him, and be encouraged by him?

The good news is that it's possible to meet with Paul. All we have to do is pick up the books he wrote, especially Ephesians, and read them. One popular Christian counseling book says, "In a pinch you could do all your counseling from Ephesians . . . [It] aims to teach you how to live."[16]

Ephesians was originally a letter to a church, and like all letters, it can get confusing unless you know a few details, such as who wrote it and to whom it was written.

The apostle Paul is a towering figure in world history. Martin Luther called him "the wisest man after Christ."[17] In roughly a decade of ministry, he walked an average of nearly twenty miles a day, preaching a message hated by most everyone. He was single, without the comfort of a wife, and he was often alone and abandoned by so-called friends. His account of his life is brutal:

> Are they ministers of Christ?—I speak as a fool—I am more: in labors more abundant, in stripes above measure, in prisons more frequently, in deaths often. From the Jews five times I received forty stripes minus one. Three times I was beaten with rods; once I was stoned; three times I was shipwrecked; a night and a day I have been in the deep; in journeys often, in perils of waters, in perils of robbers, in perils of my own countrymen, in perils of the Gentiles, in perils in the city, in perils in the wilderness, in perils in the sea, in perils among false brethren; in weariness and toil, in sleeplessness often, in hunger and thirst, in fastings often, in cold and nakedness—besides the other things, what comes upon me daily: my deep concern for all the churches. Who is weak, and I am not weak? Who is made to stumble, and I do not burn with indignation?[k]

In spite of all of this, not only was Paul filled with a seemingly inexhaustible energy, but he was also filled with the Word of God. His great intelligence can be inferred from his prestigious education under the renowned rabbi Gamaliel (Acts 22:3) as well as from his multilingualism (Hebrew, Aramaic, Greek, and possibly Latin). In his letters, Paul used more than one hundred Old Testament quotations in addition to innumerable echoes and summations of biblical themes and terms, perhaps all from memory. Paul's theology is expressed in thirteen letters, written over a period of at least fifteen years to at least seven different churches and two individuals. Biblical scholar Paul Barnett goes so far as to call Paul the "first theologian in the early church, and arguably the greatest in the history of Christianity."[18] Early church father John Chrysostom wrote of Paul, "Put the whole world on one side of the scale and you will see that the soul of Paul outweighs it."[19]

---

k. 2 Cor. 11:23–29.

According to theologian D. A. Carson, "Paul continues to minister to us today through the thirteen epistles of his that have become part of the canon of the New Testament, putting Paul just behind Luke in the percentage of the New Testament written by a single individual. And if one adds the sixteen chapters of Acts (13–28) that are almost entirely devoted to Paul, Paul figures in almost a third of the New Testament."[20] And since Luke was a disciple and traveling companion of Paul, most of the New Testament can be directly or indirectly traced to Paul. Among his letters is Ephesians, which he wrote to the churches in and around the city of Ephesus.

EXPLORING EPHESUS

Ephesus was a world-class city. In preparation for this book, I made three separate trips with scholars and guides to the ancient archaeological excavation at the city to learn all I could. On one day, we even reserved the entire ancient city for our tour so we could explore freely and examine fully.

Ephesus is in the ancient region of Anatolia. In Paul's day, Ephesus was an enormous cosmopolitan city of some 250,000 people. Travelers from all over the Roman Empire passed through because of its strategic location: a massive harbor on one end facilitated travel and trade via water, and a highway system enabled travel and trade via land. Ephesus was a highly spiritual but pagan city, which is why Paul's letter is filled with references to spiritual warfare, spiritual power, and demons. Ephesus was also known as the center of supernatural and paranormal activity for the worship of Artemis, involving demonic activity, widespread sorcery, and witchcraft. Egyptian colonists and traders also introduced the worship of Serapis and Isis to Ephesus, building beautiful temples for the deities.[21]

The city was wealthy because of its enormous trade and banking center and was a popular tourist destination because of its pagan Temple of Artemis, declared to be one of the Seven Wonders of the ancient world. Ancient reports called Ephesus "the greatest commercial center in Asia this side of the Taurus river."[22]

In addition to being wealthy, Ephesus was politically powerful and functioned as the Roman provincial capital of Asia Minor. As a powerful city, it was also a corrupt one, steeped in sexual sin. Prostitution was common, much as it was in any other major port city. Sailors incorporated sinful sex into their spirituality with the prostitutes who worked at the pagan Temple of Artemis. Archaeologists have even uncovered what they believe to be an ancient brothel connected to the library by a secret underground tunnel, thereby enabling men to commit adultery when their wives thought they were hitting the books.

Finally, Ephesus was geographically central. A recent study of Roman milestone markers demonstrates that mileage to other cities in Asia Minor was measured from Ephesus, which helps explain why Ephesus served as the administrative and commercial hub of Asia Minor.

THE RELEVANCE OF EPHESUS

Why does all of this matter? Because when we read the Bible, we tend to think of it in terms of rural rhythms, populated with fishermen and farmers who lived simple lives, far less complicated than our own. Subsequently, we wonder if the Bible can actually speak into the troubles of our time and the temptations we face. But Christianity is rooted and flourished in difficult urban contexts, where people struggled with the same things you and I do today. If ancient Rome was like New York or London, then Ephesus was like Los Angeles or Chicago.

The strategic importance of Ephesus helps explain why it also became a hub for Christian missions—particularly training leaders and sending out church planting teams.[1] Priscilla, Aquila, Apollos, Paul, Timothy, John, and Luke all worked there. The city was the headquarters of Jesus' youngest disciple, John, who had jurisdiction over the seven leading churches of Asia named in the opening three chapters of Revelation, with Ephesus being the first and most important church addressed. It's also rumored that John acquired a house

---

1. Acts 18:18–19; 1 Cor. 16:8–12; 1 Tim. 1:3; 2 Tim. 4:12.

there for Jesus' mother, Mary, although most believe she lived with her converted sons back in Israel.

John's own student, Ignatius of Antioch, wrote of the continuing fame and faithfulness of the Ephesian church. The third ecumenical council took place in Ephesus in AD 431 to condemn the heresy of Nestorius, the leader of Constantinople's church, which confused the human and divine nature of Jesus and was followed by the Ephesian church of St. Mary, the ruins of which can still be seen today.[23] The example of Ephesus is that Christianity can flourish in a difficult and pagan culture, and that Christians can maintain their identity in Christ in such cultures for generations by the grace of God.

But it also serves as a warning that faith can be lost from one generation to the next if we're not careful. Today, Ephesus is not populated and instead is a popular tourist destination, as archaeologists are uncovering the ancient city made of majestic marble. And Turkey, the country in which the city's ruins reside, is now among the least Christian nations on earth.

It's not an overstatement to say that had the gospel of Jesus Christ not taken root in Ephesus and spread from there across the Roman Empire on the trade routes and beyond, Christianity as we know it may not exist.

WHY PAUL WROTE EPHESIANS

Unlike many New Testament letters, which were written to address questions (1 Corinthians) and crises in various churches (Galatians), Ephesians was most likely written to newer Christians from pagan or Jewish backgrounds who were tempted to go back to their former sinful lifestyles. Paul's letter articulated their unified identity in Christ, reminding them to live their lives patterned after Jesus Christ in holiness and righteousness through the power of the Holy Spirit to guard them from ignoring their new identity, to keep them from pursuing their old idolatry, and to unify them as one church.

The letter, however, wasn't written solely to the church at Ephesus. The city was a headquarters from which Christian truth and training went out to a number of other churches in the region and beyond, similar to some of today's megachurches, which operate as resource centers for other congregations and even have a network of related churches. Therefore, the letter would have gone to and then through Ephesus sometime around AD 60–62, much as a newswire sends out bulletins to its subscribers everywhere today. Paul assumed that the Ephesian church would distribute his vital instruction as widely as possible.

Ephesus was an important city for Paul's ministry work, and his devotion to the gospel sparked much controversy in that city. Many citizens, especially merchants who profited from pagan temple worship, hated Paul because his converts were costing them a lot of money. They tried to run him out of town and sparked a riot against him.[m] Additionally, the majority of recent biblical scholars believe that Paul was imprisoned on more than one occasion in Ephesus for preaching the gospel of Jesus Christ and may have even written a few books of the Bible on those occasions.[24]

For what dangerous idea was Paul hated, run out of town, rioted against, and likely imprisoned in Ephesus? What truth did he tell that was so powerful that the spiritual, political, and economic leaders despised and opposed him? What did he teach that was so threatening to a culture as exalted and enduring as the Roman Empire? What made his message such a threat to the great city of Ephesus? Two words: "in Jesus"—in other words, *in Christ*."[n]

IN CHRIST

The two words "in Christ" changed the world and are the summary, essence, and totality of a believer's identity. Simply put, either our identity is in Christ or in idolatry.

In speaking of identity, Jesus said in John 15:5, "I am the vine; you are the branches. Whoever abides *in me* and *I in him*, he it is that bears

---

m. Acts 19:21–41.
n. Acts 19:4 (NASB).

much fruit, for apart from me you can do nothing" (ESV; emphasis added). Throughout Ephesians and the rest of Paul's writings, Jesus' "expression was a habit" out of which Paul "creates a symphony of language" with several variations, such as "in Christ," "in him," and "in the Beloved."[25] In Ephesians alone, Paul spoke of believers as being "in Christ" twelve times overtly and twenty-two other times in various forms (ESV).

So central to Ephesians is the idea of being "in Christ" that the letter opens with a benediction that, while serving as a praise to God, also recounts the glories of salvation *in Christ*.[26] In fact, the phrase "in Christ," or a variation of it (e.g., "in him"), saturates the section (actually one long sentence in Greek). Following is a compilation of every use in Ephesians 1:1–14 (with emphasis added):

- "To the saints who are in Ephesus, and [are] faithful *in Christ Jesus* . . ." (1:1)
- "Blessed be the God and Father of our Lord Jesus Christ, who has blessed us with every spiritual blessing . . . *in Christ*." (1:3)
- "He chose us *in Him* before the foundation of the world, that we should be holy and without blame before Him." (1:4)
- " . . . to the praise of the glory of His grace, by which He made us accepted *in the Beloved*." (1:6)
- "*In Him* we have redemption through His blood, the forgiveness of sins, according to the riches of His grace." (1:7)
- " . . . making known to us the mystery of his will, according to his purpose, which he set forth *in Christ*." (1:9 ESV)
- " . . . as a plan for the fullness of time, to unite all things *in him*, things in heaven and things on earth." (1:10 ESV)
- "*In Him* also we have obtained an inheritance, being predestined according to the purpose of Him who works all things according to the counsel of His will." (1:11)
- " . . . that we who first trusted *in Christ* should be to the praise of His glory." (1:12)
- "*In Him* you also trusted, after you heard the word of truth, the

gospel of your salvation; in whom also, having believed, you were sealed with the Holy Spirit of promise." (1:13)

Paul's "in Christ" language continues throughout Ephesians as the thread weaving together the tapestry of our identity. And although it's well beyond the scope of this book to explore in depth, it's interesting to note that Paul wrote of being "in Christ" repeatedly in his other New Testament books.[27] Two theologians examining the entire New Testament say, "The phrase 'in Christ' and its variations, such as 'in the Lord' and 'in him,' occur 216 times in Paul."[28]

The term "in Christ" is not found prior to Paul and is rare outside of his writings.[29] One respected Bible commentator goes so far as to say:

> From my perspective, "in Christ" far outstrips the term "Christian" in describing Christianity. Aside from the fact that "Christian" is only used three times in the New Testament (Acts 11:26; Acts 26:28; and 1 Peter 4:16), that title allows for an ambiguous interpretation. It can mean one who has a specific cultural affinity, or the "western tradition," or one who lives on one side of barbed wire and is killing those on the other side. But "in Christ" invites no such abuse, because it demands reflection on a dynamic, living relationship.[30]

To say the least, being "in Christ" is vital for every believer to experience and understand because being "in Christ" is the one thing that changes everything.

At the end of the day, Paul's concept of being "in Christ" is so central to a thriving and victorious life that it should go without saying that its neglect by modern-day preachers and teachers is a driving reason behind the struggles of many Christians today. It's my hope that as we study Ephesians and what it has to say about our identity in Christ, the wonderful freedom found in fully understanding and believing in faith the truth of our identity in Christ will be yours. I also hope that, moving forward in your new identity, you'll find lasting victory over your idolatry by God's grace and the power of the Holy Spirit.

HOW TO READ THIS BOOK

It's important that you read Ephesians in a readable, modern English translation (e.g., New King James Version, English Standard Version, New Living Translation, etc.). Ephesians is only 2,400 words, but those words pack a life-changing, identity-transforming, eternity-altering punch, because they are the very words of God. I encourage you to read it over and over as you read this book. Pray before you read, asking the same Holy Spirit who inspired Ephesians to help you understand it. Read carefully, stopping to highlight words, phrases, and concepts that capture your attention. Feel free to write in your Bible and make a mess of the book as needed. The old preacher Charles Haddon Spurgeon rightly said, "The Bible that is falling apart usually belongs to someone whose life is not."

Finally, as you read Ephesians, you'll notice that the book is organized intentionally and in a way that's relevant to the big idea we're studying, that before we can deal with any idolatry, we must first understand our identity. Chapters 1–3 are primarily about practical and very helpful doctrine, such as who God is and what he does for us in salvation (think of it as getting to know your dad). Chapters 4–6 are primarily about the implications of who God is and what he does for us as we live them out on a mission for him in community, for example, who we are in Christ and how God wants us to live like Christ (think of it as doing life with your dad).

Now, let's explore who we are in Christ.

3

I AM A SAINT

Paul, an apostle of Christ Jesus by the will of God, to the saints who are in Ephesus, and are faithful in Christ Jesus: grace to you and peace from God our Father and the Lord Jesus Christ.

—EPHESIANS 1:1–2 ESV

Ruth describes her past as a series of negative identities that she changed like hats. In her teen years, her identity was "rebel without a cause." As a rebel, she fought against all her parents' teachings, school rules, and her Catholic upbringing. "I had this vision of myself as unworthy, not good enough, never will be," she says. "So why try?"

The sense of hopelessness that came from her identity as a rebel eventually manifested in a devastating identity as *addict*, which culminated in an addiction to heroin. In the process, she met a man who was also an addict—and abusive. For twelve years, Ruth lived in shame and fear, looking for her next chemical hit while taking the next physical hit from her boyfriend, all the while raising her kids in this destructive environment. Out of this, Ruth developed night terrors and panic attacks, and she became embittered against her boyfriend, placing the blame of her ruined life on him, his drug habit, and his choices—and ultimately finding her identity in being a victim.

Then the unthinkable happened: Child Protective Services took custody of her two children to protect them from the domestic violence and drug use that were prevalent in her home. This shocked Ruth back into reality and compelled her to begin recovery. She left her abusive boy-friend, got her life together, was clean for several years, and eventually finished her degree.

But something was still wrong inside. "I still identified myself as an addict," says Ruth.

The sense of shame that came from carrying her identity as an addict and the damage it had caused in her life led Ruth back to the church, where she met Jesus for the first time, began a process of healing, and became involved in a community group at our church. "What I learned in community group is that I am a child of God. I am his daughter, he loves me, and Jesus has already died for my sins," she says. "I needed to drop the *addict* off my name and just be Ruth. I am so much more now without that negative title. I am no longer held in bondage by that identity."

Today, Ruth's life is dramatically different. Now that she has placed her identity in Christ, her life is unrecognizable from the one she lived years ago. "I am a child of God today," she says. "I chose to worship him and care for the gifts he has blessed me with. Today, I seek God for answers; I no longer try to numb the pain of life with drugs. God blessed me with a wonderful man who loves me and treats me with dignity. He is my 'Boaz,' and he has taken on the role of father for my two children, now fifteen and seventeen."

Collectively, Ruth and her husband now have five children, plus they've taken on a seventeen-year-old boy from the local high school who was couch surfing until graduation. Ruth describes the way she's changed as dramatic and simple at the same time. "I take my role as wife and mother seriously," she says. "I no longer need to be validated by a career, or other people outside myself. I see how important it is to serve my large, blended family and community. I am a volunteer for abused and neglected children who are in foster care as a result of parental defi-ciencies like domestic violence, drugs, and mental health [issues]. I now work hard to protect these children from a life that was similar to my own children's. I get paid nothing in money, but I feel I am doing God's work, helping children get the best possible outcome. I just feel 'lighter' having

God in my life. There is no burden too great for him, and I am learning to allow him to carry the load for me so I can continue to do his work and care for all the good things he has entrusted me to do."

Looking at Ruth's life, many today would call her a saint because of her volunteer work with abused and neglected foster children and would be surprised by her sordid past. The truth is that Ruth *is* a saint—but not because of what she does. She is a saint because of what Christ has done for her.

Like Ruth, we're also saints in Christ.

SAINT OR SINNER?

When we read the letters in the Bible, as with most letters, we tend to skip over the greeting and quickly proceed to the body of the letter. But if you do that with Ephesians, you'll miss an incredibly important truth that Paul established and that is woven throughout the letter. He referred to everyone in the church as "saints . . . in Christ Jesus" (1:1).

Saints? Everyone? Surely the churches that originally received the letter had some of the same kinds of people we do in ours—you know: the drunks, jerks, gossips, busybodies, perverts, as well as the self-righteous religious types, who proudly and wrongly think they're better than everyone else.

Yet, regarding their identity—and ours—Paul says that if we're "in Christ Jesus," which is simply a way of saying we're true Christians, then we're "saints." This word "saints" isn't there by chance. It's there by God's design, and it's presented so early in the letter because it establishes a theme explored throughout the letter.

HOW TO BE A SAINT: CATHOLIC EDITION

What do you think of when you think of a saint? Paintings of biblical figures with halos over their heads? Mother Teresa serving the needy in Calcutta, India? Billy Graham preaching to stadiums filled with people?

For me, the word *saints* conjures up images from my Catholic upbringing. My family has been staunchly Catholic for generations, all the way back to southern Ireland. I was baptized in the Catholic Church as an infant, raised in it as a boy, spent a few years attending a Catholic school, and served as an altar boy, assisting the priest with Mass. After my grandfather died, my grandmother even joined an order and became a Catholic nun.

Growing up, I was taught to venerate the saints and pray to them. We had statues and icons of saints in our church and our home. As a boy, I thought of saints as being like comic book superheroes or ancient Greek gods—somewhat human but endowed with special powers to live extraordinary lives.

The history of sainthood is curious:

The first Catholics revered as saints were martyrs who died under Roman persecution in the first centuries after Jesus Christ was born. These martyrs were honored as saints almost instantaneously after their deaths, as Catholics who had sacrificed their lives in the name of God. Over the next few centuries, however, sainthood was extended to those who had defended the faith and led pious lives. With the criteria for canonization not as strict, the number of saints soared by the sixth and seventh centuries. Bishops stepped in to oversee the process, and around 1200, Pope Alexander III, outraged over the proliferation, decreed that only the pope had the power to determine who could be identified as a saint.[1]

It was not until the seventeenth century that the Vatican's standards for sainthood were formalized. Father James Martin summarizes in ten steps the very complicated process of sainthood in the Catholic Church:

1. Be a Catholic
2. Die
3. A local "devotion" grows up around your memory
4. Your life is investigated
5. Your local bishop sends your case to the Vatican

6. Pray for a miracle
7. The Vatican investigates the miraculous cure
8. The Vatican declares you "Blessed"
9. Pray for another miracle
10. You're a saint![2]

If you make it through these ten not-so-easy steps that can easily cost upwards of a million dollars in total,

the pope declares you a saint, in a solemn ceremony known as "canonization," usually at a public Mass, perhaps in Rome but perhaps in your own diocese as a way of celebrating your heritage. You are now worthy of "public veneration" throughout the entire church, and the entire church may celebrate your feast day. Many more schools, parishes and Catholic groups will take you as their "patron," or special protector. You've made it! You're part of the great "communion of saints." But since you're infinitely happy already in heaven, it probably won't add much to your joy. In fact, you've now got more work to do, because even more people will be praying for your intercession. So you'll be very busy from now until the end of time.[3]

HOW TO BECOME A SAINT: BIBLE EDITION

The apostle Paul didn't think of saints this way. He thought of normal, average, ordinary, flawed Christians like you and me, like Ruth, and like those in Corinth, who were, for example, abusing spirit-empowered gifts, getting drunk on Communion wine, and entangled in sexual sin.[a] He called *these* men and women saints!

For Paul, sainthood was not a result of something wonderful you'd accomplished nor erased by something horrible you'd done. According to him, being a saint requires one step: be in Christ. And the total cost to you is $0. *Anyone* who is connected to Jesus by faith in his death and

a. 1 Cor. 1:2; 5:1; 6:12–20; 11:21; 14:23.

resurrection is a saint. God's saints are average and sinful people who love Jesus.

By virtue of being in Christ, we're no longer in Adam and instead are made a part of God's people. And by virtue of being in Christ, our past, present, and future sin is taken away through the death, burial, and resurrection of Jesus and exchanged for his perfection, holiness, and righteousness.

A Saint Is Sinful

God originally made humankind without sin. In Genesis 1:31, he calls his creation, including Adam, "very good." Ecclesiastes 7:29 says, "God made man upright." Therefore, all sin is fully our responsibility as rebellious sinners, not the fault of God our Creator. And the effects of sin and the curse were not originally part of the world God created for us in love. Through our first parents, sin has now infected and affected everyone and everything.

But is that the end of the story? Are we just dirty, vile, rotten sinners? Is that the sum total of our identity, even as Christians? No. In this life, even as Christians, the bad news is that we're still sinners, but the good news is that we're not *only* sinners. We also share in being image bearers of God with all men and women in God's creation.[b] We're cracked, dirty, dull mirrors—but mirrors nonetheless. And if we're in Christ, we're redeemed saints.

Tragically, most Christians I counsel don't believe they're redeemed, image bearers of God, and saints. They believe they're just sinners. Such people see themselves as little more than worthless worms, which is why their beliefs are sometimes referred to as worm theology.

Even atheist philosopher Jean-Paul Sartre mocked this erroneous Christian belief in his 1943 play, *The Flies*, with a man falling on his knees and crying out, "I stink! Oh, how I stink! I am a mass of rottenness. See how the flies are teeming round me, like carrion crows. . . . That's right, my harpies; sting and gouge and scavenge me; bore through my flesh to

---

b. Gen. 5:1–3; 9:6; James 3:9.

my black heart. I have sinned a thousand times, I stink of ordure, and I reek to heaven."[4]

This type of thinking can sadly be common in the Reformed tradition of Christian faith, of which I'm a part. For example, a summary of theological belief called the Five Points of Calvinism begins not where the Bible does in Genesis 1–2—with God, creation, and men and women created without sin as God's image bearers, and how as saints we are redeemed and restored to that status—but rather in Genesis 3, with what is called "total depravity," a doctrine that relates the helpless, sinful state of humans.

While it's true that sin has affected the totality of our persons, including our minds, wills, and emotions, we fail to say all that the Bible does regarding our identity when we place undue focus on our depravity as fallen sinners and ignore our dignity as created image bearers and our new identity as redeemed Christian saints. While a non-Christian is totally depraved, a Christian is in Christ.

Practically, focusing on just the sin aspect of our identity leads to despairing, navel-gazing Christians obsessed with their sin. Such Christians wrongly think that the best sermons are those that beat them up by reminding them of how awful they are—without any mention of their new identity in Christ. The Word of God is not a club for beating Christians until they emotionally bleed as repayment for their sin. Jesus already took our blows and shed his blood in our place. And on the cross he didn't say, "It is not finished, so beat yourself up to add to your salvation." He said, "It is finished!"[c]

This is why someone like Ruth, with a past filled with drug abuse and losing her kids to Child Protective Services, can today live free of addiction, have a healthy marriage and family, and help others who live as she once did. If she focused mainly on her sin, she'd never focus on others and minister to them through the assurance of her position as a saint in Christ.

It's wrong for Christians to simply have their identity as a sinner, nothing more and nothing less, living as pathetic people counting the

---

c. John 19:30.

miserable days until heaven, when they will finally be perfect. We're created as God's image bearers, we're fallen sinners, and if we're in Christ, we're truly redeemed, made new, and given a new identity.

It's important to note, however, that while in Christ we're genuinely new, we're not *completely* new until our resurrection. As theologian Anthony Hoekema says, "Believers . . . should see themselves and each other as persons who are *genuinely* new, though not yet *totally* new."[5] This explains why Christians aren't without sin. Indeed, 1 John 1:8 says, "If we say that we have no sin, we deceive ourselves, and the truth is not in us." A saint does sin. But a Christian is one who has *saint* as their constant identity and *sinner* as their occasional activity. For the Christian, there is a vital difference between *having* sin and *being* sin.

This explains why the Bible rarely, if ever, describes a Christian, as opposed to a non-Christian, as a sinner. Depending upon which Bible translation you read, you will hear of non-Christians referred to as sinners more than three hundred times, but only on three occasions do you find a Christian referred to as a sinner, though in each instance it may actually refer to non-Christians. Rather than sinners, the Bible overwhelmingly calls us "saints," "holy," or "righteous" more than two hundred times. Biblically, then, the primary identity of a believer in Christ is not as sinner but as saint. While we still struggle with sin in this life, as Christians, our identity is not found in our sin but in Christ's righteousness.

The recovery movement, which has the noble goal of helping people overcome addictions (drugs, alcohol, sex, gambling, food, etc.), misses the boat when it comes to identity. It's not uncommon in small group meetings for addicts to introduce themselves by their addiction, saying something like, "Hello, my name is _____ and I am an alcoholic." This is the identity that Ruth, whose story I shared at the beginning of this chapter, carried with her for many years. The problem with this is that it supplants a true identity in Christ with an identity in sin. For the Christian, our identity is not in our addiction but rather in Christ. Once you realize this—as Ruth did—your life will be changed forever.

Sin may explain some of your activity, but it's not your identity. Your identity is in Christ, and because of your new identity, by God's grace through the Holy Spirit's power, you can change your activity. Because you are a new person positionally in Christ, you can live a new life practically by the power of the Holy Spirit. This truth is deeply helpful and vitally practical.

Since a saint can act as a sinner, it's important for us to consider how we should relate to our sin.

A Saint Is Remorseful

Everyone has regrets and feels remorse. The great British preacher Charles Haddon Spurgeon said, "Few men would dare to read their own autobiography, if all their deeds were recorded in it; few can look back upon their entire career without a blush."[6] The things that make us blush—or worse—in looking back at our lives are not the moments where we lived exemplarily but rather the moments when we're steeped in sin.

As saints mature in relationship with Jesus, they often see their sin more clearly and grieve it more deeply. Paul himself, as a mature Christian, demonstrated this in looking back at his past life in comparison to the perfect life of Jesus Christ as one that had qualified him as the "chief" sinner.[d]

Remorse can be a good thing. As the Holy Spirit convicts us of sin and commends us to righteousness, just as Jesus Christ promised he would,[e] it's good for us to feel remorse for sin, confess it, repent of it, and believe in Jesus' forgiveness and cleansing from it. The Bible models godly remorse for us. Page after page is soaked in the tears of God's people who accepted the truth not only about God but also about themselves in the sight of God. For instance, the psalms of lament, such as Psalm 32, make up the largest portion of the book of Psalms. This kind of reflective, repentant remorse is a good and godly response to conviction.

Those with tender consciences, however, are prone to move from conviction to condemnation. Their tears rarely, if ever, turn to laughter. Their gaze seldom, if ever, moves from their sin to their Savior. In a word,

---

d. 1 Tim. 1:15.
e. John 16:8.

they become stuck, obsessed with, and consumed by their sin. Aware of the holiness of God and their shortcomings in life, they often move from conviction from God to condemnation from Satan, who is called a liar[f] and our "accuser."[g]

The differences between conviction and condemnation are stark.

CONVICTION . . .	CONDEMNATION . . .
is from God	is from Satan
leads to life	leads to despair
ends in joy	ends in sorrow
makes us want to change	makes us believe we can't change
leads to new identity in Christ	leads to old identity in sin
brings specific awareness of a sin	brings vague uncertainty about sin
looks to Jesus	looks to self
is a blessing	is a burden

Paul breaks through the fog of condemnation with the light of conviction in Romans 8:1, saying, "There is therefore now no condemnation for those who are in Christ Jesus" (ESV). Are you "in Christ Jesus"? If so, you have "no condemnation . . . For the law of the Spirit of life has set you free in Christ Jesus from the law of sin and death" (vv. 1–2 ESV).

A Saint Is Powerful

As saints, we're tempted to sin, just as Jesus Christ was when he walked on the earth. Yet, because we're in Christ, and Christ is in us by the presence of the Holy Spirit, we're not obligated to sinfully respond to temptation. Instead, through a changed heart and mind in Christ, we can remember our identity, say no to sin, and approach God as Jesus Christ did. As Hebrews 4:15–16 says, "We do not have a High Priest who cannot

f. John 8:44.
g. Rev. 12:10.

sympathize with our weaknesses, but was in all points tempted as we are, yet without sin. Let us therefore come boldly to the throne of grace, that we may obtain mercy and find grace to help in time of need."

In his opening lines to the Ephesians, Paul said this very same thing, that "saints" "in Christ" not only have "peace" with God but also receive empowering "grace" "from God our Father and the Lord Jesus Christ" (vv. 1–3).

Sin and temptation are two different things entirely. Jesus was tempted, but he never sinned. To be tempted is to be presented with an opportunity to either sin against God or worship God—it all depends on our response. Don't let the accuser lie to you and convince you that merely being tempted makes you guilty of sin. More important, don't believe the lie that if you're tempted, it's already too late, and you should simply give in and sin.

When you are tempted to sin, remember that you're a saint. Knowing your identity in Christ is your key to victory. Jesus models this truth for us.

Jesus' identity, given to him by God the Father, is Son of God. In Luke 3:22, before Jesus began his public ministry, the Father said at Jesus' baptism, "You are My beloved Son; in You I am well pleased." Likewise, at the transfiguration of Jesus in Luke 9:35, God the Father said of Jesus, "This is My beloved Son. Hear Him!" Satan tempted him to prove it,[h] and his enemies arrested and beat him to deny it.[i] But Jesus endured both temptation and persecution by remembering his identity and living it out in the power of the Holy Spirit. This powerful truth demonstrated in the life of Christ is also powerfully true for the life of those who are in Christ.

God the Father reminded Jesus of his identity throughout his earthly ministry, and Jesus reminded himself of his identity by stating it publicly and praying fervently, as the "Son of God," to his "Father." This helps explain how he said no to sin and yes to obedience, and why he had the

---

h. Luke 4.
i. Luke 22.

power to endure temptation, criticism, ostracism, and even crucifixion. He knew the Father, and he knew himself. As a result, he was unwavering, unflinching, and unchanging.

Jesus is the Son of God. Those who are in Christ are his holy saints, set apart to endure temptation, criticism, and ostracism just as he did. Dear saint, you must always remember who you are, especially when you need it most.

Theologians explain it in this way. The imperatives of the Bible (what you should do) flow out of the indicatives (who you are). We say no to sin because we are holy in Christ. We endure the criticism of those who hate us because God loves us in Christ. We endure ostracism from others because God welcomes us in Christ. We are not what we do. We do what we are. Our identity determines our activity. This was true for Jesus, and it's true for those who are in Christ. Our identity as new creations in Christ is the key to our victory like Christ.

A Saint Is Humble

It's helpful to think of the benefits of being in Christ as a fourfold salvation process. First, through *regeneration*, we are brought back from spiritual death resulting from our sin to new life in Christ. Regeneration brings us new desires, thoughts, and hopes to do the things of God rather than the "lusts of our flesh" (Eph. 2:3).

Second, through *justification* we're saved from the penalty of sin. Justification is the act of God declaring an unrighteous sinner a righteous saint in his sight. This is our position in Christ. As Christians, we are genuinely new, and though not yet perfectly new, we're on a path to become so as we grow in this life and are perfected after its end.

Third, journeying down this path toward God and godliness continues throughout our lives in *sanctification*. Through sanctification we're saved from the power of sin. Sanctification is both a position—we are already set apart and sanctified—and a process, in which we increasingly become more like Jesus as the Holy Spirit cleanses us and we grow in relationship with him. As a sanctified saint, we're not obligated to sin and can start enjoying holiness.

Fourth, our sanctification is completed upon death when we experience the finality of our salvation in *glorification*, through which we're saved from the presence of sin. Glorification is an eternal state of sinless perfection that culminates in resurrection from death to live with Jesus and in being like him forever.

All of this is by God's grace and for God's glory. But sometimes we as saints sin by becoming proud of the changes we've made and the things we've learned, something the Bible calls being "puffed up" (1 Cor. 13:4; 1 Tim. 3:6).

The Bible has a lot to say about the sin of pride and the virtue of humility. In our day, when the most common things posted on the Internet are photos and boastings about ourselves, the Bible's timeless words prove incredibly timely.

- Proverbs 6:16–17: "These six things the LORD hates, yes, seven are an abomination to Him: A proud look . . ."
- Proverbs 8:13: "Pride and arrogance and the evil way . . . I hate."
- Proverbs 16:5: "Everyone proud in heart is an abomination to the LORD."
- Proverbs 16:18: "Pride goes before destruction, and a haughty spirit before a fall."
- 1 Peter 5:5: "Be clothed with humility, for 'God resists the proud, but gives grace to the humble.'"

Pride is our enemy and humility is our ally. Pride compares us to other sinners; humility compares us to our sinless Savior. Pride covets the success of others; humility celebrates it. Pride is about me; humility is about Jesus and other people. Pride is about my glory; humility is about God's glory. Pride causes separation from God; humility causes dependence on God. Pride is pregnant with all sins; humility is pregnant with all joys. Pride leads to arrogance; humility leads to confidence. Pride causes me to do things in my own strength; humility compels me to do things in God's strength.

The trend of modern counseling is encouraging people to think better of themselves, to make better lives for themselves. Accordingly, the answer to what ails us is self-esteem leading to self-improvement and self-actualization. But these are just technical terms for pride. The problem with this approach is that it's only about the "self" and not about the "self" living *coram deo*, "in the face of God." We don't need to feel better about ourselves. We need the God who makes us better through himself and for himself.

Humility includes both knowing and accepting the truth about God and yourself as revealed in the Bible. A saint will grow in humility by rightly and biblically understanding identity in Christ. Knowing we're sinners saved and kept by grace will keep us from a prideful, high self-esteem. Knowing we're also saints in Christ will keep us from a painful, low self-esteem.

None of us, with the exception of Jesus Christ, can ever say we're truly humble. Instead, all we can say is that we're proud people pursuing humility by the grace of God.[7] Thankfully, this grace is freely given to all who believe in Jesus and have their identity in him.

Are you a Christian? If so, then in Christ you are a saint, redeemed and renewed in Christ, because every true Christian is a saint. Take a moment and ponder that monumental truth! It doesn't matter how you feel or what others say. God says you're a saint. Say it aloud: "I am a saint." Ask the Holy Spirit to plant that truth deep in your soul so the root of your identity in Christ will nourish the fruit of your life. As Jesus said, "Neither do I condemn you; go and sin no more."[j]

---

j. John 8:11.

4

I AM BLESSED

Blessed be the God and Father of our Lord Jesus Christ, who has blessed us with every spiritual blessing in the heavenly places in Christ, just as He chose us in Him before the foundation of the world, that we should be holy and without blame before Him in love, having predestined us to adoption as sons by Jesus Christ to Himself, according to the good pleasure of His will, to the praise of the glory of His grace, by which He made us accepted in the Beloved.

In Him we have redemption through His blood, the forgiveness of sins, according to the riches of His grace which He made to abound toward us in all wisdom and prudence, having made known to us the mystery of His will, according to His good pleasure which He purposed in Himself, that in the dispensation of the fullness of the times He might gather together in one all things in Christ, both which are in heaven and which are on earth—in Him. In Him also we have obtained an inheritance, being predestined according to the purpose of Him who works all things according to the counsel of His will, that we who first trusted in Christ should be to the praise of His glory.

In Him you also trusted, after you heard the word of truth, the gospel of your salvation; in whom also, having believed, you were sealed with the Holy Spirit of promise, who is the guarantee of our inheritance until the redemption of the purchased possession, to the praise of His glory.

—EPHESIANS 1:3–14

The first chapter of the Bible is a short and amazing account of how God created all things simply by speaking them into existence, through the power of his Word. Sadly, often missed among the mushroom cloud of controversy regarding the details of when and how God made the world is a simple phrase about what God did immediately after making our first parents: "God blessed them."[a]

Our first parents didn't ask God to bless them. He simply did so because he is gracious and good. This insight into the heart of God is radically uncommon. If you study the various world religions and supernatural belief systems, you'll be hard-pressed to find any concept of God as someone good who delights in blessing people.

Instead, the common portrait of God is that he must be manipulated and coerced into blessing people. So, people are taught that they must do something, such as suffer; fast; pray; enter an alternate state of mind; repeat a mantra; own sacred objects; make a large financial contribution; take a sacred pilgrimage; offer an animal or even human sacrifice; meet with a guru, shaman, or medicine man; cast spells; or something else to make God bless them. Whatever the method, the message is the same. You have to somehow manipulate God to bless you.

Such was the case for a young girl named Alyssa, who shared that she led a double life for over five years, having convinced her parents and friends that she was a Christian while actively practicing Wicca. "I had already been through four years of Christian education and a Lutheran confirmation class," she shared. "So I knew all the right answers without knowing Jesus."

Alyssa says that her understanding of Christ was marred by a wrong notion that she had to earn God's blessing. "The Holy Spirit showed me recently that this sprang from the lie that I could please God with my life when that's not the case at all. In reality, he is pleased when I come to him completely empty, destitute, with nothing to offer and nothing to bargain with, because he fills that emptiness with Christ and identifies me as his own. I don't have to trick God the way I trick my friends into thinking I know him!"

In Paul's time, people struggled with the same notion as Alyssa did, of needing to trick God into blessing them.[1] Ephesus was a premier city

---

a. Gen.1:28.

for religion and spirituality, and people traveled there for many festivals during the year in an effort to manipulate the spirit world for blessing. The city also practiced numerous secret occult rituals that we know very little about, commonly referred to as the "mystery rites" by scholars, and is well-known for its "Ephesian Letters" (*Ephesia Grammata*, not to be confused with Paul's letter to the Ephesians), six untranslatable words of a spell used to control and manipulate the spirit world for blessing.

These occult practices were so common that when Paul first preached the gospel in Ephesus, a near riot erupted because those profiting from the magical arts saw the gospel of grace as a threat to their economic well-being, as upon conversion, the new Christians in Ephesus brought their magical books together and burned them. Luke was clearly impressed by the amount and monetary value of the books, estimating it as equivalent to fifty thousand days' wages.[b] This environment helps explain why, percentage-wise, Paul talked about spiritual warfare, demonic power, and the victory of Jesus in Ephesians more than any other book of the New Testament.

C. S. Lewis was fond of saying that we are often guilty of "chronological snobbery." We arrogantly see people from the past as more naive, primitive, and less sophisticated than ourselves. The truth is that people have always been the same, and today, people are as pagan in their thinking as ever. From Native spirituality, to pantheistic efforts to live as one with the alleged powerful forces in nature, to positive confession in order to "manifest" reality into existence, to religious efforts to pay God back in some way, to organizing our home feng shui for positive energy, to manipulating God with promises and great acts of devotion, to run-of-the-mill superstitious behavior, people clearly still seek to manipulate the spirit realm for blessing.

Paul wanted us to know that we don't need to manipulate God to bless his people. As Jesus said, God is a good Father who delights in blessing his children with good gifts.[c] Any effort to manipulate God for blessing is as unnecessary as trying to make water wet.

---

b. Acts 19:17–20.
c. Matt. 7:11.

Perhaps this frequent misunderstanding of God as needing to be appeased is why Paul began Ephesians with one of the densest verses in the whole Bible (in the original Greek the twelve verses of Ephesians 1:3–14 are in fact one long sentence of 202 words!), exploring in depth the theme that God blesses his people.

Paul started by saying that we should bless God because God has blessed us "in Christ": "Blessed be the God and Father of our Lord Jesus Christ, who has blessed us with every spiritual blessing . . . in Christ."[d] The concept of blessing can be to "speak well of, praise, extol" or to "bestow a favor, provide with benefits."[2] Both ideas appear in Paul's opening to his letter. We are to *praise* God for the *favor* he shows us.

In recollecting God's blessings in Christ, Paul listed his blessings to us. When I read Paul's list, I'm reminded of a fireworks display where the finale has one massive, epic blast of glory after another. Before telling us what we should do for God, Paul wanted us to know what God has done to bless us.

BLESSED IN CHRIST

Paul was emphatically clear that any blessings we have are a result of being in Christ. This explains why he mentioned Jesus no fewer than fourteen times in the first fourteen verses of Ephesians. Furthermore, though "in Christ" or "in him" appears some thirty-six times throughout Ephesians, it occurs eleven times in the first fourteen verses. As theologian Thomas Schreiner has written, "The diversity of expressions to describe being in Christ in this one long sentence (Eph. 1:3–14) is astonishing, and the sheer repetition of the formula indicates that it is crucial."[3]

If a genie in a bottle promised to grant you one wish, what would you choose? Honestly, what would it be? Wealth? Power? Love? Now, consider that God has already given us himself. In this life, God may not give you health, wealth, simplicity, or ease, but he has given you himself. If you're in Christ, then you're blessed by and welcomed into community with the

---

d. Eph. 1:3.

entire Trinity—the eternal Friendship of God the Father, God the Son, and God the Holy Spirit. Nothing compares to that blessing.

In the opening section of Ephesians, the entire Trinity is mentioned as both our blessing and the source of all our blessings as we hear of the "Father," "Jesus Christ," and the "Holy Spirit" in that order. This is because every blessing originates with God the Father, is mediated and accomplished by Jesus Christ the Son, and is applied to the believer by the Holy Spirit. This blessing was planned "before the foundation of the world" (v. 4). Before God made the heavens and the earth, God planned to know, love, save, and bless you.

If we're honest, we can't conceive of the time before time, when all that existed was God. But as an eternal being who has created time, the universe, the stars, and the planets, God has eternally planned to bless us in Christ and reconcile us to himself before he even laid the foundations of creation. Yet, comically, we think we can shake the foundations of such a blessing and feel we must help God in the building of it.

There are times we don't feel blessed, but the fact is that we're always blessed. A woman who is now a deacon in our church, named Joyce, found this out through deep tragedy in her life.

"As a believing child of God," she says, "I subconsciously thought the way my life worked out was evidence of God's blessing. When my dream of a 'forever' marriage ended in divorce after twenty years, I was afraid Jesus was rejecting me as well. My next marriage was a disaster—even a court judge told me he had never seen such a skillful con man. His abuse was so sinister I was nearly killed. Over the next several months, I dealt with my husband stalking and attacking me. Even when I was terrified, I knew God was there, protecting me; but again, something didn't seem right about this horror happening to a child of God. Wasn't I supposed to be shielded from this kind of soap opera life?"

During this time, Joyce's business began flourishing and she started attending church. "I had become solely responsible for the success of my business, so I threw myself into it, believing that God would make it work because I was his child, my motives were right, and I was praying about it." Then her business fell apart, too, as a disgruntled employee sabotaged her main source of business, which affected other business ventures to the point that everything came crashing down.

"My net worth went from an impressive number to a huge negative overnight," shares Joyce. "That same week my twenty-four-year-old son died as a result of a massive seizure. The pain seemed unbearable. Then I realized that I had to move from the house where I had expected to live the rest of my life—by Friday. It felt like a tsunami of loss, and this only a few years after going through an abusive hurricane of a marriage and divorce. Where was God? On the other hand, why shouldn't I suffer in this life? He suffered, and he promised me eternal life with him, not a perfect life now. But why would he let this happen to me? I was his child, wasn't I? My thoughts were a mess."

Through all this pain and loss, God was working in Joyce's life. "I gradually realized I had believed my identity in Christ was measured by how well I did in life's circumstances, particularly financially," she says. "As I studied the theme of redemption, I realized there is no sin or circumstance that he will not forgive, nothing that can separate me from his love, nothing that can disqualify me from serving him, if I repent and allow him to use the past to glorify him. I began to realize that being a child of God doesn't mean I'm impervious to failure or harm, but it does mean that I can trust in the sovereignty of a loving God whose plans for me are good, whose presence brings me peace, and who is preparing an eternal home that will delight all my senses."

As Joyce knows, life is hard, and in the especially hard times, it's easy for us to forget that we all deserve hell, and that every good thing in our lives is a blessing not owed to us by God but graciously given to us in love. That's a lot of blessing.

Sometimes we're so focused on our desired blessings that we fail to stop and thank God by remembering the blessings we already have in Christ. Paul models this attitude of gratitude for us early in Ephesians, recounting the unbelievable eternal blessings every believer already has in Christ.

The Blessing of Holiness

For the Christian, holiness is both positional and practical. In Christ, our position before God is "holy and without blame" (Eph. 1:4). Martin Luther was fond of calling Jesus' work on the cross the "great exchange." There, our unrighteousness went to Jesus, who suffered and died in our place, and Jesus' righteousness came to us. The result is that God now graciously sees us as he sees Jesus, righteous and holy.

Practically, this means we're given new desires and empowered by the Holy Spirit to live out those desires in a holy life. This doesn't mean we live without any sin, but rather that we can live in such a way that increasingly reflects the holiness of Jesus Christ and the effects of his blessing in our lives.

In what ways has God changed you to become more holy because of Jesus' blessing? How is God inviting you to make further changes in your life to live at greater levels of obedience and holiness to reflect Christ more?

The Blessing of Predestination

Paul taught that God has chosen and predestined you to receive his love, enjoy his grace, and be his friend forever. In their Old Testament context, this idea is expressed in various forms of the words such as *plan*,[e] *purpose*,[f] and *choose*.[g] Likewise, the New Testament uses a constellation of words, such as *predestined*,[h] *elect*,[i] *chose(n)*,[j] and *appointed*,[k] to speak of God choosing to save some people but not all people.

The doctrine of predestination can understandably bring to mind a host of questions. Why does God save some people and not others? Is God unfair and unloving to save some people and not others? Is there no hope of salvation for those who are not chosen by God? Sadly, the hard questions are often debated more than the divine truth of predestination is celebrated—before time began, God predestined a plan to love and save his people. How does God accomplish this? Through Christ's work on the cross, by the power of the Holy Spirit, through the preaching of Jesus by us.

e. Jer. 49:20; 50:45; Mic. 4:12 (ESV).
f. Isa. 14:24, 26–27; 19:12; 23:9.
g. Num. 16:5, 7; Deut. 4:37; 10:15; Isa. 41:8; Ezek. 20:5.
h. Rom. 8:29–30; Eph. 1:5, 11.
i. Matt. 24:22; Rom. 8:33; Col. 3:12.
j. 2 Thess. 2:13; 1 Cor. 1:27; Eph. 1:4.
k. Acts 13:48.

The Christian is supposed to lovingly, truthfully, and humbly present the gospel of Jesus Christ to non-Christians and see what God does as a result. Rather than be a hindrance to evangelism, as some would claim, predestination frees us up to do as God has commanded all Christians to do, to preach him boldly without the worry that we somehow affect the process of salvation or can mess it up. It frees us up to be bolder in evangelism, not the opposite.

Predestination also allows people like Joyce to rest in God's sovereignty—even when the world is crashing down—because God is good and has good plans for us, even through the evil our sin and others' sin brings into the world. For the Christian, the doctrine of predestination is something to be considered and rejoiced in. God predestined our redemption "in love" (Eph. 1:4). God is obligated to no one, but he has chosen to save us. If you're a Christian, then you're on God's predestined path to relationship with him. God has chosen to know you, love you, seek you, forgive you, embrace you, and befriend you!

The Blessing of Adoption

God is a father, and in Christ you're adopted into his family. In the thirty-nine books of the Old Testament, God is referred to only as Father roughly fourteen times—and each time it's impersonally, in reference to the nation of Israel, not to individuals.

Everything radically changed with Jesus. He spoke of God as Father more than sixty times in the New Testament. No one ever spoke about or prayed to God like Jesus Christ, using a very informal and tender word that little kids call their loving dads—much as my kids call me "Papa Daddy." Following Jesus' example, we refer to God as a Father and salvation as adoption.

Charles Haddon Spurgeon contrasts God's adoption with human adoption:

A man, when he adopts a child sometimes is moved thereto by its extraordinary beauty, or at other times by its intelligent manners and winning disposition. But, beloved, when God passed by the field in which we were

lying, he saw no tears in our eyes till he put them there himself; he saw
no contrition in us until he had given us repentance; and there was no
beauty in us that could induce him to adopt us—on the contrary, we
were everything that was repulsive; and if he had said, when he passed by,
"Thou art cursed, be lost forever," it would have been nothing but what
we might have expected from a God who had been so long provoked, and
whose majesty had been so terribly insulted. But no; he found a rebellious child, a filthy, frightful, ugly child; he took it to his bosom, and
said, "[Sinful] though thou art, thou art comely in my eyes through my
son Jesus; unworthy though thou art, yet I cover thee with his robe, and
in thy brother's garments I accept thee"; and taking us, all unholy and
unclean, just as we were, he took us to be his—his children, his forever.[4]

The Blessing of Redemption

Apart from Christ we're slaves to sin, which is the Bible's language
for addiction. The imagery for slavery and redemption is birthed out of
the book of Exodus and often revisited throughout the Old Testament.[l]
Millions of Hebrew people were enslaved to an Egyptian king, called
a "Pharaoh," who ruled over what was at that time the most powerful
nation on the earth. He was worshipped as a god, and he brutally mistreated the people he enslaved.

Pharaoh repeatedly refused to repent of his ways and release his
slaves. So God sent a terrible series of judgments upon the entire nation.
The wrath of God was eventually poured out on the firstborn son of
every household, killing them in one night. The only households spared
from death to their firstborn son were those who, in faith, took a young,
healthy lamb without blemish or defect, slaughtered it as a substitute, and
covered the doorposts around the entry to their homes with its blood. As
a result of the lamb's blood, the wrath of God passed over them and was
diverted. God's people were redeemed, freed to leave their slavery and live
as free worshippers of God.[m] All of this symbolized the fact that sin rules

---

l. Ex. 15:1–18; Deut. 7:8; 15:15; 2 Sam. 7:23; 1 Chron. 17:21; Isa. 51:10; and Mic. 6:4.
m. Ex. 7–12.

over us, enslaves us, and destroys us. But Jesus was the Lamb of God, whose blood was shed that we might be spared and freed.

In Christ, you're redeemed. Whatever has enslaved you, be it drugs, alcohol, food, sex, gambling, fears, or something else, Jesus has redeemed you. You no longer have to be enslaved to such things. Because Jesus died for your sin, you can put your sin to death, walk away from whoever or whatever has enslaved you, and enjoy a new life to worship God freely.

The Blessing of Forgiveness

What deep regrets haunt you? What words have you spoken, deeds have you done, motives have you held, lies have you believed, harm have you caused, people have you grieved, and shame have you carried? What have you done to try to assuage your guilty conscience? Have you sought to deny your sin, blame others for it, minimalize it, hide it, pay God back, or punish yourself for it? How have your efforts failed?

In Christ, you are totally, completely, and eternally forgiven. It doesn't matter what you've done or will do. Jesus died for it all and lives to forgive it all. You're forgiven. God doesn't hold your sin against you, isn't going to punish you, and loves you in spite of your sin.

The Blessing of Grace

When Paul wrote of God's grace to us, he was referring to what theologians call *common grace* and *saving grace*. This grace is an outpouring of God's love. God loves all people with common grace and loves his chosen people with additional saving grace.

God's common grace allows even those who despise him to learn to make gains in areas such as science, philosophy, technology, education, and medicine. God's common grace also fuels the creative process and permits the arts and creativity of all kinds. Furthermore, God's common grace allows societies to flourish, families to exist, cities to rise up, and nations to prosper.[n]

In addition to common grace, which everyone receives, those in

n. e.g., Ex. 31:2–11; 35:30–35.

Christ also receive saving grace. Like common grace, saving grace has innumerable benefits in this life. However, unlike common grace, it also provides infinite benefits beyond this life in that it reconciles us to God through Christ, freeing us to spend eternity in his presence as holy and blameless.

Paul spoke of grace more than any other biblical writer, some one hundred times.[5] In every single one of his letters, Paul opened and closed with the grace of God. He was thus repeatedly and emphatically illustrating the truth that it's not possible to be in Christ in any way or to any degree apart from the grace of God.

In Christ, you're graced. You're chosen by grace, saved by grace, kept by grace, gifted by grace, empowered by grace, matured by grace, and sanctified by grace. You persevere by grace, and one day will see Jesus, the best friend you've ever had, face-to-face, by grace.

The Blessing of Being Sealed

In the ancient world, owners would affix a personal seal to their possessions. By placing the Holy Spirit in us, God also places his seal upon us (Eph. 1:13). We now belong to the Lord. The Holy Spirit is the beginning of the blessings that await us, as his possession, as part of our inheritance. Practically, this means that the foretastes of the kingdom we enjoy in this life are only the beginning.

Consider for a moment the joys you've had in this life from experiencing the presence of God, learning the Word of God, enjoying the people of God, and singing the praises of God. Now consider that the best days in this life are only a foretaste of the eternal life to come, an appetizer to whet our appetites for the great feast.

TO THE PRAISE OF HIS GLORY

Why does God bless us? Is it so he can glorify us? Or, is it so that he will be glorified? Paul taught that the entire point of God's blessing is his glory, writing that God's blessing is "to the praise of the glory of His grace" (Eph. 1:6), and twice saying "to the praise of His glory" (vv. 12, 14).

Paul's opening lines in Ephesians are really a lengthy prayer of praise for the innumerable blessings we receive in Christ, what is often referred to as a *benediction*. As one Bible commentator explains, "The benediction, or *berekah*, has been for centuries the most common form of Jewish prayer and central to the piety of devout Jewish living. Long before the first century, Jews used both lengthy benedictions in corporate worship and brief benedictions in daily life as a way of praising God for various gracious gifts."[6]

It would greatly benefit our souls and every aspect of our lives if we regularly prayed benedictions like Paul's. Sit down with some uninterrupted time, ask the Holy Spirit to bring to mind the ways you've been blessed by God, and simply journal them. As you do, God will grow bigger, his grace will be richer, and your troubles will become smaller.

To be sure, praying that God will answer a specific request for some blessing is acceptable, much as it's good and right for a child to make requests of her loving father, but the pattern of Paul in Ephesians is that we should first pray in thanks for the blessings we already have before asking for more blessings. At our house we call these "thankful prayers," as we note the specific ways in which God has blessed us and the reasons we're thankful.

Journaling and reflecting on God's blessing daily or weekly will keep you aware of the care and affection God has for you and fuel your worshipful gratitude in response. In times of struggling, you can go back and recollect the ways in which God has blessed you. And this record of the legacy of God's blessing in your life is the kind of thing you will want to one day hand off to your children and grandchildren. Imagine how amazing it would be if your parents or grandparents had done this and you could read in detail how God had blessed them throughout their lives.

The good news is there is a way we can all experience this blessing. Some two thousand years later, we read Paul's prayerful recounting of our blessing in Christ that serves as an example for us to emulate.

In Christ, you're blessed.

5

I AM APPRECIATED

Therefore I also, after I heard of your faith in the Lord Jesus and your love for all the saints, do not cease to give thanks for you, making mention of you in my prayers: that the God of our Lord Jesus Christ, the Father of glory, may give to you the spirit of wisdom and revelation in the knowledge of Him, the eyes of your understanding being enlightened; that you may know what is the hope of His calling, what are the riches of the glory of His inheritance in the saints, and what is the exceeding greatness of His power toward us who believe, according to the working of His mighty power which He worked in Christ when He raised Him from the dead and seated Him at His right hand in the heavenly places, far above all principality and power and might and dominion, and every name that is named, not only in this age but also in that which is to come.

And He put all things under His feet, and gave Him to be head over all things to the church, which is His body, the fullness of Him who fills all in all.

—EPHESIANS 1:15–23

In early 2012, Patrick Stump, the former lead singer of Fall Out Boy, a multiplatinum-selling pop band, posted on his blog that he was thinking of leaving the music industry. He titled the post, "We Liked You Better Fat: Confessions of a Pariah."

Stump shared that the commercial failure of his solo album, as well as the negative criticism of Fall Out Boy's latest album, left him feeling as if he had "received some big cosmic sign that says [he] should disappear." In the post, he told how once-adoring fans mocked him on the road, yelling out that they liked him better when he was fat, sending threatening letters to his home, and telling him he was nothing without his band.

He went on to say, "The reality is that for a certain number of people, all I've ever done, all I ever will do, and all I ever had the capacity to do worth a damn was a record I began recording when I was 18 years old . . . The truth is wherever and whoever I am . . . I will never be the kid from 'Take This to Your Grave' again. And I'm deeply sorry that I can't be, I truly am (no irony, no sarcasm). I hate waking up every morning knowing I'm disappointing so many people. I hate feeling like the awkward adult husk of a discarded once-cute child actor."[1]

Stump's heartfelt confession of feeling inadequate highlights the truth that no matter how famous or rich we become, we all want to be appreciated—and the feelings that come from feeling unappreciated can be devastating, crippling us and crushing our desire to move forward.

When we feel this way, we're faced with a choice. Do we believe what the world says about us? Or do we believe what God says about us? What we choose to believe can change the trajectory of our lives in dramatic ways.

YOU'RE APPRECIATED

We live in an increasingly rude world. Everyone seems to act as if they are more important and what they're doing is more significant than anyone else. Next time you're driving in traffic, leaving a crowded event, or exiting a plane, make note of how people expect to be treated like gods and goddesses while treating others like paupers and peasants. Sadly, technology has only made things worse. The more biting, harsh, and critical people are, the more followers and fans they amass online.

To varying degrees, we're all guilty of participating in our culture of rudeness. Which of us hasn't become jealous when others succeed? Yet we hate it when we're on the receiving end of this rudeness.

Ask yourself, "How does it feel to be neglected?" Are you frustrated when no one says thank you for a job well done? Are you tired of feeling overworked and underappreciated? Is getting more criticism than encouragement grinding you down? Do you wonder if all the time, energy, and money you put into church, work, and life are worth it? Do you find yourself wondering if anyone really cares?

If you're feeling this way, there's good news. God sees everything you do. God knows the sacrifices you make, the ways you're growing, the people you serve, the times you're generous, and the impact you make. And he's appreciative.

I want you to read the following verses as a message from Jesus to you through Paul: "Therefore I also, after I heard of your faith in the Lord Jesus and your love for all the saints, do not cease to give thanks for you, making mention of you in my prayers."[a] You are appreciated!

Particularly religious folks may bristle at the thought that the Lord appreciates what Christian individuals and churches do. They're prone to turn simple gratitude into unnecessarily complex theology arguments. While it may sound spiritual to say that everything that happens is solely by God and that we can take no credit and deserve no appreciation for anything we do, it's unbiblical and ungrateful. The reality is that we are God's "workmanship, created in Christ Jesus for good works, which God prepared beforehand that we should walk in them."[b] The word *workmanship* used by Paul denotes that we are God's work of art or poem. Just as we do with works of art made by artists in this world, we can take enjoyment in, praise, and appreciate the work of art itself while giving ultimate credit to the artist who created it.

To be sure, our lives and any holiness, obedience, or fruitfulness we enjoy are empowered and enabled by the grace of God through the power of the Holy Spirit. But God often chooses to work through people who desire to do his will, obey his commands, lean upon his grace, and are filled with the Spirit. Paul himself demonstrated this, saying, "By the grace of God I am what I am, and His grace toward me was not in vain; but I labored more abundantly than they all, yet not I, but the grace of God which was with me."[c]

It's grievous when, out of the good desire to reserve all glory for God, we forget to also appreciate those through whom God works. God is as equally glorified when we praise him for his unmediated grace as when

a. Eph. 1:15–16.
b. Eph. 2:10.
c. 1 Cor. 15:10.

we're thankful for those through whom he chooses to deliver it. This is why throughout Ephesians Paul not only praised God but also appreciated people. In Ephesians 1:15–16 alone, he stated appreciation for the people's "faith in the Lord Jesus" and their "love for all the saints," saying "[I] do not cease to give thanks for you." The point is clear: we're to thank God for being faithful to his people *and* to thank his people for being faithful to him.

Paul's appreciation for the people was incredibly personal. Much of his service was to the churches in and around Ephesus, which was the only city in which he ministered for an extended period of time.[d] Just before leaving Asia Minor for Jerusalem, Paul asked the Ephesian church elders to join him in the neighboring city of Miletus, where he gave a prolonged, heartfelt speech, knowing he would likely never return.[e] The love and appreciation Paul and the Christians in Ephesus shared is movingly highlighted as Paul boarded the ship to leave them: "Then they all wept freely, and fell on Paul's neck and kissed him, sorrowing most of all for the words which he spoke, that they would see his face no more."[f]

It's this sense of thankfulness that Paul expressed in his letter to the Ephesians. When Paul heard and saw of the Ephesians' continued faithfulness toward Jesus and their dedication in serving him, he was thankful. In a world where fame, reputation, envy, resentment, and hatred were the norm, Paul responded with joy and thankfulness.

Paul's appreciation to God and others for loving service appears frequently throughout his letters. His appreciation is in response to the actions of both individuals and entire churches. Read the following examples, receiving them each slowly, deliberately, and personally, as if Paul had written about you specifically:

- Romans 1:8: "First, I thank my God through Jesus Christ for you."
- 1 Corinthians 1:4: "I thank my God always concerning you."

---

d. Acts 18:19–20:1.
e. Acts 20:17–35.
f. Acts 20:37–38.

- Philippians 1:3–5: "I thank my God upon every remembrance of you, always in every prayer of mine making request for you all with joy, for your fellowship in the gospel from the first day until now."
- Colossians 1:3: "We give thanks to the God and Father of our Lord Jesus Christ, praying always for you."
- 1 Thessalonians 1:2–3 (ESV): "We give thanks to God always for all of you, constantly mentioning you in our prayers, remembering before our God and Father your work of faith and labor of love and steadfastness of hope in our Lord Jesus Christ."
- 1 Thessalonians 2:19–20: "For what is our hope, or joy, or crown of rejoicing? Is it not even you in the presence of our Lord Jesus Christ at His coming? For you are our glory and joy."
- 1 Thessalonians 3:9–10: "For what thanks can we render to God for you, for all the joy with which we rejoice for your sake before our God, night and day praying exceedingly that we may see your face and perfect what is lacking in your faith?"
- 2 Thessalonians 1:3: "We are bound to thank God always for you, brethren, as it is fitting, because your faith grows exceedingly, and the love of every one of you all abounds toward each other."
- 2 Thessalonians 2:13: "But we are bound to give thanks to God always for you."
- 2 Timothy 1:3–4: "I thank God, whom I serve with a pure conscience, as my forefathers did, as without ceasing I remember you in my prayers night and day, greatly desiring to see you, being mindful of your tears, that I may be filled with joy."
- Philemon 4–5: "I thank my God, making mention of you always in my prayers, hearing of your love and faith which you have toward the Lord Jesus and toward all the saints."

How encouraged are you when you read those verses? What things did the Holy Spirit bring to mind as specific examples of ways in which God is appreciative of you?

Paul was keenly aware that none of his suffering or service to God was unseen by God. Simply and significantly, he knew that he was appreciated. This allowed him to press forward in spite of harsh criticism, lonely ostracism, and brutal opposition. It also made him more appreciative of servant-hearted Christians and compelled him to encourage them by saying often that both he and God appreciated them.

Appreciated People Exchange Grumbling for Praying

When we feel neglected, taken advantage of, and taken for granted, we can fall prey to grumbling. The Bible is clear that grumbling is a sin,[g] but how do we stop grumbling? Do we just stuff our frustration, pretend we're happy, and fake joy? No. Instead, we must stop looking to people for appreciation and start looking to Jesus.

Far from being appreciated, Jesus was disrespected, neglected, and murdered. The crowds didn't cry out, "Appreciate him." Instead they cried, "Crucify him." Yet, rather than grumbling, Jesus spent his time praying both in the Garden of Gethsemane before he was arrested and from the cross as he was dying. He didn't just pray for himself but also for those who hated him, asking, "Father, forgive them, for they do not know what they do."[h] Jesus endured this because he was certain that he was doing the Father's will. He knew that the Father was pleased with him and appreciated his obedience. At his baptism, he latched onto the Father's words, "This is My beloved Son, in whom I am well pleased."[i] In Christ, God is also pleased with you. You now enjoy Christ's righteousness as your own. In Christ, the Father also appreciates your obedience to his Word and will.

When Paul thanked people, he mentioned that he was praying for them. Certainly the churches to which Paul wrote had problems and difficult people. But rather than grumbling over what was wrong, Paul commended what was right and prayed that they would continue to know God more and become more like Jesus.

How about you? When frustrated, annoyed, or feeling unappreciated,

g. James 5:9; Jude 1:16–19; 1 Peter 4:9.
h. Luke 23:34.
i. Matt. 3:17.

do you respond with grumbling or with praying? Practically speaking, as you think of past examples in your own life, how has grumbling only made the situation worse? What if you exchanged grumbling for praying? By praying, we talk to God rather than gossip to others, and we invite God to help us, to protect our hearts from bitterness and anger, and to change not only our circumstances externally but also our hearts internally. If you're not already, start praying for others today.

Appreciated People Exchange Competing for Celebrating

When we're unappreciated, we're prone to engage in unhealthy competitiveness. While there is a healthy kind of competition, where we "spur one another on toward love and good deeds,"[j] seeking to motivate one another in love to be more faithful and fruitful for God's glory and others' good, many times our competitiveness isn't godly or gracious. Rather, the focus becomes showing our superiority over others, seeking to outperform others to achieve power, status, praise, and reward.

When even godly things are done with the underlying motivation of ungodly competition, it leads to ungodly behavior. Sinful spiritual competition is when we compete against others to defeat them rather than compete with others to become more like Jesus. We become jealous of others, speak ill of them or even malign them, question their motives, obsess over defeating them, and rejoice if they fail or suffer humiliation.

Knowing God appreciates us liberates us from wrongly competing with others and allows us to instead celebrate them and their successes. This is precisely what Paul modeled for us in Ephesians 1:15–16: "After I heard of your faith in the Lord Jesus and your love for all the saints, [I] do not cease to give thanks for you." Paul didn't compare their works to his or even make any mention of his many accomplishments. Instead, he celebrated the evidence of God's grace in their lives.

How about you? Do you celebrate others' success? How could a deeper understanding that God celebrates your successes in your life help you do the same for others? With whom have you wrongly competed that God is

---

j. Heb. 10:24 (NIV).

now convicting you to start celebrating? How can you do that practically? If you're not already, start celebrating others today.

Appreciated People Exchange Bitterness for Thankfulness

When we forget that God appreciates us and we don't feel appreciated by others, we can become bitter against both people and God.

Some bitter people stop serving altogether. They simply give up, saying things like, "If no one appreciates what I do, why try?" Or, "If people are going to be ungrateful, they can do it themselves." Others continue serving but do so with a grumbling spirit. They let everyone know how hard their task is, how much work they're doing, and in effect beg people to tell them how much they're appreciated.

The truth is that God appreciates everything good that every one of his children does by the power of the Holy Spirit. In Christ, you're appreciated. This fact allows you to exchange bitterness for thankfulness. Paul demonstrated this, saying, "[I] do not cease to give thanks for you."[k] Appreciated people can be thankful for God's grace in their own lives, and in the lives of others.

Are you bitter against God or someone else because of the gifts, opportunities, blessings, or fruitfulness that you covet for yourself? How has that bitterness soured your soul and negatively affected your friendship with Jesus and others? How can knowing the truth that you are appreciated by God set you free from the lie that you're not? Start being thankful for people today.

Appreciated People Exchange Performing for Serving

Throughout Jesus' earthly ministry there was a running argument among the disciples as to which of them was the greatest.[l] What's interesting is that rather than rebuking his disciples, Jesus redirected their aspirations, saying they should aspire to be great servants.

Jesus himself came to the earth as a humble servant.[m] In the

---

k. Eph. 1:16.
l. Matt. 18:1–6; Mark 9:33–37; 10:35–45; Luke 9:46–48; 22:24–30.
m. Isa. 42:1–4; 49:1–7; 52:13–53:12; cf. Phil. 2:1–11.

upside-down kingdom of God, greatness is determined not by how many people serve you, but by how many people you serve. This is what Jesus meant when he said, "Whoever desires to become great among you shall be your servant."[n] And this also explains why Jesus is the greatest person who has walked or ever will walk the earth. He "did not come to be served, but to serve, and to give His life a ransom for many."[o] Following his Master's example, Paul also referred to himself as a servant.[p]

Knowing God appreciates us allows us to exchange our performance for service. Performance is done for the sight and approval of others. Service is done knowing that God is watching and approving whether or not anyone else is. Performance causes us to be enslaved to others' opinions, unable to say no, and prone to being overworked. Service frees us to do what God wants, thereby saying no as needed. Performance presses us toward perfectionism, where we seek to do everything just right so others will praise us. Service allows us to do our best, knowing that God's appreciation of us is secure regardless of our performance. Performance causes us to focus on the "big" things and only do what is highly visible or significant. Service allows us to do simple, humble, and menial tasks—the "little things"—knowing that the peasant Jewish carpenter we worship equally appreciates them both. Paul models this for us by serving those who read his letter, including us, in love.

How about you? Are you prone to perform, or serve? How could a deeper understanding of God's appreciation for your works free you from the pressures of performing to the satisfaction of serving? Start serving others today.

Appreciated People Exchange Boasting for Encouraging

Some years ago we held a conference at our church. At the conclusion of the first day, numerous staff and volunteers were talking about one of the speakers. There was an absolute buzz about not his preaching, but his appreciation. They felt so loved and encouraged by him that they

---

n. Mark 10:43.
o. Mark 10:45.
p. 1 Cor. 4:1; 9:19.

were excited to work hard, faithfully serving those attending the event. The next day, doing my best ninja impersonation, I followed the speaker around at a distance to see what I could learn from him.

What I witnessed was simple and powerful. He was genuinely interested in everyone who served and in what they were doing. He took time with seemingly every person who served at the event. He looked them in the eye, sincerely thanked them, and encouraged them by explaining the difference they were making to him and how much he appreciated their service. He was genuine. He was attentive to the detailed ways each person served. It was no wonder they loved him so much, and now, some years later, these folks continue to remember him fondly.

Unappreciated people can resort to boasting in an effort to earn others' appreciation. This is an unhealthy, unholy, and unhappy path to venture down. We can become obsessive about making known what we've done and are doing, exaggerating the facts, and even lying to impress others and feel appreciated.

The underlying hope is that when people hear about the great things we've done and the sacrifices we've made, they'll be grateful and appreciative. Instead, most people find such boasting off-putting, arrogant, and repulsive. Why? Because when one unappreciated person boasts to another unappreciated person, the result isn't appreciation; it's jealousy.

If we truly believe that God appreciates our service, we can stop boasting and start encouraging. When we boast, we use people for appreciation. When our appreciation comes from God, we can start loving people, sharing the ways both God and we appreciate them. Paul demonstrated this by encouraging others, thanking them for what they'd done by God's grace, rather than boasting in his many accomplishments. Our conference speaker had the same mentality, and it changed everything for our volunteers and convicted me.

One of the most revealing ways to discover whether or not we truly believe God appreciates us is to consider our prayer life. In its most general sense, prayer simply means communicating with God. This can be done audibly, as God hears our words, or silently, as God knows our thoughts. Prayer can include singing, journaling, or letter writing. Praying is the primary way we engage in relationship with God, and just as communication is key to interpersonal relationships, it's vital to our relationship with God.

Those who know that God appreciates them pray frequently and differently. They pray frequently because they're aware of God's work in the lives of others, giving them more to pray about. And they pray differently because they're focused on others and their needs, giving thanks for the work of God's people instead of focusing on themselves. This explains why roughly half of Ephesians is composed of prayer. One author wrote, "Ephesians is a book of prayer. Literally, it is a book of prayer. Do you realize that about half of the Book of Ephesians is prayer? Prayer reports, prayer requests, and invitations to prayer . . . even outlines of prayers that Paul has prayed for the Ephesian Christians and for you and me."[2]

One example is found in Ephesians 1:15–23, where Paul quite simply prays that Christians who already knew God, had been under good Bible teaching (Paul, Timothy, John, and Luke all taught in Ephesus), and had been enjoying a growing ministry would know God better.

One pastor and Bible teacher says, "We might very well ask, 'What do you mean, Paul, when you pray that the Ephesians might come to know God better? You have taught them all these things already. Do you mean that they do not know them? Or that there is some hidden, esoteric information still to come?' 'No,' Paul would answer. 'You have misunderstood me. I am not praying that the Ephesians might come to know more *about* God, though they probably do have a great deal more to learn, but rather that they might know *him*. Knowing him and knowing about him are quite different.'"[3]

My wife, Grace, and I enjoyed our first date on March 12, 1988. From that first time together, I have known her, but I'm still learning to know her better all the time, and will for the rest of my life. So it is to an even greater degree in our relationship with the infinite God of the Bible. He knows us intimately and perfectly. We, however, always have more to learn about him as we get to know him. Our relationship with God needs to be continually nurtured.

In thinking of service, has anyone in your life ever served you as Paul served the Ephesian church? Is there anyone who appreciates you, encourages you, teaches you, and prays for you? If so, perhaps you could return the favor by sharing with that individual why you appreciate him or her and the thankful prayers you pray to God for this friend. If not, then let Paul's words in Ephesians be a gift of appreciation and prayerful encouragement to you. Receive them as your own, commit them to memory, display them in your home, and carry them in your heart. In Christ, you're appreciated.

Finally, commit by God's grace to being an appreciative person to others. With your family, friends, and coworkers, strive to make more deposits in the account of appreciation than withdrawals from criticism. To whom does God want you to communicate your appreciation? What specific ways have they been helpful to you and/or others? In what ways are you encouraged by what you see in their lives? What would be the most effective way of communicating your appreciation of them? Perhaps you could, as Paul did, write a letter of appreciation to them, sharing a prayer of thanksgiving to God for them and the ways you're asking God to help them.

Such a letter would be a gift, likely one they would treasure and keep, not unlike Paul's letter to the Ephesians, which we still open a couple thousand years after it was written. That is the power of appreciation.

6

I AM SAVED

And you He made alive, who were dead in trespasses and sins, in which you once walked according to the course of this world, according to the prince of the power of the air, the spirit who now works in the sons of disobedience, among whom also we all once conducted ourselves in the lusts of our flesh, fulfilling the desires of the flesh and of the mind, and were by nature children of wrath, just as the others.

But God, who is rich in mercy, because of His great love with which He loved us, even when we were dead in trespasses, made us alive together with Christ (by grace you have been saved), and raised us up together, and made us sit together in the heavenly places in Christ Jesus, that in the ages to come He might show the exceeding riches of His grace in His kindness toward us in Christ Jesus. For by grace you have been saved through faith, and that not of yourselves; it is the gift of God, not of works, lest anyone should boast. For we are His workmanship, created in Christ Jesus for good works, which God prepared beforehand that we should walk in them.

—EPHESIANS 2:1–10

When Bill was saved at twenty-one, he didn't understand what it really meant other than that he now had to go to church and try to live a better life. As a result, most of his Christian life was spent trying to measure up. "I grew up in a home where measuring up meant trying to receive affirmation and 'attaboys' from my dad," Bill says. "Unfortunately, when I got saved, I projected my understanding of a father onto God based on what I grew up with. I therefore continually struggled with the idea that God was pretty much displeased with me most of the time."

Bill's desire to make God proud of him ended up pushing him to do some good things for all the wrong reasons. In 1994, he left a lucrative, full-time position as an engineer to pursue full-time vocational pastoral work. Looking back, he realized his motives were to impress God, not serve him. "I believed that my identity was in the things I did—not who I was in Christ," says Bill. "So here's the problem with having your identity wrapped up in the things you accomplish: your accomplishments become your god. However, the god of accomplishments only works as long as things go well. When the wheels start to come off, you are left again with nothing but the old, familiar image of an angry guy shaking his head in disappointment."

And in 1996, things went wrong. Bill was diagnosed with a Parkinsonism called progressive supranuclear palsy (PSP), with a life expectancy of about five years. "Here I was, serving God, raising a family, being faithful to my wife," says Bill, "in other words, doing all the right things! Yet, God allowed me to get sick."

In 2000, God miraculously healed Bill of his physical illness, but Bill still struggled with finding his salvation in his works rather than in Jesus. That same year, God blessed Bill's family with a seventh child, Annie, whom Bill viewed as a response to God's blessing in his life. "She was an amazing, lovely, graceful—her middle name was Grace—little girl," says Bill. For three years, everything was great as Bill pastored at a church and watched his family grow. Then, the unthinkable happened.

At the age of three, Annie suffered a seizure resulting from an undiagnosed malady affecting her adrenal glands—Addison's disease. The lack of oxygen from the seizure caused Annie to suffer permanent brain damage. She could no longer talk, walk, or understand most of what was said to her. Additionally, she couldn't eat and had a permanent tube placed into her stomach so she could be pump fed.

"I could not understand God's purposes in this tragedy," shares Bill. "Because my identity was wrapped up in my identity as a pastor, a husband, and a father, I was devastated. I felt like a hypocrite working as a pastor when I had my own questions about whether God was really good or not. My faith was in the toilet. So I resigned.

"Everything I had built up in an effort to please God—my work and my family—was crumbling down around me," says Bill. "Watching Annie suffer had a devastating effect on our whole family."

Annie died this past March, at age seven. Bill and his family knew after her seizure that she might not live a long life. Still, he says, "Her life was far too short. We miss her every day, all day."

Through all this tragedy, Bill has grown in his understanding that he was saved by Jesus, not by what he did for Jesus. "Understanding that my identity is in Christ and not in the things I do, allows me to finally embrace the knowledge that I have a Father who loves me unconditionally," says Bill. "He could not love me any more, and he will not love me any less. He has things he wants to see me accomplish for his glory, but his favor is not based on my ability to please or impress him. How sad that I've only begun to understand this freedom at fifty-three. But the past is the past. How I look forward to doing great things only for his glory—not my résumé!"

God saved Bill at twenty-one. God is still saving Bill today. And one day, God will save Bill and make him fully like Jesus. The same is true for us.

GOD SAVES

Christians often use the word "saved" as a shorthand way of speaking of salvation. Like many Christian colloquialisms, it's a word more often uttered than understood. The word is specifically used twice in Ephesians 2:1–10,[a] but the entire section is really an explanation of what it means to be saved. In one sense, "saved" is a simple summary of the gospel message: you were dead in sin, living in it, headed toward final judgment, and God "saved" you. In another sense, you could mine its riches forever. It's "one of the clearest, most expressive, and most loved descriptions of salvation in the New Testament."[1]

Generally, when we tell people we're saved, we do so using the past tense. In the New Testament, Paul used the term in a much richer and fuller context, employing the past, present, and future tenses of the same

---

a. 2:5; 2:8.

root word. According to Paul, we have been saved,[b] we are being saved,[c] and we shall be saved.[d] As noted theologian A. W. Pink has written,

> In the New Testament "salvation" is threefold in its scope—past, present, and future; and it is threefold in its character—from the penalty of sin, from the power of sin, and from the presence of sin. Every believer *has been saved* from the penalty of sin. . . . But we *shall yet be saved* from the very presence of sin. . . . At our Lord's return we shall be completely emancipated from the dominion and pollution of sin.[2]

It is helpful to understand that though we are positionally righteous before God in Christ (have been saved), we may also struggle with sin because we are being made new and like Christ daily (are being saved). But we have hope, as Christians, that one day we will be perfect like Christ (shall be saved). The best part is, the past, present, and future work of salvation in our lives is all the work of Christ in us. Along every step of salvation, we are brought along by Jesus and lovingly empowered by his Holy Spirit.

In everyday life, when we speak of someone being saved, we communicate two basic things: One, someone was in danger and unable to rescue himself from a terrible fate. Two, someone else rescued, redeemed, and delivered him.

Sandra McCracken, on her album *Live Under Lights and Wires*, shares a story of two young boys in Missouri who spent their summer playing by some sandbag levees that had held back some of the extreme flooding that happened over the past decade on the Mississippi River. Tragically, the two boys found themselves in some quicksand resulting from a breach in the levy. When rescue workers finally found them and came to them, they found only the younger boy standing in the sand.

"Where is your brother?" asked one of the rescuers.

"I'm standing on his shoulders," answered the young boy.

The older brother had sacrificed his life to save his younger brother.

b. Eph. 2:5; Rom. 8:24.
c. 1 Cor. 1:18.
d. Rom. 5:9.

Just as this young boy needed saving, we, too, were once sinking in the sand of our sin, and it took our older brother Jesus to sacrifice himself so we could be saved. And like the little boy, we are still in the sand of sin but saved from the death it would cause, and one day, the rescue worker Jesus will come and pull us out completely. This is the basic sense of what the Bible means when it says that we're saved in Christ.

SAVED FROM WHAT?

A fellow schoolmate was the first person to ever ask me if I was saved. Truthfully, I didn't understand what he meant. I said something like, "I believe in God." I wasn't a Christian, but I believed there was a God of some kind, and I tried to live a good life as a good person.

At that time, I had no deep awareness of God's holiness, my sin, and, as a result, no sense of urgency to learn more about God or make any major changes in my life. I was like a man caught in quicksand, but I didn't notice I was sinking, so I didn't feel that I needed a savior. I certainly saw other sinners who needed Jesus, but I felt I was a good person and was okay. Since that time, I've met enough people to know that the erroneous beliefs I held are widely believed by many other people.

Before we can understand and embrace our identity in Christ, we must first accept our identity apart from Christ. Becoming a Christian is not merely accepting the truth about Jesus as our Savior. It's also accepting the truth about ourselves as needy sinners.

In Ephesians 2:1–3, Paul says, "And you He made alive, who were dead in trespasses and sins, in which you once walked according to the course of this world, according to the prince of the power of the air, the spirit who now works in the sons of disobedience, among whom also we all once conducted ourselves in the lusts of our flesh, fulfilling the desires of the flesh and of the mind, and were by nature children of wrath, just as the others." In Christ, we're saved from six things: sin, death, worldly living, Satan, our old nature, and the wrath of God.

In Christ, We're Saved from Sin and Death

Death is first and foremost the penalty for sin. Because of sin, death entered the world[e] and spread to all.[3] It may be obvious, but death separates us from the source of life. What is not so obvious for many people is that God is the source of all life. So death, in a very real sense, is a separation from God, both spiritually and physically. In this life, death is the fundamental characteristic of the spiritual life of those not in Christ. In this sense, every non-Christian is a "dead man walking," separated from the life of God because of his "trespasses and sins."

Thankfully, in Christ, we're saved from our sins and the consequence of death. Because Jesus died, each of us can live a new life as a new person with new desires for the things of God, free from the penalty and power of sin. Because Jesus rose, we live spiritually alive and will one day rise physically from death, like Jesus, to be with him and like him forever.

In Christ, We're Saved from a Pattern of Worldly Living

Consider for a moment who you would be and what your life would be like had God not saved you. What patterns of thought and action did your family, friends, and culture have that you wouldn't have questioned without a new mind in Christ and new authority in Scripture?

For most people, a truthful look at who they could have been is horrifying. For the Christian, it becomes more so as we understand the severity of all our sins—not just the "big" ones. To fully appreciate our Savior, we must first fully acknowledge our sin, remembering, as Paul wrote, the way "in which [we] once walked according to the course of this world" (Eph. 2:2).

Imagine for a moment, physically speaking, how far you would travel from home if every day you simply walked in the same direction down a well-worn, popular path. Spiritually, the life of a non-Christian is like that. With one's back toward God and his face toward selfishness and sin, the sinner daily walks deeper into darkness, devastation, and death, what Paul calls "the course of this world"; that is, the pursuit of power, money,

---

e. e.g., Gen. 2:16–17; 3:3–4; Deut. 30:17–19; Rom. 1:32; 5:12–14, 18–21.

companionship, significance, control, beauty, and more, instead of God and the things he'd have for you.

The Christian is one who repents, which literally means turning his back to sin and his face toward God, and walks with Jesus as his new identity. In Christ, we're saved from a worldly way of living and transformed to a holy way of living. In God's grace, this can establish a new pattern for generations to come as our children and grandchildren are encouraged to follow in our proverbial footsteps with Jesus.

In Christ, We're Saved from Satan

In Ephesians 2:2, Paul spoke of the non-Christian walking "according to the prince of the power of the air," who is the "spirit who now works in the sons of disobedience." The phrase "prince of the power of the air" refers to Satan, and "power of the air" is a shorthand way of referring to the spiritual realm in Paul's culture.

Satan is the prince, ruler, power, and authority of the dwelling place of demons. This is why in Luke 4:6 the devil tells Jesus that he will give him all his "authority" if Jesus worships him. Satan has authority over the spiritual forces that play out their diabolical schemes in and through humanity and the kingdoms of the world, and "although the ruler of this world has been defeated (cf. Eph. 1:20–22), he is not surrendering without a struggle and without still making his powerful influence felt."[4]

Thankfully, Jesus rules above Satan and demons, and has defeated their hold on us through his sinless life, substitutionary death, bodily resurrection, and exaltation to the throne. He sits in heaven today, where he rules over everyone and everything—including Satan and demons. While Satan is ultimately defeated, he is still trying to war against us and against God, much like a foreign king who has lost the war but has not yet surrendered. Skirmishes continue as enemy soldiers and snipers continue their assault, but in Christ, we do not have to be defeated, as his victory and authority are our victory and authority. We get into trouble when we forget this fact and instead give Satan a foothold, inviting him to have authority in our lives.

In Christ, We're Saved from Our Old Nature

Speaking of those not in Christ, Paul wrote of the "spirit who now works in the sons of disobedience." The phrase is Hebrew in nature and found in other places in the New Testament, such as Mark 3:17, Luke 10:6, and Acts 4:36.[5] It denotes "men and women whose lives are characterized by disobedience," which includes a rejection of the gospel but also a general disregard for God and his will.[6]

Importantly, Paul pointed out that such people are those "among whom we all once lived in the passions of our flesh, carrying out the desires of the body and the mind, and were by nature children of wrath, like the rest of mankind" (v. 3 ESV). That we all come from the same plight of an old nature should move us toward compassion for those not in Christ. Our old way of life was in one sense unavoidable for us before Christ and is so for those presently without Christ. It is who we are "by nature," a "condition or circumstance as determined by birth."[7] According to the Bible, we're born anything but good people with good hearts. Rather, we're sinners by nature and choice, as sin is both a nature we inherit and a lifestyle we choose.

As such, we deserve justice, condemnation, and hell. But in Christ, we're saved from our old nature, which is dethroned from the center of our lives, and given a new nature that desires love for Jesus, love for others, love for the truth, and love for holiness. In Ephesians 2:1–10, Paul contrasts our old nature with our new nature in this way:

OLD NATURE	NEW NATURE
Separated from Christ	United to Christ
Dead	Alive
Disobedient	Obedient
Ruled by spiritual evil	Sharing in Jesus' rule over spiritual evil
Objects of God's wrath	Objects of God's affection
Brings vague uncertainty about sin	Brings specific awareness of a sin
Walking in sin	Walking in good works
Destined for hell	Seated with Christ in heaven

If you're having a hard time believing your new identity in Christ, it may be beneficial to take this list drawn from Paul's letter and tape it to your mirror to remind yourself in the morning that you're saved from sin and death, worldly living, Satan, and your old nature. You're a new creation in Christ, with a new identity.

SAVED BY WHOM?

What we don't need in this world is more politics, spirituality, morality, or religion. We don't need more sinners trying to act like a savior. We need a Savior.

The answer to the question of who saves us is simple: Jesus. Or, as I like to say, "It's all about Jesus!" We see these ideas in Ephesians 2:4–5, 8–10, where Paul wrote, "But God, who is rich in mercy, because of His great love with which He loved us, even when we were dead in trespasses, made us alive together with Christ (by grace you have been saved.) . . . For by grace you have been saved through faith, and that not of yourselves; it is the gift of God, not of works, lest anyone should boast. For we are His workmanship, created in Christ Jesus for good works, which God prepared beforehand that we should walk in them."

The theme of these verses is unmistakably clear: God saves us through Jesus as an act of mercy, love, and grace. The grace of God is a theme that runs throughout Ephesians, as is the love of God. Paul's emphasis is that all of salvation is a gift. Some bristle and say that salvation by the lavish love and grace of God is too easy. We do this overtly with our words and rejection of Jesus or inadvertently, like Bill, who through his constant striving to find identity in work believed his sacrifice needed to be added to Jesus' sacrifice on the cross. But the truth is that though salvation by grace seems simple, it's actually hard because it requires that we humbly come empty-handed to God. We earn nothing. Jesus earns it all. We boast in nothing. Jesus gets all our boasting. We don't save ourselves. Jesus alone saves us.

The word *savior* appears twenty-four times in the New Testament, with eight occurrences referring to God in general and sixteen referring to Jesus in particular. In fact, the name Jesus means "God saves." An angel declared that Jesus would be born to "save His people from their sins."[f] At the birth of Jesus, an angel also declared that "a Savior" had been born.[g] Upon seeing the newborn Jesus, the godly, old man Simeon, who had been longing for the Savior's coming, held the baby Jesus in his arms and said, "My eyes have seen Your salvation."[h] In addition to the word *savior*, related words, such as *save* and *salvation*, also appear frequently throughout the New Testament. They, too, point to Jesus as our God and Savior.

Jesus alone is the only Savior, and apart from him no one is saved. This is why Paul said that our salvation is only "in Christ" no fewer than three times in Ephesians 2:1–10.

SAVED FOR WHAT?

Once we become Christians, the natural question is then, "Now what?" What did God save us for? And what does God have for us next?

Ephesians 2:5–6 says that God "made us alive together *with* Christ," he "raised us up *with* him," and he "seated us *with* him in the heavenly places" (emphasis added). Each verb Paul used has "with" attached to it. All of what God does in us happens "with" Christ through his resurrection from the dead and his exaltation at the right hand of God. While this is almost too magnificent to believe, it is nonetheless true: "What God has accomplished in Christ he has also accomplished for believers."[8] Paul described the glorious victory in which believers share as they are in Christ.

After establishing our victory in Christ, Paul gave us the reasons why God does this for us. God desires to "show the exceeding riches of His grace" that he has toward us (v. 7). Our God is a wealthy Father who is rich in grace and who loves to lavish upon us the gift of grace. This inspires deep praise from us to the Father for his mercy for all eternity. A Bible commentator says,

---

f. Matt. 1:21.
g. Luke 2:11.
h. Luke 2:30.

In 2:4–7 Paul paints a bright portrait of God's grace that stands in dramatic contrast to the dark landscape of human sin in 2:1–3. By giving believers life with Christ, raising them with Christ, and seating them with Christ in his place of victory, God has demonstrated the overwhelmingly merciful, loving, and gracious nature of his character. This demonstration of his character was not something that happened as a side effect of his gracious saving work, but was the very purpose for which he did this work. He rescued those who are in Christ from the domination of the world, the devil, and the flesh so that he might demonstrate forever the overwhelmingly gracious nature of his character.[9]

As Paul expounded on the concept of God's grace in verses 8–10, he ended the whole section by talking about how we are God's workmanship, saved *for* good works. Paul wasn't suddenly making a switch from grace to works here. Rather, he meant that even our works are empowered and made possible by God's grace for us, in us, and through us. We are *his* workmanship—his "work of art, his masterpiece"[10]—*created* in Christ Jesus for good works, which *God* prepared beforehand.

Man-made religion in its various forms seeks to have human works entirely or at least partially involved in salvation. In Buddhism, ceasing desire saves you. In Confucianism, education, self-reflection, self-cultivation, and living a moral life save you. In Hinduism, detaching from your separated ego and making an effort to live in unity with the divine save you. In Islam, living a life of good deeds saves you. In Orthodox Judaism, repentance, prayer, and working hard to obey the Law save you. In New Ageism, gaining a new perspective, through which you see how you're connected to all things as a divine oneness, saves you. In Taoism, aligning yourself with the Tao to have peace and harmony saves you. What nearly all religions and spiritualities hold in common is the theme that, if there is a savior, it's the person we see in the mirror every morning.

Christianity is also a religion of works—just not our own works. Only by the work of Jesus Christ are we saved. Only through faith in his sinless life, substitutionary death, and bodily resurrection can anyone be saved. Jesus saves us, which then results in our good works—what Jesus also often refers to as the "fruit" of his already accomplished work of salvation in us. This is a vastly different way of looking at the world than any other religion. Our works don't justify us. Rather our works are an act of worship to a God who has already made us new.

MAKE A DIFFERENCE

Being saved to a new life in Christ is meaningful, valuable, and purposeful. The world is filled with sin and death, and God's people are part of God's mission to see sinners saved and all things made new. What we do makes a difference, glorifies God, is good for others, and brings us joy. Christians should care about justice, the poor, the marginalized, the oppressed, and the suffering because God cares for people and has prepared good works for us to walk in on his behalf. These works include preaching the gospel, planting churches, feeding the hungry, visiting the imprisoned, praying for the sick, giving to the poor, teaching the Bible, comforting the broken, contending for justice, and so much more.

They also include the normal, everyday stuff of life. Jesus is now ascended back into heaven, where he rules over all of creation. Even so, a theologian insightfully says, "There is not a square inch in the whole domain of our human existence over which Christ, who is Sovereign over all, does not cry: 'Mine!'"[11] Therefore, there is no such thing as "secular" and "sacred" works. Anything and everything we do in Christ, for Christ, and like Christ is a sacred work. Practically, this means that even the most menial and mundane tasks of life are infused with meaning, as in Christ they become the good works God has prepared for us. We see this in Jesus' own life: the second member of the Trinity spent many years as a carpenter as part of his life of good works.

In closing, Martin Luther provides plain sense insight about how in Christ our good works are not those merely done in the church, but also those done when we wash dishes in the kitchen, fold our laundry, rake our leaves, and change our kids' diapers.

Now observe that when that clever harlot, our natural reason (which the pagans followed in trying to be most clever), takes a look at married life, she turns up her nose and says, "Alas, must I rock the baby, wash its diapers, make its bed, smell its stench, stay up nights with it, take care of it when it cries, heal its rashes and sores, and on top of that care for my wife, provide for her, labor at my trade, take care of this and take care of that, do this and do that, endure this and endure that, and whatever else of bitterness and drudgery married life involves? What, should I make such a prisoner of myself? O you poor, wretched fellow, have you taken a wife? Fie, fie upon such wretchedness and bitterness! It is better to remain free and lead a peaceful, carefree life; I will become a priest or a nun and compel my children to do likewise."

What then does Christian faith say to this? It opens its eyes, looks upon all these insignificant, distasteful, and despised duties in the Spirit, and is aware that they are all adorned with divine approval as with the costliest gold and jewels. It says, "O God, because I am certain that Thou hast created me as a man and hast from my body begotten this child, I also know for a certainty that it meets with Thy perfect pleasure. I confess to Thee that I am not worthy to rock the little babe or wash its diapers or to be entrusted with the care of the child and its mother. How is it that I, without any merit, have come to this distinction of being certain that I am serving Thy creature and Thy most precious will? O how gladly will I do so, though the duties should be even more insignificant and despised! Neither frost nor heat, neither drudgery nor labor, will distress or dissuade me, for I am certain that it is thus pleasing in Thy sight."[12]

You are saved by Jesus to glorify God through the good works he's prepared for you. Infuse each moment of your day with the grace shown to you by Christ. There is nothing more powerful in this world than a Christian rightly understanding the grace of God and applying that grace to all facets of life. By doing so, we show Christ to our spouses, our children, our friends, our family, our coworkers—even our enemies—that many may be saved.

7

I AM RECONCILED

Therefore remember that you, once Gentiles in the flesh—who are called Uncircumcision by what is called the Circumcision made in the flesh by hands—that at that time you were without Christ, being aliens from the commonwealth of Israel and strangers from the covenants of promise, having no hope and without God in the world. But now in Christ Jesus you who once were far off have been brought near by the blood of Christ.

For He Himself is our peace, who has made both one, and has broken down the middle wall of separation, having abolished in His flesh the enmity, that is, the law of commandments contained in ordinances, so as to create in Himself one new man from the two, thus making peace, and that He might reconcile them both to God in one body through the cross, thereby putting to death the enmity. And He came and preached peace to you who were afar off and to those who were near. For through Him we both have access by one Spirit to the Father.

Now, therefore, you are no longer strangers and foreigners, but fellow citizens with the saints and members of the household of God, having been built on the foundation of the apostles and prophets, Jesus Christ Himself being the chief cornerstone, in whom the whole building, being fitted together, grows into a holy temple in the Lord, in whom you also are being built together for a dwelling place of God in the Spirit.

—EPHESIANS 2:11–22

Dr. John Perkins knows a few things about suffering. Born in 1930 on a plantation near New Hebron, Mississippi, John watched from a young age as his mother died of malnutrition and his father left him to find work fifty miles away. Growing up with his grandmother in this small,

Southern town, he witnessed the painful and sinful consequences of racism.

"Bigoted whites were systematic in maintaining control over blacks with dehumanizing rules designed to take away any sense of manhood or personal identity," shares John. "We were addressed as 'nigger' or 'boy'—elderly black men might be addressed as 'good ol' nigger.' When approaching a white man on the street, we were to step off the sidewalk into the gutter, keeping our heads lowered and eyes averted."[1]

Those in the black community who avoided being "uppity" were generally left alone, though not always. Those who defended themselves or others faced serious consequences—sometimes even death.

At age sixteen, Dr. Perkins witnessed firsthand the terrible effects of hatred and racism when his brother, Clyde, a decorated war hero, was waiting in line for the theater with some friends. Clyde and his friends were having some fun and horsing around when the sheriff, who was nearby, warned them to quiet down. When Clyde tried to talk to the sheriff, he was promptly clubbed with the sheriff's baton. When Clyde tried to grab the baton in self-defense, the sheriff stepped back and shot him two times in the stomach.

John rode with his brother to the nearest hospital—sixty miles away—watching him slowly die.

"Then sixteen-year-old John tried to rub his dying brother's head, but Clyde pushed his hand away. 'I don't know why he did that,' John says, 'but I've never forgotten it.'"

The car sped over nearly twenty miles of gravel road to reach the main highway. When they finally arrived at the hospital, Clyde was placed, unconscious, on a gurney, with a blood pressure cuff and an IV drip, then left there to die. "As John looked on helplessly at his brother's nearly lifeless body, an unfamiliar rage welled up inside him."

Knowing this rage grew inside John, along with a desire to exact a revenge that would land him on death row, or worse, John's family convinced him to move out of the state, to which he agreed, eventually moving to California.

In California, Dr. Perkins built a new life with a promising career and a beautiful wife. Yet something still didn't seem right. "Though John had achieved much in his life, he'd never given himself permission to rest. He'd never understood the concept of God's grace. His was a life fueled by anger, ambition, and the need to succeed in the white man's world."

Dr. Perkins's wife was a devout Christian; he was not. While he attended church sometimes, he never understood the grace of God through Jesus. This began to change as he saw his three-year-old son, Spencer, come home from Sunday school quoting verses. He became impressed and intrigued.

In the midst of this, a friend of John's invited him to his church, and for the first time, "something took."

"Only on that day, when he and his family stepped inside Bethlehem Church of Christ Holiness, would John finally discover the peace and unconditional love his spirit had hungered for all those years. The church embraced John and Vera Mae [his wife] immediately, taking them to their hearts.

"'For the first time in my life,' John says, 'people actually accepted me and made me feel I belonged.'"

This awakening to Jesus sparked something in John's soul, and he began studying the Bible and the great Christian leaders therein. Out of this was birthed a new calling to bring racial reconciliation through the gospel.

In 1960, leaving everything behind in California, John and his family moved back to Mississippi. They rented a small, two-room house in Mendenhall, and opened the Fisherman's Mission in a small storefront building next door.

Times were changing in Mississippi. The birth of John's ministry coincided with the rise of the civil rights movement. John and Vera Mae discovered a new unrest as blacks began to assert their identity, demanding freedom from Jim Crow laws and white supremacy.

Though his initial mission centered on Bible teaching and child evangelism, John soon realized that in order to be fully effective in his ministry, he must attend as much to people's physical and emotional needs as to their spiritual needs. He understood that if people don't have proper nutrition, Bible teaching alone will not sustain them. This was his "whole person" ministry philosophy.

Over the next few years, thanks to dedication, imagination and the ongoing contributions of white supporters back in California, John and Vera Mae's outreach expanded to include literacy classes, children's nutrition programs, job training, and a farm co-op.

These were hard times of ministry for John that culminated in a tragic event in which he was set up by white supremacists, abducted, and beat mercilessly for a full night to the point of death.

During the beatings "a strange lucidity came over him—as if he were seeing these men for the first time. An unfamiliar, unexpected emotion gripped him: pity.

"John felt pity for these men, so imprisoned by their own hate. He began to pray for them—and for his own depraved soul. As the blows continued to rain down on him, he uttered a silent prayer: *Lord, if you will let me survive this, I will devote my life to bringing the races together in love and service to You.*"[2]

To this day, John has kept that promise. Over the years, he founded the Spencer Perkins Center for Reconciliation and Youth Development in Jackson, Mississippi, "which oversees a retreat center, urban recreation facilities, low-cost housing and programs designed to minister to felt needs *and* hungry souls desperate for God's Word.

"Dr. Perkins is also chairman emeritus of the Christian Community Development Association (CCDA), headquartered in Jackson. CCDA is dedicated to improving the quality of life for those in urban areas through Dr. Perkins's philosophy of Christian community development. His '3 Rs' of relocation, reconciliation, and redistribution are considered a model for urban community."[3]

The mission of his foundation is "to develop the lives of youth, leaders and underprivileged in our community and around the world by setting an example of God's love to further his Kingdom."[4]

John's life could've been one of bitterness, hatred, and retaliatory violence. Instead, Jesus captured his heart and used him to lead on the front lines of the gospel's mission of reconciliation of all men and the world in Jesus. Now John understands deeply, perhaps more than anyone, the power of the gospel to transform lives and communities—to reconcile all men to Christ.

John is reconciled in Jesus. And so are we. John is being used by Jesus to bring his reconciliation to the world. And so should we.

SEPARATING WALLS

Growing up next to the airport, I'd often watch the airplanes come and go, rumbling overhead and shaking the windows of our house, wondering where they were going. I really wanted to see the world, experience new things, and meet new people. I often dreamt of flying on those planes going over my house as a kid, but though I lived spitting distance from the airport, I never flew on one until I was a teenager heading out of state to play in a baseball tournament. In college, I was only on a few planes. It wasn't until I started traveling some as a pastor in my late twenties that I began flying regularly.

Now, years later, God has been gracious to me, and I've seen some amazing parts of the world. In my travels I've noticed one common thread in many diverse cultures—dividing walls separating people groups who have a long and tense conflict. In South Africa, the black townships are surrounded with high walls separating them from their more affluent white neighbors. In Belfast, Northern Ireland, enormous concrete walls with chain-link fences and barbed wire atop them separate the Catholic from the Protestant quarters. But nothing compares to Israel.

In Israel, enormous walls are everywhere, with the biggest and most secure separating Abraham's children through Hagar (Arab Muslims) from Abraham's children through Sarah (Jews). As my family and I traveled to cities that are considered more Christian, like Bethlehem, we had to change drivers, vehicles, and tour guides, as our Jewish hosts were not allowed to accompany us. We then passed through gates guarded by armed soldiers and made our way through town by going around the enormous walls intended to keep out gunfire and suicide bombers. These regions have a long history of such separation.

A wall separated people in the days of Jesus and Paul as well. The Jewish historian Josephus (AD 37–ca. 100) described the dividing wall, saying that the temple was "encompassed by a stone wall for a partition, with an inscription which forbade any foreigner to go in under pain of death."[5] In another work, he wrote of this wall as "a partition made of stone all round, whose height was three cubits. Its construction was very elegant; upon it stood pillars at equal distance from one another, declaring the law of purity, some in Greek and some in Roman letters, that 'no foreigner should go within that sanctuary.'"[6]

Spiritual Separation

To this day, the world is filled with physical walls that separate people. And in the spiritual realms it's no different.

At the beginning of this book, I talked about identity idolatry and how if we idolize our tribe (e.g., our nation, race, class, generation, subcultural grouping, or people of the same gender or marital status), we invariably demonize those unlike us. This simple concept explains the "isms" of our world (nationalism, racism, classism, sexism, ageism, etc.). This also explains why most religions and spiritualities are tribal—their god is for them and against people unlike them. Their enemies have the same idolatry but a different deity.

The world changed, however, following the resurrection of Jesus Christ. Historically, God's people were the Israelite Jews, starting with Abraham, whom they looked to as the father of their faith. It was his descendants through his grandson Jacob, generally speaking, who alone worshipped the God of the Bible. Upon occasion, non-Israelites would convert, but they became both spiritually and culturally Jewish.

Though God designated the Jews as his people, he did so in order that they would be a blessing to the world, and he was clear in the generations leading up to the coming of Jesus Christ that his heartfelt intent was to save people from every nation, race, and culture. God said to Abraham in Genesis 12:3, "In you all the families of the earth shall be blessed." In

Genesis 17:4, he told him, "Behold, My covenant is with you, and you shall be a father of many nations." Not only did Moses marry an Ethiopian[7] woman,[a] he also led people out of slavery in Egypt to worship the God of the Bible, and their number included a "mixed multitude" outside of the Jews.[b] And when the Temple was opened, David's son Solomon uttered this Spirit-inspired prayer:

> When a foreigner, who is not of your people Israel, comes from a far country for your name's sake (for they shall hear of your great name and your mighty hand, and of your outstretched arm), when he comes and prays toward this house, hear in heaven your dwelling place and do according to all for which the foreigner calls to you, in order that all the peoples of the earth may know your name and fear you, as do your people Israel.... [c]

God's plan was that through the Jews would come one Jew in Jesus Christ who would reconcile people to God and one another. Jesus was Jewish while on the earth. His disciples were Jewish, as were his first converts. The early church that met in the Upper Room, as well as the first converts on the day of Pentecost early in Acts, were Jewish too. But then, Gentiles (non-Jews) started converting to Christianity in large numbers.

Questions arose concerning whether Gentiles could just be Christians who followed Jesus or if they had to also culturally convert to Judaism and start circumcising their men, changing their diet, observing new holidays, and so forth. Nearly all of the New Testament letters speak to these issues either directly or indirectly, with some, such as Galatians, focused nearly entirely on it.

By the time Paul wrote Ephesians, many of these debates were theologically settled, but practically there was still a lack of racial and cultural unity in the church between Jews and Gentiles. Two thousand years later, the problem persists among various groups.

---

a. Num. 12:1.
b. Ex. 12:38; Num. 11:4.
c. 1 Kings 8:41–43 (ESV).

Rather than addressing the issue of racial and cultural reconciliation in a gospel-centered way, as Paul did in Ephesians, some Christian leaders have instead promoted the "homogeneous unit" principle, which states that since people like being with their own kind (nation, culture, subculture, race, class, generation/age), we should have churches for various kinds of people and not expect Christians to interact much with those different from them. This only perpetuates identity idolatry. Even worse, many churches are so deep in their identity idolatry that they're homogeneous not by intention but by lack of intention. They simply don't think of racial and cultural reconciliation.

THE PROMISE OF RECONCILIATION

The separation between Jew and Gentile in the early church is not merely some antiquated problem. The names may have changed (black and white, rich and poor, single and married, suburban and rural, young and old, etc.), but the problem of separation still persists. Sometimes it's the result of unexamined preferences. Other times it's the result of deeper cultural prejudices. We all have them. Those who have been the outsiders and mistreated see this more clearly than those of us who have been in the majority or the ones with power. The result is a "wall" of separation and division between people.

But one day the local church as we know it will be replaced by the kingdom of God. The picture of worship in that eternal future is incredibly and gloriously diverse, according to Revelation 7:9–10: "After these things I looked, and behold, a great multitude which no one could number, of all nations, tribes, peoples, and tongues, standing before the throne and before the Lamb, clothed with white robes, with palm branches in their hands, and crying out with a loud voice, saying, 'Salvation belongs to our God who sits on the throne, and to the Lamb!'"

Since all of God's people, regardless of their differences and preferences, will be together forever in his kingdom, the gospel of Jesus Christ and our witness to the world as his church require reconciliation in this life.

Paul's timeless words on reconciliation in Ephesians 2:11–22 are as timely as ever. As one Bible commentator says, "This paragraph provides one of the most wonderful descriptions of peace and reconciliation . . . where believers 'come near' to God and to one another (Gentiles and Jews) through the saving death of the Lord Jesus Christ."[8] In Christ, all things are reconciled to each other and to God. As the church of Christ, we must exhibit this gospel-centered reconciliation in our lives both corporately and individually.

All of the talk about diversity and racial and cultural reconciliation in our day is in fact quite old. A few thousand years ago, Paul explained how Jesus is the answer for human divisions. Once reconciled to God, we can then understand living reconciled lives with other people.

Jew and Gentile Are Reconciled in Christ

Anytime there is an extended conflict between groups of people, you can be sure there's a complicated history that must be understood for the sake of context. Without that understanding, the entire conflict can be easily misunderstood, misdiagnosed, and mistreated. This was true in Paul's day between Jews and Gentiles. Their rift could be traced all the way back to Abraham, in the first few dozen pages of the Bible.

God told Abraham—formerly Abram—to leave his homeland to journey to a new land that God would show him, promising him that though Abraham's wife was barren, he would be a father. He was promised to be a great nation, blessed by God to be a blessing to the nations of the earth through one of his offspring or seed. This promised "seed" is singular, meaning Jesus, and not the plural seeds that would become Israel.[d] Galatians 3:16 connects the promise of Abram's "seed" with Jesus Christ: "Now to Abraham and his Seed were the promises made. He does not say, 'And to seeds,' as of many, but as of one, 'And to your Seed,' who is Christ."

In this way, God promised that the nation of Israel would come through Abraham, and like Mary, be the "womb" through which Jesus

---

d. Gen. 13:15; Matt. 1:17.

would come as a blessing to all nations. This fact is significant, and its implications are found in Galatians 3:8–9: "And the Scripture, foreseeing that God would justify the Gentiles by faith, preached the gospel to Abraham beforehand, saying, 'In you all the nations shall be blessed.' So then those who are of faith are blessed with believing Abraham."

In faith, Abram believed and obeyed God, doing as God commanded at the age of seventy-five, along with his wife, Sarai. Genesis 15, one of the Bible's most important chapters, focuses on God's covenant with and through Abraham. In this chapter the vital themes of grace, faith, and covenant appear. There, God poetically promises to be Abram's protector and provider, and that though Abram was childless and his wife was barren, they would have a son, and that through that son a nation of people would be born. Genesis 15:6, among the most significant verses in the Bible, reports Abram's response to God's Word: "And he believed in the LORD, and He accounted it to him for righteousness."

This verse is central to the New Testament doctrine of faith in general, and Paul's doctrine of justification by faith alone in particular.[e] Additionally, Jesus' brother James quoted Genesis 15:6 to teach that true faith in God results in a life of good works.[f]

God's covenant with Abram was confirmed with a sacrifice and the shedding of blood. This act foreshadowed the new covenant of our salvation, which was confirmed with Jesus' sacrifice of his own life on the cross and the shedding of his blood.

In studying Abraham's story, we find a man who is inherently relatable to us. Though he is one of the most significant characters in the Bible, he is also a royal screwup. Following God's momentous covenant with Abram in Genesis 15, Abraham's faith faltered and, rather than trust God, he took matters into his own hands and slept with Sarah's servant, Hagar, resulting in the birth of Ishmael in Genesis 16. But as is always the case, when we fall short of our covenant promises to God, he is faithful to us. God renewed his covenant with Abraham through the sign of circumcision.

e. Rom. 4:3; Gal. 3:6.
f. James 2:23–24.

When Abram was ninety-nine, God changed Abram's name to Abraham, meaning "father of a multitude," and commanded him and his men to be circumcised as a covenant sign. Circumcision was performed either with a sharp knife or a stone, and was very painful for adult males. Yet Abraham immediately obeyed God, as Genesis makes clear with the phrase "that very same day."[g] Ever since this occasion, Jews have circumcised their sons on the eighth day, as that was the day chosen for their father Isaac.[h] "In ancient Jewish beliefs, non-Jews could never participate in the fullness of the covenant without circumcision, although they could be saved by keeping some basic commandments. To be circumcised was to be grafted into the community of Israel, to become part of God's covenant people."[9]

This history explains what Paul meant when he said that the Jews referred to themselves as "the Circumcision" and used the derogatory slang term "Uncircumcision" to refer to the Gentiles. In our day, the slurs may have changed, but the underlying issue has not. We humans have always been creative in inventing language to tear down others and exalt ourselves.

The truth is that we all come from a line of godless pagans if we trace our history back far enough. Any progress we've made is solely by the grace of God and should cause us to be humble and compassionate toward others rather than haughty and condemning.

Paul reminded the Jews of this. When Abram was called by God to become the father of a new nation, the prototype of a life of faith, and one of the most important men in the history of the world, he was just another sinner living among the scattered pagan nations.[i] Since Nehemiah 9:7 and Acts 7:2–3 seem to indicate that God in fact called Abram while he was still living in Ur of the Chaldeans, a place the Chaldeans would name "Babylon" centuries later, Abram may have been an ancestor of the godless Babylonians whom God judged.[j] Amazingly, he found gracious favor in the eyes of the Lord.

---

g. Gen. 17:26.
h. Gen. 17:12.
i. Gen. 12:1–4.
j. E.g., Isa. 13:19; 48:14; Jer. 24:5; 25:12; 50:1; Ezek. 1:3; 12:13; 23:15.

My Irish ancestors were pirates whose most legendary acts revolved around seizing ships transporting wine. Apparently everything beyond thievery, piracy, and lunacy in my life is the result of the grace of God. So I, as one example, have only Christ to boast in. How about you? What does your family history look like if you trace it back far enough? How has Jesus been gracious to redeem your past and give hope for your future? In Christ, we're all made part of his holy family, regardless of our backgrounds.

You and God Are Reconciled in Christ

Paul taught that the non-Christians' identity is "Gentiles in the flesh," or "Uncircumcision," "without Christ," "aliens from the commonwealth of Israel and strangers from the covenants of promise, having no hope and without God in the world," "far off," living in "separation" with "enmity," because they are "strangers and foreigners."[k] That is as bleak, dark, and grim an identity as one could possibly have.

Conversely, now consider Paul's words describing your identity in Christ as a Christian: "brought near by the blood of Christ," "peace," "new man," "reconcile[d]," "access by one Spirit to the Father," "fellow citizens with the saints and members of the household of God," "holy temple in the Lord," and "a dwelling place for God by the Spirit."[l] If you truly, deeply, and continually believe even a fraction of what the Spirit is saying through Paul, you'll never see yourself the same way again. Neither will you doubt God's love for you after comparing who you were apart from Christ with who you are in Christ. Apart from Christ you are farther from God than you feared. In Christ you are nearer to God than you hoped. Through faith in the truth about who God is and who he's made you to be, you're reconciled to God in Christ.

You and Others Are Reconciled in Christ

Through Christ we're reconciled to God, and we're also reconciled to one another. When there are two cultures of people in conflict (e.g., Jew

---

k. Eph. 2:11–19 (ESV).
l. Eph. 2:11–22 (ESV).

and Gentile, black and white, rich and poor, young and old), the battle rages over which group will win and which will lose. Yet the Scriptures completely alter how we deal with diversity.

Paul wrote that "in Christ" there is a "new man." This "new man" refers to an entirely new group of people with a new identity who make up a cultural grouping among people from every culture. Various Bible teachers refer to this group as a third race, new humanity, and new race. This new group is Christians, making up the church of Jesus Christ.

Practically, this means that when we become Christian, we may retain our cultural affinity, but it's no longer our primary identity. Rather, our primary identity as Christians is in Christ. In him, no matter what our history, culture, and position in life, we're closer to one another than we are to those of our same history, culture, and position. In Christ, an old, suburban, Jewish, Christian woman is closer to a young, urban, black man than she is to her unbelieving, Jewish father because the woman and the young man are in fact part of the "new man."

This changes how we should relate to one another as the people of God, both on an individual and a collective level. So as not to miss the magnitude of our identity in Christ and how it supersedes our idolatry of tribe, consider this:

> The Jew had an immense contempt for the Gentile. The Gentiles, said the Jews, were created by God to be fuel for the fires of hell. God, they said, loves only Israel of all the nations that he had made . . . It was not even lawful to render help to a Gentile mother in her hour of sorest need, for that would simply be to bring another Gentile into the world. Until Christ came, the Gentiles were an object of contempt to the Jews. The barrier between them was absolute. If a Jewish boy married a Gentile girl, or if a Jewish girl married a Gentile boy, the funeral of that Jewish boy or girl was carried out. Such contact with a Gentile was the equivalent of death.[10]

In Christ, such thinking is nailed to the cross, thereby ushering in an entirely new social structure modeled by the church because of the reconciling power of Jesus Christ.

The timing of Paul's words is particularly insightful. "Around the time Paul was writing these words, arguing for racial unity in Christ, Jews and Syrians were massacring each other in the streets of Caesarea, a city where he had been not long before (Acts 23:23). Here, Paul does not simply mimic a common stand against racism in his culture; he condemns racism and segregation of a religious institution even though he has to challenge his culture to do so."[11]

Paul had himself idolized his heritage, culture, and race to the degree that he idolized his people and demonized other people, even murdering at least one man who disagreed with him.[m] Yet despite his prejudiced past, after becoming part of the third race in Christ, Paul suffered imprisonment for being falsely charged with taking a non-Jew inside the temple of Jerusalem, "an important breach of Jewish law that the Romans even permitted Jewish leaders to execute violators of this law. Paul's readers in Ephesus and Asia undoubtedly know why Paul is in prison (Acts 21:27, 29); thus for them, as well as for Paul, there can be no greater symbol of the barrier between Jew and non-Jew than 'the dividing wall' of verse 14. But Paul says that this dividing wall is shattered in Christ."[12]

Paul's letter to Ephesus is somewhat similar to Martin Luther King Jr.'s "Letter from a Birmingham Jail," written during the civil rights movement of the early 1960s. While King's work is not sacred Scripture, it's interesting that both men wrote their letters while imprisoned for being ministry leaders connected to the cause of reconciliation. Paul proclaimed the reality of the unity of Jew and Gentile in the person and work of Jesus Christ, and Martin Luther King Jr. pleaded with the white church in America to recognize the brotherhood of African-Americans. He stated, "In the midst of a mighty struggle to rid our nation of racial and economic injustice, I have heard many ministers say: 'Those are social issues, with which the gospel has no real concern.' And I have watched many churches commit themselves to a completely other worldly religion which makes a strange, un-Biblical distinction between body and soul,

---

m. Acts 7:1–8:1.

between the sacred and the secular."[13] Both Paul and Martin fought for racial reconciliation in Christ, and both men died fighting that battle in faith.

A Christian friend and I had an interesting conversation about the practical and social implications of this idea of a third race called Christian. His non-Christian, white father is deeply racist, and upon hearing that his Christian son was going to adopt a black child, he essentially disowned my friend and refused to even meet the child. My friend's father felt betrayed by his son, couldn't understand his desire to adopt and raise a black child, and basically told his son to remain true to his race and heritage. Despite his natural father's rejection, my friend adopted the black child. Why? He is in Christ, and he no longer considers his identity to be determined by such things as skin color or even his natural family ties. He is part of a new people group called the church, where blacks and whites are closer by the blood of Christ and their new birth spiritually than blood family of physical birth. In Christ, we receive a new Father, a new family, and a new identity as part of a new people group comprised of staggering diversity held together by the unity of being in Christ.

Our cultural differences may distinguish us, but they do not define us and should not divide God's people or allow them to accept the social structures and idols that wrongly divide people. In Christ, while we have great diversity, we ought to live in even greater unity because how we do life is far less important than how Jesus has reconciled us to God and one another. I encourage you to each and every day pray and contend for the unity that you have and that is found in Christ Jesus.

8

I AM AFFLICTED

For this reason I, Paul, the prisoner of Christ Jesus for you Gentiles—if indeed you have heard of the dispensation of the grace of God which was given to me for you, how that by revelation He made known to me the mystery (as I have briefly written already, by which, when you read, you may understand my knowledge in the mystery of Christ), which in other ages was not made known to the sons of men, as it has now been revealed by the Spirit to His holy apostles and prophets: that the Gentiles should be fellow heirs, of the same body, and partakers of His promise in Christ through the gospel, of which I became a minister according to the gift of the grace of God given to me by the effective working of His power.

To me, who am less than the least of all the saints, this grace was given, that I should preach among the Gentiles the unsearchable riches of Christ, and to make all see what is the fellowship of the mystery, which from the beginning of the ages has been hidden in God who created all things through Jesus Christ; to the intent that now the manifold wisdom of God might be made known by the church to the principalities and powers in the heavenly places, according to the eternal purpose which He accomplished in Christ Jesus our Lord, in whom we have boldness and access with confidence through faith in Him. Therefore I ask that you do not lose heart at my tribulations for you, which is your glory.

—EPHESIANS 3:1–13

Maaz comes from a long and important line of Muslims. His family moved to Palestine around AD 700, and in the 1100s, King Saladin gifted the only house on the compound of the Dome of the Rock to his distant grandfather. His ancestors continued to serve as muftis and imams of Jerusalem until his grandfather broke the legacy, starting the first local travel agency in Israel. Maaz's father married an American and moved to the United States, where Maaz was born.

Though living in America, Maaz's family remained Muslim. But as Maaz was exposed to Christianity, the Holy Spirit began to work in his life. "I was born here in the States, where the idea of converting religiously is common and okay culturally, though it was not for my family," he says. "Jesus saved me after showing me the true depravity of the world, which is quite evident in American culture."

Converting to Christianity had strong and painful implications for Maaz, having come from a deeply connected and powerful Islamic family. "I knew that converting would get me in a good amount of trouble with the family," says Maaz, "but I also knew that I would be in worse trouble if I didn't. God quickly taught me how to depend on him and act out of a love for him.

"My dad disowned me and did not communicate with me for a while. But the Spirit pushed me to seek after my dad and show him the love that Allah or any Muslim had never shown him."

Today, while Maaz's father isn't a Christian, there has been some reconciliation. His father no longer holds to Muslim religious beliefs and is talking with Maaz again. In the process, God has used Maaz's suffering to grow him for the good of others: "The Holy Spirit also has shown me how to evangelize to Muslims and be bold for the mission and glory of God. I've learned that there really aren't intimidating people—only lost people."

YOU WILL SUFFER

If we're in Christ, we should expect to suffer like Christ and for Christ. We worship a God who came to the earth and was afflicted. And throughout the Scriptures and the history of the church, those who have served him most faithfully have been afflicted most painfully. Among the most legendary is Paul.

Before his new identity in Christ, Paul harassed Christians, such as the early church deacon Stephen, whose murder he oversaw.[a] Once born again in Christ, Paul went from afflicting Christians to being afflicted as a Christian, even writing some of his New Testament letters, such as Ephesians, while in prison.

Paul knew what it was like to be afflicted, and he knew what it was like to watch the affliction of others whom he loved. Subsequently, he had a clarity and credibility regarding suffering that was battle-tested and tearstained. His words are perception-altering and life-giving for those who are afflicted.

Oftentimes we're so consumed with our own feelings about our suffering that we fail to think deeply about it as the Bible does, which has much to say about and model on affliction. For instance, laments or groaning amid difficulties accounts for roughly a third of the prayers and songs that comprise the book of Psalms. The entire book of Lamentations is a painfully honest journaling in the midst of affliction. And every Old Testament prophetic book but Haggai includes a lament on affliction.

Without a fully biblical understanding of affliction, we wrongly diagnose the troubles we (and others) face, and in so doing misdiagnose both the cause and the cure of affliction. This inevitably occurs when we take only some of what Scripture says on an issue and then wrongly apply it to all situations. Perhaps the most legendary example of this is when Job's friends only understood his suffering as God's punishment for his sin. Thus, rather than comforting him, they rebuked him unjustly.

Affliction in the Scriptures, like our own affliction, isn't neat, tidy, or systematic. Life is often more complex than clear. While there is no way to answer all the questions for those who are afflicted, I thought it might be helpful to pull back and look at fourteen kinds of affliction seen throughout the Scriptures.

Fourteen Kinds of Affliction in Scripture

1. Adamic Affliction: When Adam sinned, all of us were implicated,

---

a. Acts 7.

and we inherited a sin nature[b] and were born into a fallen world.[c] As a result, some affliction is simply the result of being part of Adam's race. Everyone will suffer to varying degrees and ways because of Adam's sin, our sin, the sins of others, and the curse that permeates all of creation. This will remain the case until Jesus returns, removes the presence of all sin and its effects, resurrects Christians from death, and ushers in a new creation. Subsequently, we must accept that suffering is part of life on this side of the kingdom.

2. Punishment Affliction: God judges unbelievers and punishes them for sin. Biblical examples include God's judgment on Sodom and Gomorrah and on Pharaoh and Egypt. This kind of punishment reveals God's justice. It brings the work of horrendous sin to an end so that those suffering at the hands of evildoers are given reprieve, reveals to unbelievers the urgent need to repent of sin and place their faith in God to avoid eternal punishment, and encourages believers that God will not be mocked and that faith in him is not in vain. It should be noted that God does not punish those in Christ in the same sense that he punishes non-Christians, because Jesus already paid the penalty for his people's sins. Therefore, God would be unjust to also condemn Christians to death. Subsequently, even though a Christian and a non-Christian may endure the same suffering, there is a different use by God for each.

3. Consequential Affliction: Sometimes we suffer because of foolish decisions. We see examples of this throughout Proverbs: the lazy become hungry, adulterers reap what they sow, fools suffer harm, and poor financial stewards are impoverished. Practically, much of life's suffering is consequential, resulting from our decisions.

4. Demonic Affliction: Because Satan is alive and at work in the world, demonic affliction is very real. This includes torment,[d]

b. Rom. 5:12–21.
c. Rom. 8:18–23.
d. Acts 5:16.

physical injury,[e] deception arising from false miracles,[f] accusation,[g] and even death.[h] Sometimes demonic suffering can be difficult to discern; unfortunately, Satan is too often blamed for suffering when we're really experiencing consequential affliction from our own decisions. Nonetheless, demonic affliction is real for some and therefore should not be discounted just because some people wrongly blame shift everything to Satan.

5. Victim Affliction: Victims endure affliction by being sinned against. This is a constant and heavy part of pastoral ministry. Since I started Mars Hill Church in the fall of 1996, I can't recall a week in which I haven't heard a devastating story about someone who was beaten, raped, molested, stolen from, cheated on, and the like. A recent example is a woman who lost her virginity at the hands of her father, who raped her. All I could do was weep as she told me of the violence she endured. Those who aren't on the front lines of ministry can't imagine the amount of pain people carry as a result of sin committed against them. Evil is real, and its devastating effects are evident in the lives of many.

6. Collective Affliction: Sometimes we suffer as a result of being part of a people who are suffering. A biblical example is the Old Testament prophets' frequent repentance of not only their own sins but also the sins of their forefathers and their nation as they lamented the suffering God had permitted to come upon them for chastisement. We're not isolated, autonomous individuals. We're members of families, nations, and cultures—all of whom suffer. Subsequently, we can suffer simply because of family ties or our nationality. Likewise, those born into poverty, famine, hardship, war, and the like experience suffering simply because of where and when they were born.

7. Disciplinary Affliction: God chastens believers in order to mature

---

e. Acts 8:4–8.
f. 2 Thess. 2:9–10.
g. Rev. 12:10.
h. John 8:44.

them. Examples can be found in such places as the Wisdom Literature,[i] the Prophets,[j] and the New Testament.[k] The Scriptures are clear that discipline comes from God, who loves us and is like an honorable father who corrects us to mature and save us from the harm that sin causes. While this kind of suffering is not pleasant at the time, we later see the effects of God's work and thank him for continually working for our growth in holiness and fruitfulness.

8. Vicarious Affliction: Sometimes those in Christ suffer because the ungodly oppose them. Examples include the Old Testament prophets and the New Testament apostles. Vicarious affliction comes in varying degrees, from opposition to persecution. Physical persecution causes some to painfully die for Christ, whereas those who experience verbal opposition painfully live for Christ, as they are maligned, lied about, falsely accused, mocked, and harassed. Such was the case for Maaz, whose story I shared at the beginning of the chapter. He was born into a culture hostile to the gospel and suffered by virtue of his devotion to Jesus in a family that opposed him and disowned him.

9. Empathetic Affliction: This is the suffering that comes when someone we love is hurting. The Bible says this will be common in the church because when people we love suffer, we suffer as well.[l]

10. Testimonial Affliction: Some suffering is a demonstration of the gospel so that others will have a deeper appreciation and understanding of Jesus. This kind of suffering tests our identity in Christ, confirms to us that we are true believers, strengthens our fellow Christians, and evangelizes non-Christians. The classic example is Hosea's marriage to Gomer. God called the prophet to marry and stay married to an unfaithful woman as an example of Jesus' devotion to the church.

11. Providential Affliction: Some of us suffer to teach a lesson about

---

i. Prov. 3:11; 13:24; 15:5.
j. Zeph. 3:7.
k. Heb. 12:7.
l. Rom. 12:15; 2 Cor. 2:4.

God so that worship of him increases. Examples include Joseph's imprisonment in Egypt, where his suffering resulted in many people being saved physically from starvation and spiritually from sin. The truth is that God can have more purposes for allowing some suffering than can be easily discerned at first glance.

12. Preventative Affliction: Sometimes suffering warns us of greater suffering that will happen if we don't heed God's warnings. This kind of suffering is indicative of the very loving nature of God, who, for instance, allows us to experience lesser degrees of pain (e.g., an ache in our side) in order to warn us of greater degrees of pain (e.g., a burst appendix).

13. Mysterious Affliction: Sometimes God, in his providence, has chosen not to reveal why we suffer. As Scripture says, we know in part.[m] Job is the most obvious example of this kind of suffering, because during his trouble he was unaware of what was occurring between God and Satan. I believe that this category is incredibly important because, if we are humble and honest, the truth is that life is often not as clear as the categories listed above.

14. Apocalyptic Affliction: The Bible speaks of increased suffering that will signal the end of this age, as seen in the prophecies of the Old Testament[n] and of Jesus.[o] While we don't know when the end of this age will be or when Jesus will return, we do know that Christians living in the final chapter of human history will suffer greatly as a result of being in Christ. While we shouldn't live in fear of this future, nor seek to predict its timing, these scriptures will serve as a particularly helpful guide when they are needed most.

How about you? How have you experienced affliction in your life? Based on the categories I've just presented, what do you believe is the cause of your suffering, and what could God be teaching you through it? How are people you know experiencing affliction, and in what ways

m. 1 Cor. 13:9.
n. Isa. 24–27; Jer. 30–33; Ezek. 33–48; Dan. 2–12; Zech. 12–14.
o. Matt. 24:3–44; Mark 13.

could you comfort and counsel them? In what ways have you wrongly understood your difficulties and misunderstood God in the midst of your suffering?

EXCHANGING "WHY" FOR "WHO"

All too often, when we suffer, we question whether God is sovereign or good. Some of us are prone to believing the sovereignty of God while diminishing his goodness. The result is a cold, distant God who can't be our comforter. Others of us lean toward downplaying God's sovereignty while retaining his goodness. The result is a false view of a God who doesn't want suffering to occur but is powerless to stop it. Sadly, when either the sovereignty or goodness of God is questioned, we're left without comfort or help because our pain distorts our perspective of God.

The Bible repeatedly reveals that God is both sovereign and good. For those in Christ, this means that everything in life, including our suffering, either comes from or passes through his hand. Further, God uses suffering for our good, even if it was intended for evil. Theologically, this is what Paul meant when he stated in Romans 8:28 that "all things work together for good to those who love God." And this is precisely what Joseph said in Genesis 50:20 to his brothers who sought to destroy him: "You meant evil against me; but God meant it for good."

The Bible does not promise that we will immediately see God work all affliction for his glory and our good—or even see it in this life—but for those in Christ, it's guaranteed that whether in this life or the life to come, the promise of God will come to pass.

Until that day, it's often difficult for us to believe in God's goodness and sovereignty when we suffer. We're prone to ask God *why*, which is dangerous because it puts us in a judge's chair and puts God on trial. Admittedly, sometimes this is simply an emotional response from a hurting person and even has biblical precedent. In such cases, we want to help those who are suffering, not condemn them. But as in Scripture, it's important for us when suffering to move from asking *why* to asking *who*.

The "who" question does not seek answers from God as much as it seeks God himself. The one who asks *who* seeks to grow in deeper understanding of who God is and who we are, because when we're suffering, what we need more than answers—even helpful, biblical ones—is God and an assurance of our identity in Christ. This is why the Psalmist, even when asking *why* concerning his suffering, moves to affirming *who* by exclaiming what he knows of God: "I will speak of Your testimonies also before kings, and will not be ashamed. And I will delight myself in Your commandments, which I love. My hands also I will lift up to Your commandments, which I love, and I will meditate on Your statutes. Remember the word to Your servant, upon which You have caused me to hope. This is my comfort in my affliction, for Your word has given me life."[p]

DON'T LOSE HEART

Christians often get discouraged because of affliction, and we feel guilty and unsure what to do about it. After all, we know that God is good, loves us, and gives us grace. But sometimes Christianity can seem as if it's not "working" because we are suffering.

While life in Christ doesn't prevent us from facing affliction, it does empower us to endure whatever we may face by God's grace and for his glory and our good. One example of such endurance is found in Ephesians 3:1–13. From this passage of scripture, we learn about not only Paul's conviction but also his compassion.

The Christians scattered in churches in and around the city of Ephesus were in a season of discouragement. They experienced collective, vicarious, empathetic, testimonial, demonic, and providential affliction. Their pastor, Paul—who planted the first church in their region, labored for years to train other leaders in their church, and loved them well—was imprisoned far away in Rome and experiencing at the least Adamic, demonic, victim, collective, vicarious, testimonial, and providential affliction. Sitting imprisoned alone, likely cold, and hungry in what was

---

p. Ps. 119:46–50.

perhaps a literal hole in the ground turned into a cell, their pastor could have easily been discouraged as well. He was not suffering merely as a Christian but for being a Christian, calling himself "a prisoner for Christ Jesus" (v. 1 ESV).

Paul suffered because of his love for Jesus. As a result, he couldn't enjoy the companionship of fellow Christians back home. The example for Christian discouragement in Ephesians 3 comes from the pen of a man perhaps lying on a cold floor in the dark with an aching body from repeated beating, truthfully speaking of his "tribulations" while exhorting his brothers and sisters in Ephesus to "not lose heart" (v. 13) during theirs.

How can we, like Paul, suffer affliction without losing affection? What is the secret to avoiding discouragement, bitterness, unbelief, anger, sullenness, indifference, or rebellion? How do we as victims of gossip, abuse, assault, betrayal, mockery, abandonment, theft, slander, adultery, and the like "not lose heart" while suffering?

Paul didn't give us pithy steps to victory. He didn't put on the tough-guy act, saying we need to simply toughen up, move on, and stop being babies. He didn't assume the hyper-spiritual stance, quoting lots of Bible verses promising nothing but blessing and protection for those who love God. He didn't give us the ever-smiling optimist routine, glibly promising that God must have something better for us. He didn't dish out the bony-fingered "Repent!" treatment, assuming that suffering is the direct result of our sin, which we need to uncover and repent of if we hope to stop suffering. He didn't give us the guilt routine, reminding us that someone, somewhere has it far worse. And he didn't do the Eastern religion thing, saying suffering is simply an illusion.

Instead, Paul modeled deep thinking about suffering while himself deeply suffering. He opened Ephesians with reflections on suffering, introducing himself as, "Paul, a prisoner for Christ Jesus" (v. 1 ESV) and closed chapter 1 by saying, "Therefore I ask that you do not lose heart at my tribulations for you, which is your glory."

Because afflictions cost us so much, they are too precious to waste. Though God may not cause your affliction, he can use your affliction for his glory, others' good, and your growth, if you are in Christ. Only by trying less to dissect and avoid our sufferings and instead embracing them as opportunities in Christ to grow, glorify God, and share the gospel will we begin to "not lose heart," and instead find joy in our circumstances, whatever they may be.

Afflicted for God's Glory

Paul wasn't afflicted because he sinned, but rather because others sinned against him. The Roman Emperor Nero held Paul in prison, but ultimately Paul knew that Jesus Christ the King of kings reigned above Nero. And as he suffered, Paul's thoughts weren't consumed with himself but rather his Suffering Savior. That is why he spoke of being "the prisoner of Christ Jesus." This is key.

As we suffer, we must think deeply about Jesus' suffering so we don't waste our suffering, but rather use it for God's glory. Our God didn't suffer so that we wouldn't suffer. He suffered so that when we do suffer, we can become more like him and point more people to him.

One example is my friend, Pastor Matt Chandler, who is the president of the Acts 29 church-planting network. Young and healthy, with a beautiful family and a fast-growing church, he blacked out, hitting his head on his fireplace mantel, and awoke in a hospital to hear he had a brain tumor. Despite his affliction, he has continued to preach the gospel and love his family with full devotion. When a reporter from a major media outlet called to interview me regarding a story about Matt, I asked him what he learned being around the Chandler family. The man was not a believer, but he reported that he was very impressed with their faith in God, humility, love for people, and authenticity. Why? Because Matt didn't waste his affliction.

Becoming like Jesus in suffering requires first reflecting on Jesus' own suffering. After eating the Last Supper, Jesus was so distressed about his impending crucifixion that, while his friends fell asleep and failed him, he remained awake late into the night, sweating drops of blood in stress-filled prayer in the Garden of Gethsemane.

He was betrayed by one of his closest friends, Judas. He was arrested on trumped-up charges and brought forth by false witnesses. A mob of angry men beat him severely, and he was stripped in shame and whipped. The soldiers used a *flagrum*, a torture tool with a handle from which proceeded strips of leather with weights affixed to the ends, in order to tenderize Jesus' back, legs, and buttocks. Its hooks sank deeply into his flesh, ripping off skin, muscles, tendons, and bones.

Jesus' body shook violently from the trauma. His blood loss was severe. His tormentors then pressed a crown of thorns into his brow in mockery. On his back they dropped a heavy, rough-hewn crossbar, which he was forced to carry through a mocking crowd to his place of cruci-fixion. Jesus fell under the weight of the cross, crushing his chest on the pavement under the perhaps one hundred pounds of weight, possibly puncturing his heart sac.

After getting help carrying his cross, Jesus arrived at Golgotha, where the soldiers and crowd disrespectfully pulled out his beard, spat on him, and mocked him in front of his family and friends. The equivalent of railroad spikes were nailed through his hands and feet, containing the most sensitive nerve centers in the human body. As he was lifted up, the mob cursed him as his body convulsed, blood and sweat dripping off him. Soon after, Jesus gave up his spirit and died. To ensure his death, a soldier ran a spear through his side, puncturing his heart, and blood and water poured from his side.

Jesus suffered greatly for our sins. He was afflicted both by us and for us. Our sin killed God, but his death brought us life. His affliction was for our salvation. But beyond that, the primary purpose of his suffering was to glorify God the Father by at once perfectly revealing true justice and mercy. If you're in Christ, you can endure affliction as he did, to the glory of God.

Afflicted for Others' Good

When Paul faced persecution, rather than asking, "Why?" he asked, "Who?"—namely, "Who am I in Christ?" In doing so, what would oth-erwise be misery became ministry. Paul explained that his ministry was about proclaiming a mystery—"that the Gentiles are fellow heirs, members of the same body, and partakers of the promise in Christ Jesus through the gospel."q

For those who haven't heard the gospel, Jesus remains a "mystery." Paul's life—and ours—existed for the purpose of letting others know that the one Savior has opened the one path to salvation for everyone in every nation. Therefore, even though he suffered for his devotion to Christ, Paul wasn't discouraged but rather encouraged because the gospel was proclaimed. We, too, may face affliction as we preach that same good news, just as Maaz suffered at the hands of his Muslim family. This makes our suffering meaningful, purposeful, and valuable, because Jesus invites us to participate in his good work to see lives changed and healed by the power of the gospel.

In affliction, we become discouraged when we can't have what we consider most dear. Paul's affliction was both evil and painful, but he was not disheartened or disappointed, because he didn't lose what he counted most dear—friendship with Jesus.

Afflicted for Your Growth

When we suffer, we have a divine appointment to learn three things about affliction that help us grow as Christians.

First, we gain a deeper understanding of how humble and gracious God is to serve us as our Suffering Servant, Jesus Christ. God came not in glory but in humility to serve, not to be served. That truth should astonish us every time we ponder it. And that God sends us the Holy Spirit as our "Helper" is staggering.

Second, we learn to better love and appreciate those who serve us. We discover how deep some people's love for us truly is when we are hurting, needy, and inconvenient. Those who reflect the character of Jesus to us most clearly become the greatest gifts in seasons of suffering.

Third, as Jesus and others serve us, we learn new ways to serve those who suffer. We can easily become consumed with our own lives and callous to the needs of others. But through affliction God teaches us to

q. Eph. 3:6.

open our hearts, eyes, and finances to meet the needs of others who are afflicted.

Afflicted for Credibility

When we're afflicted, we have a unique credibility to speak about difficult subjects in a way that helps bring healing and life to others facing the same afflictions. For instance, a dear friend of ours was repeatedly raped growing up, and now speaks to rape victims about the healing and hope in Jesus Christ. Though her experiences were tragic, an authentic credibility with those she counsels could not likely be had any other way.

Perhaps the most perplexing verse about Jesus in all of Scripture, Hebrews 2:10, says that Jesus was "perfect through sufferings." This doesn't mean that Jesus was sinful before his sufferings, but rather that his sufferings allowed him to fully identify and sympathize with ours. Furthermore, through his suffering, he obtained our salvation, and one day he'll return to put an end to all sin and suffering.[r] Until then, through our sufferings, we're gifted a divine appointment to become more like Jesus. We become more captivated by love toward him, whom we caused to suffer, more compassionate for those who suffer, and more committed to justice and alleviating the injustices others face.

How about you? How has suffering made you more like Jesus? How have others noticed a change in you through your trials? How has God used your distress for your growth and others' good?

For those who are afflicted and in Christ, Jesus is a God to whom you can speak personally. You can run to him and walk with him. Jesus Christ didn't sit back in his heavenly ease and from a safe distance give us mere counsel for our suffering. Instead, he entered into human history to identify with us. He was tempted. He wept. He was poor and home-less. His family rejected him. His friends abandoned him. His disciples betrayed him. His enemies falsely accused him. The government unfairly tried and condemned him. The soldiers mercilessly beat him beyond

---

r. Rev. 21.

recognition. He bled, suffered, and died in shame. And he did it all for God's glory and your good.

Jesus is our sympathetic High Priest, who gives grace to the hurting and promises justice to the unrepentant. He is preparing a place for us, and he's given us God the Spirit as our Comforter until he returns, so we can live out of our identity in Christ.

One day, we will see Christ face to face. Our faith will be sight. His nail-scarred hands will wipe our tears away. *One day,* all who are in Christ will sing his praises and see his glory together forever. *One day,* he will work out all things for the good of those who love him. *One day,* all our questions will be answered, our hopes will be realized, and our fears will be forgotten. Until that day, we will be afflicted, but our identity in Christ need not be affected.

9

I AM HEARD

For this reason I bow my knees to the Father of our Lord Jesus Christ, from whom the whole family in heaven and earth is named, that He would grant you, according to the riches of His glory, to be strengthened with might through His Spirit in the inner man, that Christ may dwell in your hearts through faith; that you, being rooted and grounded in love, may be able to comprehend with all the saints what is the width and length and depth and height—to know the love of Christ which passes knowledge; that you may be filled with all the fullness of God.

Now to Him who is able to do exceedingly abundantly above all that we ask or think, according to the power that works in us, to Him be glory in the church by Christ Jesus to all generations, forever and ever. Amen.

—EPHESIANS 3:14–21

Some dear friends of our family have a very cute little girl named Ruby. One day, I knelt down to speak with her, saying, "Hi, Ruby!"

"Hi, Amen!" she replied. Because her parents occasionally say, "Amen!" during my sermons, she thought that was my name.

It was one of the cutest and funniest moments I can remember. It also illustrates an important principle: children learn to speak by listening to their elders. Similarly, new Christians learn to speak to God, or pray, by listening to those who are older in faith.

Who taught you how to pray? I was raised Roman Catholic and memorized the prayers of dead people, like Francis of Assisi, as well as rote prayers, such as the Hail Mary and the Act of Contrition. While there's nothing wrong with praying scripted prayers, I didn't know how to speak to God personally and conversationally. I thought prayer was basically a formal meeting with a stodgy, old man named God, who lived far away and demanded to be spoken to like a foreign dignitary. As a result, I prayed very infrequently and rarely, if ever, about the practical stuff of my life.

Then God saved me at the age of nineteen. Suddenly, I had new desires. I wanted to learn the Bible, so I began reading it. I wanted to talk to God, so I started trying to figure out how to pray. And I wanted to be with God's people, which led me to a great church.

Excited to learn, I joined my first small group. Everyone was nice, and we began our time in prayer. But in what can only be described as an oops moment, the leader asked me to open the group in prayer since I was new. It was incredibly embarrassing to inform the group that I didn't know how to pray, had never prayed in a group, and had only ever prayed formal, written prayers memorized for participation in a Mass.

Thankfully, he quickly saw my embarrassment and led the group in praying aloud. I listened carefully. I wanted to hear how other people prayed so I could learn to pray, and I noticed that they prayed to God not as Mr. Stodgy, Faraway, Old Man but as a lovingly concerned "Father." They also used everyday language and spoke to God as if he were with them and wanted to hear about the stuff of their lives. I don't remember what our Bible study was about that night, but I do remember walking away mesmerized by prayer and with an idea of how to begin praying.

Christians learn how to pray by listening to other Christians who are mature in the faith, both in the church and in the Scriptures. This helps explain why the Bible is filled with prayers such as Psalms. Other books of the Bible have prayer as an overarching theme. One of them is Ephesians. Nearly half of Ephesians is composed of prayer.

The God of the Bible is a trinitarian community of Friends. The Father, Son, and Spirit have spoken and listened to one another for all eternity. We see this, for example, in Jesus' prayer life, in which we observe conversations within the godhead. This leads us to an exciting truth: if you are in Christ and Christ is in you, then God hears you!

For those who are in Christ, he serves as a mediator, bringing our prayers to God. And since God the Holy Spirit dwells in those who are in Christ, our prayers are by the Spirit, through the Son, to the Father. He hears your spoken words, unspoken thoughts, and unclear longings. This one fact is utterly astonishing. God's heart is always inclined toward you, his face set toward you, and his ear open for you. This explains why the Bible invites us to "pray without ceasing"[a] about anything, anytime, and anywhere.

The Christian life can become overly complicated, and we can overlook the majesty of simplicity. As a reminder that God is our friend, to whom we should talk regularly, not because we have to but because we get to, the Bible includes prayers. One example is Paul's prayer in Ephesians 3:14–21, of which one theologian has said, "No prayer that has ever been framed has uttered a bolder request."[1]

Imagine sitting with Paul in his jail cell. Picture him rubbing his aching joints and scarred body as he gets down on his knees in a wet, cold, filthy hole in the ground, and raises his voice in prayer. To listen in on Paul's prayer life as he speaks from his heart amid great suffering and prays for Christians, including you, to understand the depths of God's love and be filled with the fullness of God, reveals to us who he truly was. By eavesdropping on his conversation with God, we discover six principles of prayer: Personal, Relational, Asking, Yearning, Expecting, Revealing.

PRAYER IS PERSONAL

At perhaps eleven years old, my oldest daughter, Ashley, sat on the coffee table in front of me and explained some distressing relationship troubles she was going through with friends. When I asked her what I could do to serve her, she said, "Pray for me," knelt in front of me, bowed her head, and waited for me to place my hand on her head to pray over her as her father to "Our Father."

Because Ashley had a personal relationship with me, she trusted, honored, invited, loved, needed, welcomed, respected, and submitted to

---

a. 1 Thess. 5:17.

me with the simple, silent act of kneeling and asking for prayer. I laid a hand on her head and prayed for her while also thanking God for the honor of being her "Papa Daddy."

Famed preacher Martyn Lloyd-Jones once wrote: "Prayer is beyond any question the highest activity of the human soul. Man is at his greatest and highest when upon his knees he comes face to face with God."[2] Kneeling for prayer was rather uncommon throughout the Bible, as most people stood to pray.[b] Therefore, kneeling to pray is an unusual and humbling act.

Paul, prompted by the same Holy Spirit as Ashley was, tells us that while praying, he knelt before the Father.[c] Kneeling must have been difficult for Paul in light of his health, as he had suffered much in his service to Christ. Yet he did so humbly and happily.

Praying is one of the most edifying and humbling activities we can do. In prayer, we lay out our deepest desires, fears, emotions, pain, joys, thanksgivings, and more to the God of the universe. It's deeply personal.

To be fair, it's perfectly acceptable to pray to God while standing, sitting, or even lying in bed, and the Bible gives examples of each of these methods. Still, we must never forget or neglect the importance of at least occasionally kneeling before the Father—not so he will hear us, but because we know he does. Not because he requires it, but because he deserves it. By kneeling with our hands raised in prayer, we appear like soldiers in surrender and children reaching out to their father, which in many regards is what prayer is all about—surrendering to your Father.

PRAYER IS RELATIONAL

Throughout the gospels, Jesus called God "Father" some sixty times. Jesus may not have been the first Jew to call God his Father, but he was the first to do so as his primary means of speaking to God.[d] To call God Father was not commonplace in ancient religion but rather a new understanding

---

b. Mark 11:25.
c. Eph. 3:14.
d. Matt. 11:25; Mark 14:36; Luke 23:46; and John 17:1.

of the nature of God. Jesus taught his followers to call God their Father.[e]
So, like Jesus, Paul prayed to God as Father.[f]

An understanding of God as Dad is primary to prayer. If we understand that God is Dad, then we will naturally speak to him anytime about anything because we know we're loved, cared for, and safe with him. He's not negligent. He's present.

Do you want to learn how to pray? Then don't focus on prayer. Prayer is a means by which we see God as Father. Watch children who have a good dad and see how they interact with him. By watching kids talk to their dad who loves them, you will understand the key to prayer.

If you've had an awful dad, it will be more difficult for you to relate—or want to relate—to God as Dad. Please don't judge God by the standard of your earthly dad. Judge your earthly dad by the standard of God the Father. The Father chooses us to be his kids and, through the work of our big brother Jesus, adopts us into his family because he loves us.

As a dad to five kids, I learn a lot about prayer from my children. They continually initiate with me to talk, ask questions, and make requests. They don't give much thought to it. They just walk right up and speak to me, assuming I will acknowledge them, hear them, and answer them with a "Yes," "No," or "Later."

Since God is an infinitely more loving, powerful, generous, patient, forgiving, caring, encouraging, and fun Father than any earthly father, it follows that his children would talk to him all the time about everything. This is exactly what Paul modeled for us when he prayed to God as "Father." He knew that the God who is our sovereign Creator, King, and Lord is also, by grace, our Dad.

Because God our Father has adopted us into his family, we have what the Bible commonly refers to as spiritual "brothers" and "sisters" that comprise the church. As we live in community with the rest of God's family, hear what his other children are learning, and see how they change, we learn more about our Father and his purposes for us. Additionally,

---

e. Matt. 6:9.
f. Eph. 3:14.

because we have brothers and sisters in Christ, we can be in prayer with them and bring our requests to God together. This is why Jesus said, "For where two or three are gathered together in My name, I am there in the midst of them" (Matt. 18:20). By doing so, we encourage one another toward Christ, and we're able to help each other discern what God is saying to and doing among us as a family.

One day there will be a family reunion in Jesus' presence, where all of God's people are together forever. In the meantime, we come to know more of our Father from his other children as we read their biographies, live in community with them in our church, and cultivate friendships with Christians from various denominations, networks, and groups. As John Stott said, "It takes the whole people of God to understand the whole love of God; all the saints together—[Christian] Jews and [Christian] Gentiles, men and women, young and old, black and white—with all their varied backgrounds and experience."[3]

PRAYER IS ASKING

Unlike God, who is independent, self-sufficient, and lacking in nothing, we need. Thankfully, our Father is a generous giver who welcomes us to ask for anything. Consequently, in a distinctively trinitarian prayer, Paul asked God the Father to empower Christians through the Holy Spirit so Jesus Christ would dwell in their hearts and meet their deepest spiritual needs.[g] There are two big ideas to unpack here.

First, God the Holy Spirit is the means by which the power of God—achieved for us through the life, death, resurrection, and ascension of Jesus—is available to those whose faith is in Jesus. Living the Christian life requires power, not so we can avoid all suffering, domineer over others, or achieve our own selfish desires, but so we can become increasingly like Jesus Christ in such things as truthfulness, holiness, love, wisdom, courage, humility, and perseverance. The Bible teaches that Jesus was filled with the Holy Spirit and that it's impossible to become like Jesus without

---

g. Eph. 3:16–17.

the work of the Holy Spirit.[h] Therefore, when the Bible speaks of being Spirit-filled, it's simply another way of saying that we can live like Jesus by the Holy Spirit's grace and power. The Christian life is not a life lived for God, but the life of God lived in us, through us, with us, and sometimes in spite of us by the power of the Holy Spirit.

Second, Paul prayed that Christ would dwell in our hearts. Curiously, this is the only place in the Bible that speaks of Jesus living in our hearts, and Paul's words are directed toward Christians, which seems odd. As D. A. Carson has rightly observed, "At first sight it seems strange for Paul to pray that Christ may dwell in the hearts of believers. Did he not already live within them? In answer, it is noted that the focus of this request is not on the initial indwelling of Christ but on his continual presence. The verb used in this prayer is a strong one, signifying a permanent indwelling rather than some temporary abode."[4]

To help explain what Paul means, I'll tell you about places I've lived. In college, I lived in a fraternity for about one week, hated it, and then moved to a dorm for one school year. The following two years, I lived with college buddies in different rental homes decorated with what was once furniture, long before it got to us, and dirty dishes stacked up to what Paul called the third heaven. Going into my senior year of college, I married Grace, and in the first years of our marriage, we moved many times and never settled anywhere. She did her best to make the places feel like home, with no money and no long-term commitment to stay there.

Then we bought a home. We painted every room, got new furniture, put in lighting, erected a fence, built a play area, finished the space above the garage for my office, added a deck, plugged in a hot tub, and planted flowers. Now we even watch those home-improvement shows on television to see what to work on next. Why? Because, as Paul said, it's the place where we plan to "dwell."[i]

By praying that Jesus would dwell in our hearts (literally, "inner being"), Paul was asking that Jesus would make our lives his home and

h. Luke 4:1, 14, 18; 10:21.
i. Eph. 3:17.

keep working on all the broken, dirty, disorganized, foolish, and deadly things so we would have an ever-improving home.[j] He also prayed that we wouldn't lock some of the doors in our lives to Jesus in rebellion and unrepentance but rather that we would open every aspect of our lives to his cleansing and renovation.

PRAYER IS YEARNING

Jesus loves you. How do you feel when you read that? Do you doubt it because you're suffering? Do you disbelieve it because there's great sin in your life? Do you disregard it because it seems trite, overly simple, and not something you have truly plumbed to its depths? Do you dismiss it because you're so busy with life and its cares that you don't have time to dwell on deep truths?

If so, then Paul prayed, not only for the Ephesian church but also for you, saying, "I pray that you, being rooted and established in love, may have power, together with all the saints, to grasp how wide and long and high and deep is the love of Christ, and to know this love that surpasses knowledge—that you may be filled to the measure of all the fullness of God."[k]

Paul prayed that we'd know the staggering enormity of God's love, and his prayer is evidence of God's love for us too. Not many people pray, and most who do pray mainly for themselves, but, in love, Paul prayed for the church and us while sitting in a jail cell, suffering and alone.

Paul didn't doubt that God loves you, but he did doubt that you'd truly know it, really believe it, and deeply receive it in a passionate, experiential, and personal way. Many Christians know that God loves them, but they know it like someone who takes a driver's education class but never drives a car.

Paul wanted God's love to be set firmly in our minds, like the foundation

---

j. Ibid.
k. Eph. 3:17–19 (NIV).

of a building. But he wanted more. He wanted the love of God, like a plant rooted deeply in nourishment and able to flourish, to be the deep root in our soul. He wanted us, along with "all the saints," to know that God's love is wide enough to welcome anyone anywhere, long enough to stretch from the beginning of time to the end, deep enough to reach down to the worst of sinners, and high enough to transport us to God's heavenly kingdom. Because God's love is boundless, infinite, unending, and something we can know truly but not fully, Paul strained to find the words to explain it.

Remember Paul's audience—Christians scattered in churches throughout the city of Ephesus, in what is modern-day Turkey. These Christians intellectually knew God loved them, but they needed—as do we—to fully know the truth of God's love, not in the way we know the directions to our homes, but in the way dearly loved children know it when they hear their father call their name, inviting them to run to him as he smiles and laughs with arms outstretched, ready to catch them, hold them up, and kiss them on the forehead.

God wants us to know that he loves us like that. Paul prayed that we would "grasp" this love.[1] That word is a curious one, meaning "to take or seize eagerly," "to clasp or embrace, especially with the fingers or arms," or "to lay hold of with the mind." Too many Christians pit knowledge against experience and the head against the heart. The truth is, both are needed to grasp God's love. The love of God is what happens when the truth in our heads captivates the affections of our hearts, which spurs us on to grasp the love of God in our lives.

As the love of God increasingly captivates our hearts and we grasp onto his love, we're changed and become increasingly mature in Christ because our affections determine our actions. As we're rooted and grounded in love, we begin to love what God loves, and subsequently hate what God hates, namely, sin. This transforming of our affections results in the transforming of our actions. The truth is that there is one answer to all our problems—a full understanding of God's love for us. Therefore, the experiential love of God is something we must pray for and pursue

---

1. Eph. 3:18 (NIV).

by the power of the Holy Spirit, both for our church and ourselves, just as Paul did.

Unexpectedly, it's often in times of suffering that God's love becomes fully known. Don't just read the words of Paul's prayer, but remember that they were written while he was in prison, hungry, hurting, suffering, and likely writing by candlelight on a dirty floor, yearning that we would experience the love of God as deeply and passionately as he did.

How could he do this? In his suffering, Paul was continually reminded of the greatest act of love the world has ever known—the death of Jesus in our place for our sins as our Suffering Savior. Indeed, to speak of the love of God is to speak of the cross of Christ. Paul's life illustrates the fact that, in the kindness of God, some of our most painful seasons teach us the most about the love we enjoy because of the suffering Jesus endured.

PRAYER IS EXPECTING

Paul prayed because God "is able to do immeasurably more than all we ask or imagine."[m] *More* is a vital word. God isn't only powerful; he is also generous. Do you believe God can do anything? The true test of your theology is not just what you say, but also how you pray.

If others listened in on your prayer life, would they hear you praying the kind of prayers that could only be answered if God really showed up in a big way? Do you truly believe down deep in your gut that God can do more than you can ask or imagine? Pray as big as your Dad.

Not only is our all-powerful, mind-blowing, creation-ruling, crazy-generous God at work; he is "at work within us."[n] And God's power working in us gives us hope. We can change when God powerfully and continually transforms us by captivating us with his love. Paul modeled prayer that expected God to continue working in us by the power of the Holy Spirit. In light of God's power at work in us, we should pray expecting to be heard, if we pray within God's will, which is how Paul closed his prayer.

---

m. Eph. 3:20 (NIV).
n. Ibid.

PRAYER IS REVEALING

You can learn a lot about people when you listen to them pray. You learn who or what is on their hearts and minds, what they care about, and where their passions lie. You can also learn a lot about yourself by listening to how you pray. In prayer, your heart, motives, desires, false gods, and functional saviors are exposed.

Paul's prayer (as all prayer should) begins and ends with God. It begins by speaking of and to God as Father and ends with the glory of God revealed through the person of Jesus Christ and through the witness of his church. It's fitting that Paul would end his prayer with the glory of God, because that is the purpose of all things.

God is glorious and deserving of glory. The "glory of God" speaks of the splendor, beauty, magnificence, radiance, heaviness, weightiness, prominence, preeminence, luminescence, splendor, majesty, holiness, purity, worthiness, and superiority of the God of the Bible.

We exist to glorify God as fish exist to swim and birds exist to fly. The glory of God is a mega-theme in the Bible, appearing about 275 times in various English translations, including some 50 times in the book of Psalms alone. When people encounter God's glory, they respond in fear, awe, wonder, worship, dread, respect, conviction, repentance, and humility. God is big; we're small. God is good; we're bad. We exist for God; God doesn't exist for us. Yet, he hears us and loves us.

Jesus Christ is the glory of God. He perfectly, continually, and obediently revealed the Father. This is why Jesus said that if we see him, we see the Father,[o] and why we're told he is "the radiance of the glory of God."[p] In suffering, loneliness, singleness, poverty, betrayal, and even death, Jesus perfectly and continually lived to the glory of the Father.

Similarly, the church exists to glorify God. As the church, we're made to cheer, sing, and brag about our God, and to reflect his glory by living like him to show his character and love to the world. Often,

---

o. John 14:9.
p. Heb. 1:3 (ESV).

this God-given passion to worship is misdirected toward idolatry and the worship of created things, like sex, fame, and food, rather than God. But when God's glory is the true north on the compass of our lives, everything, including our prayer life, is God-directed and God-centered.

In his book *The City of God*, Augustine rightly determined that everything flows from the issue of glory. Once the issue of glory is settled—that is, where glory is going and who and what deserves it—then everything else is decided. Once we determine in our souls that God's glory is our goal, we then stop taking the path of least resistance and start taking the path of most glory to God.

Arguably the greatest theologian America has ever produced, Jonathan Edwards, made the glory of God the center of his theological studies. He often explained that the trinitarian God of the Bible is infinitely happy living to glorify one another in perfect love. Edwards went on to teach that the glory of God is a shorthand way of speaking of who God is and what God does in totality, saying, "All that is ever spoken of in the Scripture as an ultimate of God's works is included in that one phrase, 'the glory of God.'"[5]

God does not need us, but he wants us, which is far better. He welcomes us into relationship to know his glorious joy and make it known. As the Westminster Catechism says, "Man's chief end is to glorify God, and to enjoy him forever."[6] Making an important modification for what he calls "Christian Hedonism," John Piper wrote, "The chief end of man is to glorify God *by* enjoying Him forever."[7]

For God's glory to be revealed in the church, as Paul prayed, we must be satisfied in him individually and collectively, though we also long for the day we see Jesus face to face (Ex. 33:18; 1 Cor. 13:12). This means enjoying him as our greatest treasure, knowing beyond knowing that he loves us, being captivated by and grasping his love, living in a maturing relationship with him, repenting of our sin, growing to glorify him more and more by grace with joy, sharing his fame with others, humbly serving those in need as he has served us, singing of his love, and praying for his church. The life lived to reveal the glory of our Father God results in our joy and others' good as we become more like Jesus by the Spirit's power.

You Father is waiting. You will be heard.

10

I AM GIFTED

I, therefore, the prisoner of the Lord, beseech you to walk worthy of the calling with which you were called, with all lowliness and gentleness, with longsuffering, bearing with one another in love, endeavoring to keep the unity of the Spirit in the bond of peace. There is one body and one Spirit, just as you were called in one hope of your calling; one Lord, one faith, one baptism; one God and Father of all, who is above all, and through all, and in you all.

But to each one of us grace was given according to the measure of Christ's gift. Therefore He says:

"When He ascended on high,

He led captivity captive,

And gave gifts to men."

(Now this, "He ascended"—what does it mean but that He also first descended into the lower parts of the earth? He who descended is also the One who ascended far above all the heavens, that He might fill all things.)

And He Himself gave some to be apostles, some prophets, some evangelists, and some pastors and teachers, for the equipping of the saints for the work of ministry, for the edifying of the body of Christ, till we all come to the unity of the faith and of the knowledge of the Son of God, to a perfect man, to the measure of the stature of the fullness of Christ; that we should no longer be children, tossed to and fro and carried about with every wind of doctrine, by the trickery of men, in the cunning craftiness of deceitful plotting, but, speaking the truth in love, may grow up in all things into Him who is the head—Christ—from whom the whole body, joined and knit together by what every joint supplies, according to the effective working by which every part does its share, causes growth of the body for the edifying of itself in love.

—EPHESIANS 4:1–16

When I was a little boy, I loved it when I was able to work with my dad, Joe, who was a construction worker. I'd put on steel-toed boots, overalls, a white T-shirt, and a hard hat, just like my dad. I'd even carry a thermos and a lunch box for our breaks and had my own little bucket of tools. My dad could've done all the work without me, and in fact, it would've been a lot easier. But I think my dad took me to work so I'd know him better.

God is a Father, and ministry, which every believer does, is like going to work with your dad. As Jesus said, "I must be about My Father's business."[a] The majority of Jesus' ministry years were spent as a carpenter, glorifying God and serving people by working with his adoptive father, Joseph. He spent the last three years of his life preaching, teaching, healing, feeding, evangelizing, leading, and more, and then died on the cross for our sins, was buried, rose from the dead, and ascended back into heaven, from which he rules today, still doing ministry.

The ministry of Jesus continues on the earth today through his people. Through the Holy Spirit, Jesus empowers our gifts and talents,[b] which enable us to do meaningful ministry for Jesus. Spirit-empowered gifts are given solely by God's grace, and we can't get a gift unless God gives it.[c] Because God knows what people need, what the future holds, and where particular churches are deficient, he gives us specific gifts needed for the health of the church. Practically, this means that you're gifted by Christ and needed in the church.

The Scriptures often refer to the necessity of every person in a church as being like the parts of a human body, connected together in purposeful unity.[d] This makes it clear that if you're a Christian, you're gifted to serve the body of Christ.

Not every Christian is called to full-time *vocational* ministry, but every Christian is called to the "work of ministry." This ministry work includes your job, your family, church, and community, loving and serving people in your life on behalf of Jesus Christ.

As a gifted person, Paul suggested that when you serve your church, many things happen. You:

---

a. Luke 2:49.
b. 1 Cor. 12:11; Heb. 2:4.
c. Rom. 12:6; 1 Cor. 12:4–7, 11.
d. Col. 1:18, 24; 2:19; Eph. 1:22–23; 4:4, 12, 16; 5:30; 1 Cor. 12:12–31; Rom. 12:5

- contribute to "the unity of the Spirit in the bond of peace";
- edify "the body of Christ";
- encourage "unity of the faith and of the knowledge of the Son of God;"
- help people grow to the "fullness of Christ";
- increase the number of biblically mature people who are no longer "tossed to and fro and carried about with every wind of doctrine";
- learn to both give and receive "the truth in love";
- grow to appreciate different Christians as your work together causes you to be "joined and knit together";
- see "growth of the body"; and
- help the church grow "in love" for both those in the church and those who do not yet know Jesus.

In Christ, you have both a new identity and a new community where you learn more about your new identity as you use your gifts to serve and are served by the gifts of others. Sometimes, Christians shy away from involvement in a local church because they see faults with the church. Ironically, the fact that they see a lack may indicate that there's a need for them and their gifts. Rather than complaining, it's better to humbly start serving to meet a church's needs and invite others to also help.

Four separate lists of Spirit-empowered gifts appear in the New Testament, including Ephesians 4:1–16.[e] Since no two lists of gifts in the New Testament are the same, it's unlikely that even combining all the lists gives us a complete picture of all the gifts that we are given and which the Spirit empowers. For instance, many people have gifts such as artistic skill, musical ability, athletic prowess, and so forth, which the Holy Spirit can use to serve the church and bring glory to God. It's likely that simply any ability used by a Christian to serve the cause of the gospel counts as what some call "spiritual gifts." Both supernatural and natural talents are God-given gifts to "do the work of the ministry," and in the end what matters most is that God is glorified and your church is edified by God's

---

e. 1 Cor. 12:8–10, 28–30; Rom. 12:6–8; Eph. 4:11; 1 Peter 4:11.

grace through you as you "walk worthy of the calling with which you were called." Because God has gifted you, the church needs you.

SPIRIT-EMPOWERED GIFTS

The remainder of this chapter will focus on various Spirit-empowered gifts that are listed in the Scriptures. As you read through, pray and think about where you're gifted and how you might serve the body of Christ with your gifts.

Before we jump into various gifts, however, a few introductory thoughts may be helpful.

- We're given differing portions of a gift or talent. For example, some are gifted in leadership to lead dozens, others to lead thousands or more.
- Our gifts need cultivation and maturity through discipleship and growth. For example, you may be gifted to teach but might need years of studying before formally teaching the Scriptures to large groups.
- Be willing to serve outside of your area of giftedness, at least for a season, to fill a need until a more gifted person comes along. In this way a church is much like a family, where the members pitch in to help as needed.
- There's a difference between giftedness and maturity. We should cultivate not only our gifts by the grace of God but also our maturity. Sometimes gifted people aren't mature people, which is deceptive to them and dangerous for others.
- The best way to discover our gifts is simply by trial and error. Find a place to serve in a church that interests you, and see how it goes. If it's not a fit, don't get discouraged. Rather, try something else until you find your place.

As we examine the gifts listed in Scripture, I hope you find it exciting. God has given you a gift to do a little bit of what Jesus did, which is a great honor and opportunity. Also, for those wanting to study more in the area of spirit-empowered gifts, there are good resources available.[1]

Wisdom (1 Cor. 12:8)

Those with the gift of wisdom have extraordinary insight into people and situations, combined with an understanding of what to do and how to do it. They not only see but also apply the principles of God's Word to the practical matters of life by the "Spirit of wisdom"[f] and often function well as coaches, counselors, and consultants.

Do you have this gift?

1. When studying God's Word, do you find that you discover the meaning and its implications of a passage before others do?
2. Do you understand things about God's Word that other believers with the same background and experience don't?
3. Are you able to apply biblical truth in a practical way to help others make good life choices?
4. Do you get frustrated when people make foolish decisions because you know what they should have done instead?
5. When people have important decisions to make, do they come to you for prayer and biblical counsel?

Knowledge (1 Cor. 12:8)

Those with the gift of knowledge research, remember, and make effective use of information on a number of subjects. They love to study and learn, and aren't content with a surface-level knowledge. They're compelled to thoroughly research and compile their findings for others' benefit. People with this gift love God with "all [their] mind."[g]

Do you have this gift?

1. Do you love to study and have a good memory?

---

f. Eph. 1:17.
g. Mark 12:30.

2. Have others pointed out your ability to know and understand God's Word?

3. Do people come to you with difficult problems and questions from the Bible, seeking your insight, because they know you'll have the answer or find it?

4. In studying God's Word, have you found that new insights and understanding of difficult subjects is easy for you?

5. Are you frustrated when you hear bad teaching from people who've not done their homework?

Faith (1 Cor. 12:9)

Faith is the ability to envision what needs to be done and to trust God to accomplish it, even if it seems impossible to most people. Those with the gift of faith trust God in difficult—even impossible—situations when others are ready to give up and are often visionaries who dream big dreams, pray big prayers, and attempt big things for Jesus. They're also persuasive about Scripture because they are convinced of the truth and power of God and his Word.

Do you have this gift?

1. Do you see obstacles as opportunities to trust God for the impossible?

2. Do you find yourself frequently boasting about the power of God and what you have seen him do?

3. Does it bug you when someone says something can't be done or accomplished?

4. When other believers face overwhelming trials or tasks, do they come to you for encouragement and prayer?

5. Have you seen many wonderful answers to prayers that were impossible from the human point of view?

Healing[2] (1 Cor. 12:9)

Healing is the ability to call on God through prayer in faith to heal the sick through supernatural means for the purpose of revealing God. Those with the gift of healing see healings as signs God uses to reveal his power so that many will come to believe in Jesus. This doesn't mean, however, that every time those with the gift of healing pray, others are healed. God alone sovereignly decides whether to heal someone or not.[h]

Do you have this gift?

1. Do you have a deep compassion for people who are sick?
2. Do you have a deep conviction that God can heal anyone he chooses?
3. Do you enjoy praying for people who are sick, and have you seen people healed when you do so?
4. When God heals someone, are you excited because it helps reveal his power to others?
5. Do you long for the coming of God's kingdom, when there will be an end to all sickness?

Miracles[3] (1 Cor. 12:9)

The gift of miracles is the ability to call on God to do supernatural acts that reveal his power. People with the gift of miracles see God show up in extraordinary ways from little events to major public displays. Examples from the Bible include casting out demons, causing nature to obey God's authority, and raising the dead. Obviously, miracles are uncommon and don't happen regularly. Otherwise they wouldn't be viewed as miraculous. People with this gift should not chase signs and wonders, but they should expect them to follow God's people.

Do you have this gift?

1. Do you truly believe that God can do the impossible?
2. When you read of the many miracles in the Bible, are you encouraged because you love to see God made known in ways that can't be ignored?
3. Have you seen someone freed from demonic oppression?
4. When you hear of or see miracles, is your faith in God greatly increased?

---

h. e.g., Gal. 4:13–14; Phil. 2:27; 1 Tim. 5:23; 2 Tim. 4:20.

5. Do you use stories of God's miracles to help prove to others that Jesus is God?

Discernment (1 Cor. 12:10)

Discernment is the ability to quickly perceive whether something is from God or from Satan. People with the gift of discernment know that Satan and his demons disguise themselves as holy,[i] that he empowers counterfeit miracles to deceive people,[j] and that he empowers false teachers, prophets, apostles, and doctrines.[k]

Do you have this gift?

1. Have you felt a special responsibility to protect the truth of God's Word by exposing error?
2. Do you often make a swift evaluation of someone or something that others did not see but that proved to be correct?
3. Do you have a solid understanding of Scripture and sensitivity to the leading of God the Holy Spirit?
4. Are you keenly aware of moral sin and doctrinal heresy?
5. Can you read a book or hear a teacher and almost immediately uncover any false teaching?

Apostleship (1 Cor. 12:28; Eph. 4:11)[4]

The gift of apostle can be confusing because there is sometimes a failure to distinguish between the office of Apostle (big *A*) and the gift of apostle (little *a*). The office of Apostle refers to the early apostles chosen by Jesus.[l] The requirements for the office included witnessing the life and resurrection of Jesus and miraculous power.[m] "Big A" Apostles don't exist today (e.g., writing books of the Bible), although the function of their office continues in a limited sense. For example, apostleship in a

---

i. 1 Cor. 11:14–15.
j. Ex. 7:11–22; 8:7; Matt. 7:21–23; 2 Tim. 3:8; 2 Thess. 2:9.
k. 2 Peter 2:1; Matt. 7:15; 2 Cor. 11:13; 1 Tim. 1:3; 6:3.
l. Matt. 10:1; 19:28; 20:17; Mark 3:13–19; 6:7; 9:35; 10:32; Luke 6:12–16; 8:1; 9:1; 22:19–30; John 6:70–71; Rev. 21:14.
m. Acts 1:21–26; 2:43; 5:12; 8:18; 2 Cor. 12:12; Heb. 2:4.

secondary sense applies to such people as Barnabas, Apollos, Sosthenes, Andronicus, Junias, James, Silas, and Timothy.[n] They, like apostles today, were gifted individuals sent out to plant local churches,[o] raise up leaders, and minister cross-culturally.[p] Today, church planters and missionaries often operate out of a gift of apostleship, as well as Christian leaders God raises up to lead and influence multiple churches and pastors. These people often have a number of gifts, such as evangelism, teaching, leadership, faith, and exhortation, and are motivated by difficult new tasks.

Do you have this gift?
1. Can you effectively minister cross-culturally?
2. Are you called and qualified to plant a church?
3. Can you start a church from nothing?
4. Are you an entrepreneur?
5. Has God given you leadership and influence over multiple churches as a movement leader?

Teaching (Rom. 12:7; 1 Cor. 12:28; Eph. 4:11)

Teaching is the ability to understand and communicate biblical truth in a clear and relevant manner that results in understanding and application. Those with this gift enjoy studying and learning new information and find great joy in sharing it with others. Teaching opportunities vary from one-on-one discipleship to formal classes, informal Bible studies, large groups, and preaching.

Do you have this gift?
1. Do you enjoy studying and researching?
2. Do you enjoy imparting biblical truth to others?
3. Do others come to you for insight into Scripture?
4. When you teach, do people "get it"?
5. When you see someone confused in his or her understanding of

---

n. Acts 14:3–4, 14; 1 Cor. 4:6–9; Rom. 16:7; Gal. 1:19; 1 Thess. 1:1; 2:6.
o. Acts 13:3–4.
p. Acts 10:34–35; Eph. 3:7–8.

the Bible, do you feel a responsibility to speak to that person about their misconceptions?

Helps and Service (Rom. 12:7; 1 Cor. 12:28; 1 Peter 4:11)

The gift of helps and service is the ability to joyfully work alongside another and help that person complete a God-given task. People with this gift generally prefer to humbly work behind the scenes and find joy in identifying and helping alleviate others' burdens and responsibilities. They demonstrate a servant attitude, loyalty, attention to detail, and responsiveness to the initiatives of others, and they function well in positions of detail and assistant leadership.

Do you have this gift?

1. Do you enjoy helping others become more effective in their work?
2. Do you prefer to labor behind the scenes?
3. When someone is doing a job poorly, is your first instinct to help instead of criticize?
4. Do you prefer to work in a supportive rather than a leadership capacity?
5. When someone asks for your help, do you have difficulty saying no?

Administration (1 Cor. 12:28)

Administration is the ability to give direction and make decisions on behalf of others that result in efficient operation and accomplishment of goals. The mark of an administrator is his or her ability to accomplish things in a "fitting and orderly way,"[q] and administrators often have a keen eye for detail, resulting in natural talents of organization, observing and using details, problem solving, and reasoning.

Do you have this gift?

1. When things are poorly organized, do you get frustrated and want to help fix them?

---

q. 1 Cor.14:40 (NIV).

2. Can you bring order out of chaos?
3. Do you naturally organize your life, schedule, finances, priorities, etc.?
4. Do you become energized when working on tasks and projects?
5. Do efficiency and promptness matter more to you than they do for others?

Evangelism (Eph. 4:11)

Evangelism is the ability and passion to boldly and clearly communicate the gospel of Jesus Christ to non-Christians. Evangelists feel compassion for the lost and seek to earnestly understand their questions and doubts so they can provide compelling answers. They generally prefer being with people in the outer culture rather than hanging out with Christians in the church.

Do you have this gift?

1. Do you enjoy being with non-Christians and sharing the gospel?
2. Can you effectively communicate to non-Christians?
3. Does a person's conversion bring you profound joy?
4. Do you feel frustrated when you haven't shared your faith for a while?
5. Do you enjoy teaching others how to share their faith?

Pastoring/Counseling (Eph. 4:11)

In one sense, pastoring is a function of the office reserved for those who meet the biblical criteria of elder.[r] In another sense, there is a pastoral gift, also commonly known as *shepherding* or *counseling*, that God gives to people in the church. Those with a pastoral gift have a deep love for people that compels them to protect, guide, counsel, and disciple other people. People with this gift find great joy in seeing others mature in their faith to overcome sin and discouragement.

---

r. 1 Tim. 3:1–7; Titus 1:5–9.

Do you have this gift?

1. Do you have a deep love for people that compels you to care for them?
2. Do you enjoy meeting with people to listen to their life stories and provide biblical counsel to help them mature in faith?
3. When you hear that someone is hurting, is your first instinct to try to be of help?
4. Are you able to point out sin and folly in people's lives in a loving way that they receive as helpful?
5. Do people pursue you for counsel and instruction?

Encouragement (Rom. 12:8)

Encouragement (also called *exhortation*) involves motivating, inspiring, and consoling others so they mature in their walk with Jesus. Christians with this gift have an unusual sensitivity, patience, and optimism for those who are discouraged or struggling, and people pursue them for healing words, gracious truth, and compassionate counsel. They may have a knack for one-on-one relationships and prefer working with individuals or small groups.

Do you have this gift?

1. Do people seek you out for advice and encouragement?
2. Do you enjoy walking with someone through difficulties?
3. Are you drawn to those who are hurting and needy?
4. Are you patient with people?
5. Would you rather speak personally with people about their problems than send them to someone else for help?

Giving (Rom. 12:8)

Giving is the ability to be generous with wealth to joyfully and wisely meet others' needs and support ministries. People with this gift view their treasures, talents, and time, regardless of the amount, as on loan from God, enjoy giving of themselves and what they have, and are often moved to meet the physical needs of others. Even if they do not possess the resources to help, they earnestly pray for those needs to be met.

Do you have this gift?

1. Do you see the needs of others more than most people?
2. Do you enjoy giving your time, talent, and treasure to others?
3. Do you see giving to a worthwhile project as an exciting honor and privilege and seek those projects out without being asked?
4. Do you give to the church regularly, cheerfully, and sacrificially?
5. Do people often say that you're a generous person?

Leadership (Rom. 12:8)

The gift of leadership is found in people who have a clear, significant vision from God and are able to communicate it publicly or privately in a way that influences others. Those gifted in leadership gravitate toward the "point positions" in a ministry, have trust and confidence in their abilities, and best serve others by leading them in the purposes of God.

Do you have this gift?

1. Do others have confidence in your ability to lead?
2. Do you enjoy having the overall responsibility for the direction and success of a group or organization?
3. When a difficult situation or major decisions arise, do others look to you for input and leadership?
4. Do you usually take leadership in a group where none exists?
5. Do you find leadership enjoyable rather than frustrating and difficult?

Mercy (Rom. 12:8)

Mercy is the capacity to feel and express unusual compassion and sympathy for those in difficult or crisis situations and provide them with the necessary help and support to see them through tough times. Those gifted in mercy can "walk in another's shoes" and feel the pain and burdens of others, desiring to make a difference in hurting people's lives without being judgmental.

Do you have this gift?

1. Are you drawn to people who are needy, hurting, sick, disabled, or elderly?

2. Do you often think of ways to minister to the suffering?
3. Do you have great compassion for people having personal and emotional problems?
4. Does visiting the suffering bring you joy rather than depress you?
5. Do you respond to people out of compassion more than judgment?

Hospitality (Rom. 12:13)

Hospitality is the ability to welcome strangers and entertain guests, often in your home, with great joy and kindness so they become friends. Hospitality includes one's family, friends, Christians, and strangers who may not be Christians,[s] but *not* false teachers and the like, who are a danger.[t] Those who are hospitable tend to have "open homes" where others are welcome to visit, and exhibit such natural talents as interior design, cooking, and event planning.

Do you have this gift?

1. Do you enjoy having people in your home?
2. Do you enjoy watching people meet and have fun at parties and events you helped plan and host?
3. Is your home the kind that most people feel comfortable in and drop by to visit unannounced?
4. When you think of your home, do you view it from the perspective of guests who will visit?
5. Do you consider your home as a place of ministry?

Tongues (1 Cor. 12:8–10, 29–30)[5]

The word *tongues* is best translated "languages" from the Greek. The confusion regarding tongues is that at least three different uses of the gift are mentioned in Scripture. One, there is a private prayer language, which Paul wrote of in 1 Corinthians 14:14, saying, "I pray in a tongue." Two, there is a missionary gift that enables someone to speak the gospel of

---

s. 1 Tim. 5:8; Prov. 27:10; Gal. 6:10; Lev. 19:34.
t. 2 John 10–11.

Jesus in a way that foreigners hear it in their native language even when the speaker does not know that language. Acts 2:1–13 records just such an occasion, when three thousand people were saved in one day as the gospel was preached through the early Christians. Three, there is a revelatory language whereby a message of God is spoken in a language unknown to the speaker that must be translated into the native language of the people in the church so they can understand what is being said. This use of tongues, therefore, also requires the assistance of someone with the gift of interpretation.[u]

Those with a private prayer language feel closely connected to Jesus through the ministry of the Holy Spirit as they enjoy intimate time with God. Those with a missionary or revelatory gift of tongues see God use them to communicate the gospel to people they otherwise could not because of language barriers.

Do you have this gift?

1. Do you have a private prayer language that helps you connect with God?
2. Has God used you to communicate the gospel to those who do not share your language?
3. Has God used you to interpret the tongue speaking of someone else?

Prophecy (Rom. 12:6; 1 Cor. 12:10, 28; Eph. 4:11)[6]

Much like the gifts of apostleship and pastor, there is both an office of prophet that is limited to a few people and a gifting of prophecy that is open to all. In the Old Testament, the title "prophet" refers to the office of the person chosen by God to both hear from and communicate for him.[v]

Today, prophets who are the original source of inerrant Scripture no longer exist. There remains, however, the gift and ministry of prophecy. Those with the gift of prophecy easily spot compromise, sin, and error, and desire immediate change and action for Christ. They tend to be bold, sensitive to sin, and place a very high value on urgent biblical obedience.

---

u. 1 Cor. 12:10.
v. 1 Sam. 3:20; 1 Kings 18:36; 2 Kings 6:12; Hag. 1:1; Zech. 1:1.

Like tongues, prophecy is spoken of in various ways throughout Scripture. Importantly, the New Testament doesn't elevate prophecy to the highest level of authority as the Old Testament does. Each potential prophecy is supposed to be tested and approved by church leaders, such as the elders.[w]

Modern-day prophecy is sometimes the teaching ministry of preaching the Bible as God's Word in the church,[x] sometimes a revelation about a future event that God intends to reveal to the entire church that is authenticated by coming true,[y] and sometimes a word from God for an individual.[z]

Do you have this gift?

1. Do you feel compelled to proclaim the Word of God boldly?
2. When you see sin or errors, do you feel compelled to confront them?
3. Are you capable of detecting and refuting false teachings?
4. Are you bold for Christ?
5. Do you love people and seek their best in Christ?

THE MORE EXCELLENT WAY

In this chapter, we've covered a number of spirit-empowered gifts. It's my hope that as you've read, the Holy Spirit has helped you come to a fuller understanding of your gifts and how they may be used to build up the church.

But it should be noted that, while gifts are important, they aren't the most important thing. According to Paul, love is more excellent than all gifts, and those gifts, if not used in love, are worthless.[aa] So, we should all the more earnestly pray that God would give us his heart to love and serve the church with those gifts as our "work of ministry," just as Jesus did for us.

---

w. 1 Cor. 14:29–32; 1 Thess. 5:19–22.
x. 1 Cor. 14:4–7, 24–25.
y. Acts 11:28–29; 1 Cor. 14:6.
z. Acts 21:10–11.
aa. 1 Cor. 13:1–3.

From the preceding pages, what gift(s) sounded like it may be yours? Every one of us has gifts from God that the Holy Spirit empowers to bring glory to God and to serve the church. Your life matters. You are needed. You are gifted. God wants you to share in his joy of seeing people saved, churches planted, Christians grow, and congregations flourish. To help you discover where your "work of ministry" may be, consider the following:

1. Whom/where do you have a passion to serve?
2. What do you have a burden to do?
3. What needs do you see in the church?
4. What do you find joy in doing for others?
5. What opportunities has God already provided for you to serve others?
6. What things are you best at and have the most success in?
7. What have godly people commended you for doing?
8. What acts of service have given you the deepest sense of satisfaction and joy?

11

I AM NEW

This I say, therefore, and testify in the Lord, that you should no longer walk as the rest of the Gentiles walk, in the futility of their mind, having their understanding darkened, being alienated from the life of God, because of the ignorance that is in them, because of the blindness of their heart; who, being past feeling, have given themselves over to lewdness, to work all uncleanness with greediness. But you have not so learned Christ, if indeed you have heard Him and have been taught by Him, as the truth is in Jesus: that you put off, concerning your former conduct, the old man which grows corrupt according to the deceitful lusts, and be renewed in the spirit of your mind, and that you put on the new man which was created according to God, in true righteousness and holiness.

—EPHESIANS 4:17–24

Hannah grew up in a Christian home. Her dad was a worship pastor and, like many pastors' kids, she was heavily involved in church. But after a fallout with the lead pastor at the church in which she grew up, her parents stopped going to church during her high school years.

This drastic change, coupled with the fact that Hannah's parents wanted her to have her own faith and didn't, as she puts it, "force any theology or basic knowledge of Christianity," left Hannah struggling to find her identity during her formative teen and college years.

"I found my identity in boys and my worth when they worshipped my body," says Hannah. "I struggled with sexual acts but believed Satan's lie that it wasn't a big deal. I didn't bear the mark of a Christian. My faith was conditional, and repentance was minimal."

138

Her junior year in college, God brought Hannah to Mars Hill Church and began a long and difficult process of pulling back the layers of her identity. "I heard for the first time that I was a sinner," says Hannah. "I grew up understanding God's love for me and that Jesus was a really incredible God, but the gospel of what Jesus Christ had done for me was never clearly said. God opened my eyes and revealed to me the truth, and I saw for the first time what I had done to Jesus. I was a wretched sinner."

For nine months, Hannah wrestled, confessed, repented, and surrendered her sin to Jesus. "My pride was humiliated, my foundation was crumbled, and my idols were cast down," she says. "I saw myself as a prostitute and sexually impure. But this is where the devil had a hold on me. I forgot the good news that we are sinners and through Jesus there is no condemnation, but grace."

Hannah had switched from an identity in body image and boys to an identity as a condemned sinner, both of which were lies of the enemy. For months she struggled with feelings of guilt and inadequacy, but during her senior year, while attending a college conference, the Holy Spirit used a pastor's prayer to speak truth into her life.

"He was transparent in his prayers," says Hannah. "First, he listed off why he was unworthy, stating his most intimate sins. Then he proclaimed the truth of God's grace."

For Hannah, something clicked that night and she fully understood the whole gospel story. She wasn't just a sinner condemned by God. She was once a sinner, now saved by grace and made new in Christ as a child of God.

"God's grace was a new revelation for me," she says. "The Holy Spirit filled me up and I clearly felt his love and saw that I am adopted as his daughter, reconciled, and a part of the family of the church. Most important, through the power of Christ I am victorious over Satan, sin, and death. I am freed from my sins! I have never felt so liberated in my life. My bondage from sin was broken, and the enemy cannot condemn me, because I was set free through Christ and his redemptive act. This is the good news: all my sin went to Jesus as my substitute because I deserved that death, but he paid my penalty, then gifted me his righteousness. That is undeserved, unearned grace."

The result of this revelation of grace for Hannah was a completely changed outlook on life and a new way of living. "I was regenerated, completely and utterly transformed by the Holy Spirit," she shares. "I had new desires. I hated sin and loved godliness. To me, it felt like I was born again, because God changed my identity and changed me from the inside out." She was new.

ARE YOU NEW?

Most people want to be someone new. This is why seemingly every cover of the most popular magazines and books, the topics of the most popular radio and television shows, and the most trafficked blogs and websites are about one thing—becoming a new you.

Most everyone, even if they don't use the biblical language of sin and redemption, knows something is wrong, that we're not entirely who we could or should be, and that making changes would be a good thing. Using biblical language, we want to be "saved" from the consequences of our sin and the effects of sin and be "justified" or declared good by whomever or whatever we worship, which can range from Jesus to a false deity, friends' opinions, parents' approval, or even ourselves.

As humans, we are religious by fallen nature, which means we think we can be justified in one of four ways.

First, loosely religious people *assume they're good enough* and that no spiritual devotion or extra effort is required for God to be pleased with them. Such people make moderate life corrections and learn occasional new life lessons, but for the most part they believe that only "really bad" people—and not themselves—need to be made new. Basically, they're already saved and justified in their own minds.

Second, secular religious people *work very hard at social causes* because they think they're good and need to overcome evil with their good. These people tend to see others' problems more than their own and smugly think they're God's gift to the world, here to change it and make it new. They justify themselves by saving the rest of us.

Third, non-Christian, "spiritual" people *try to change themselves with vaguely spiritual self-help insights*, wanting to become new but not understanding how to achieve that in Christ. They follow the trendy books and ideas about loving oneself as the means by which one can unleash her potential and change her life. For them, God gives us principles to save and justify ourselves and only helps those who help themselves.

Fourth, devoutly religious people *work hard at keeping the rules* of a particular religion in an effort to justify themselves as good and obedient people in God's sight. Such people try very hard to do the right thing so God will love them and be pleased with them. This thinking is pernicious, and likely most common for the kind of people who would read this book—and its author.

Paul was a man just like this until he became a Christian and put off his old religious identity and put on his new identity in Christ. In Philippians 3:5–6, he listed his impressive religious performance résumé: "circumcised the eighth day, of the stock of Israel, of the tribe of Benjamin, a Hebrew of the Hebrews; concerning the law, a Pharisee; concerning zeal, persecuting the church; concerning the righteousness which is in the law, blameless." One Bible commentator rightly says, "Paul's point was that he had an outwardly perfect record!"[1] By the religious rules of his people, he would've been considered nearly perfect. Of course, inwardly he was filled with the sins of pride and self-righteousness.

Though Paul looked perfect on the outside, he declared his noble birth, impeccable education, tireless work, clean lifestyle, and unprecedented religious devotion to be "rubbish" compared to his new identity and "righteousness . . . through faith in Christ."[a] The Greek word for "rubbish" is used only once in the Bible, and various English translations call it rubbish, garbage, refuse, filth, dung, and dog dung.[2] It's a strong word that reflects Paul's strong feelings about his former life. After having a new identity "in Christ," Paul found every previous effort and accomplishment to be as worthless as stinky trash and as disgusting as a steaming pile of dog dung. Yes, that's how disgusting an identity apart from Christ is.

---

a. Phil. 3:8–9.

Speaking from his own experience and identity "in Christ," Paul explains how we live out our new identity in Ephesians 4:17–24. Repentance is explained in terms of walking down a different path than we have been, by putting off our old self (or old man) and putting on our new self (or new man).

Practically, this means we no longer think, desire, or act according to our old identity as someone disconnected from Jesus Christ. Instead, we have a new identity "in Jesus" and become a new person "created according to God, in true righteousness and holiness." Paul says this new identity has to be put on like clothing. Therefore, it's a good idea every day as we dress ourselves physically to also pray that God would dress us spiritually to live out our identity in Christ throughout the day. The question becomes, how do we put off our old self and put on our new self? The answer is found in the effects of Christ's work on the cross for us: justification, regeneration, and glorification. Justification makes us externally new. Regeneration makes us internally new. Glorification makes us eternally new in Christ.[b]

Externally New: Justification

God is a holy and just king who rules over creation and judges everyone according to his or her works.[c] As Paul taught earlier in Ephesians, apart from Christ's forgiveness and righteousness, we're "dead in trespasses and sins," "sons of disobedience," "by nature children of wrath," "aliens from the commonwealth of Israel and strangers from the covenants of promise, having no hope and without God in the world," and "strangers and foreigners."[d]

How, then, can God justify us—declaring us righteous—without himself becoming unjust by overlooking sin?[e] Since all unrighteous people deserve judgment and wrath in hell, God could've declared that no one would be justified. God would've remained perfectly just in handing

---

b. Phil. 3:9–11.
c. Gen. 18:25; Ps. 50:6; 96:13; 2 Tim. 4:8.
d. Eph. 2:1–3; 12–13; 19.
e. Ex. 23:7; Prov. 17:15.

down a death sentence to everyone who ever lived, because not one of us is righteous.[f] Although God does indeed justly condemn some people, in his loving mercy he also justifies some people in Christ.

The Bible teaches that unjust sinners can be declared righteous in God's sight by being justified or obtaining *justification*.[g] This legal term appears some 222 times in various forms throughout the New Testament and refers to a double transaction whereby God takes away our sinful unrighteousness through Jesus' substitutionary death in our place and imputes to us Jesus' righteousness in place of our unrighteousness.[h]

Second Corinthians 5:21 describes this work of God: "For He made Him who knew no sin to be sin for us, that we might become the righteousness of God in Him." Martin Luther rightly called this the Great Exchange. On the cross Jesus took our sinful unrighteousness and gave us his sinless righteousness. In this, we have imputed righteousness and imparted righteousness. In the former, we are declared holy in the sight of God. In the latter, we are empowered to live holy lives by the Spirit of God after being born again to live a new life in Christ. It's this truth that allows someone like Hannah to be free from the horror of her past apart from Christ, and to look with hope to her future with Christ.

We can't justify ourselves, though many people exhaust themselves trying to do so. We're justified by grace alone, through faith alone, because of Jesus Christ alone. As Paul wrote, "For by grace you have been saved through faith, and that not of yourselves; it is the gift of God, not of works, lest anyone should boast. For we are His workmanship, created in Christ Jesus for good works."[i]

To make this as simple as possible, let me say it this way: justification is all about Jesus. Jesus' work, not our works, saves us. Jesus' life, not our own life, is our hope. Jesus' death, not our religious works, is our payment. Jesus alone forgives sin. So, we're to repent of our sin to Jesus. Jesus alone gives righteousness. So we trust in Jesus for our justification. Our

---

f. Rom. 3:10.
g. Rom. 2:13; 3:20.
h. Rom. 3:21–22; 4:4–6; 5:12–21; 10:4; 1 Cor. 1:30; 2 Cor. 5:21; Phil. 3:8–9; 1 Peter 2:24; 3:18.
i. Eph. 2:8–10.

justification is not accomplished in any part by our own work, morality, or religious devotion. Justification is accomplished by Jesus plus nothing, and Jesus plus anything ruins everything.

Justification is something that happens externally from us. It's accomplished by the sinless life, substitutionary death, and bodily resurrection of Jesus Christ in our place, for our sins, as our Savior. It's a legal transaction in the sight of God for those whose faith is in Christ. Practically, this means you're righteous in Christ. God can't love you any more, and he will never love you any less. You don't have to be perfect, because Jesus is. You don't have to pay God back, because Jesus has. You don't need to suffer for your sins, because Jesus did. You are free to stop working for your righteousness and start working from Jesus' righteousness.

Internally New: Regeneration

In her story, Hannah shared that she was completely changed by the Holy Spirit through regeneration. Regeneration is the internal application of our external justification. Regeneration is the Holy Spirit's application of Jesus' work in us.

While the word *regeneration* only appears twice in the Bible,[j] it's described in both the Old and New Testaments by a constellation of images. Examples include "partakers of the divine nature,"[k] "new creation,"[l] and "new heart."[m] In Ephesians, regeneration is spoken of as becoming a "new man,"[n] made "alive together with Christ,"[o] and "created in Christ Jesus."[p] Each signifies a permanent, unalterable change in us at the deepest level.

When we're "sealed with the Holy Spirit"[q] as regenerated Christians, there are eleven fundamental and life-altering changes that take place.

---

j. Matt. 19:28; Titus 3:5.
k. 2 Peter 1:4.
l. 2 Cor. 5:17.
m. Ezek. 36:26.
n. Eph. 2:15; 4:24.
o. Eph. 2:5; Col. 2:13; 1 Peter 1:3, 23; 1 John 5:1.
p. Eph. 2:10.
q. Eph. 1:13.

1. New Birth

To be born again as a new person with a new heart and new nature means that at the deepest level you have a new identity and new passionate desires for God's Word and will, just as Hannah did. This change is so deep that the Bible, including Ephesians, uses the language of being "born again."[r]

This term likely comes from Jesus telling the Old Testament scholar Nicodemus that a person must be born again to enter the kingdom of God. Jesus meant that we're each sinners born physically alive but spiritually dead.[s] To be spiritually alive, we must experience a second birth of our spirits—in other words, be born again—which occurs by the work of God the Holy Spirit, as Jesus told Nicodemus.

The Bible often renamed people once they were regenerated as a tangible illustration of God's internal work in their lives. For example, Abram became Abraham, Cephas became Peter, and Saul became Paul. They were transformed at the deepest levels.

Hannah also changed her name due to the deep work of God in her life. "I was so overwhelmed by his grace and love and so moved by his calling for me to be a new creation in him," she says, "that I felt called to change my name to represent the enormous heart change God has done in me. It is by his grace I am able to share my testimony openly and honestly without shame or condemnation. I belong to him, I declare Jesus as Lord and Savior, and I am here to speak of his grace in my life. So it is by his grace I can now be known as Grace."

Every Christian illustrates the significance of regeneration and new birth through baptism. In baptism, we show that Jesus lived, died, and rose for us as we're dunked under the water and rise up out of it as a demonstration that our old self has died with Christ and our new self is raised with Christ.

First Peter 2:2 encourages born-again people to, "as newborn babes, desire the pure milk of the word, that you may grow thereby." An indicator

r. John 3:3.
s. Eph. 2:1, 5; Col. 2:13.

that we've experienced new birth is that we begin craving the nourishment of Scripture as newborn babies crave milk. Learning the Bible isn't something you do as a duty, but rather something you, as a new person with a new mind, do as a delight. You have a new birth in Christ.

2. New Lord

Satan and sin no longer dominate regenerated people. Instead, we're born again to a new life with God, who is our new Lord and who rules over all of our life. In Ephesians, Paul welcomed us to know the Lord Jesus Christ better throughout life even though we've already "heard Him and have been taught by Him."[t]

Jesus isn't just a theological concept. He's a risen, living person who reigns now and forevermore. Your new Lord loves, forgives, serves, gifts, hears, empowers, and indwells you. He will never fail, leave, or forsake you. Your new Lord defeated Satan, your old lord, so that you no longer have to believe his lies, succumb to his temptations, or serve his mission. Among the wondrous benefits of having Jesus as a new Lord is that other previous and false lords used by Satan, such as an abusive boyfriend, parent, or spouse, are dethroned. You have a new Lord in Christ.

3. New Heart

In Scripture, the *heart* is the symbolic seat and center of our identity, which is expressed outwardly in our words and deeds. The word *heart* occurs more than nine hundred times in various forms (e.g., "hearts," "hearted") throughout the Scriptures.

Jesus said that words,[u] lusts,[v] how we spend our money,[w] evil thoughts, sexual immorality, theft, murder, adultery, greed, malice, deceit, lewdness, envy, slander, arrogance, folly,[x] good and evil,[y] sinful grief, anxiety,

---

t. Eph. 4:21.
u. Matt. 12:34.
v. Matt. 5:28.
w. Matt. 6:21.
x. Mark 7:21–23.
y. Luke 6:45.

and drunkenness all come out of our hearts.[z] And the Old Testament frequently speaks of regeneration in terms of a deep work in our hearts.[aa] When we're born again and Jesus becomes our new Lord, the deepest desires of our hearts change, and we have new hearts for the things of God.

God says it this way, "I will give you a new heart, and a new spirit I will put within you. And I will remove the heart of stone from your flesh and give you a heart of flesh. And I will put my Spirit within you, and cause you to walk in my statutes and be careful to obey my rules."[ab] You have a new heart in Christ.

4. New Creation

As regenerated people, we are changed so deeply that the Scriptures call us a "new creation." As 2 Corinthians 5:17 says, "Therefore, if anyone is in Christ, he is a new creation; old things have passed away; behold, all things have become new."

Practically, this means that if there is to be any true holiness in us, change in our behavior must be preceded with a change in our nature by the Holy Spirit. On this point, Galatians 6:15 says, "For in Christ Jesus neither circumcision nor uncircumcision [both outward acts] avails anything, but a new creation [an inward act]." Sadly, we often forget this wonderful benefit of regeneration and instead try to change our outward behavior, forgetting that change begins deep inside us and works its way out into our daily actions.

God desires for each of us to be born again in him and to live a new life as a new person in relationship with him rather than seeking to be transformed by our outward and religious efforts. God doesn't want to simply improve the old you. He wants to make an entirely new you. You're a new creation in Christ.

5. New Mind

As new persons in Christ, God gives us new minds to think as he

---

z. Luke 21:34.
aa. Deut. 30:6; Jer. 24:7; 31:31–33; 32:39–40; Ezek. 11:19–20.
ab. Ezek. 36:26–27 (esv).

thinks and love what he loves. This doesn't mean that we're smarter than non-Christians, or that non-Christians are unable to come to great insights in areas such as medicine or engineering. However, it does mean that without a new mind in Christ, the things of God aren't naturally perceived and embraced. For example, apart from the Holy Spirit, Jesus as fully God and fully man is not understood, and the fact of his death in our place for our sins sounds like foolishness apart from a new mind in Christ. First Corinthians 2:14–16 says that "the natural man does not receive the things of the Spirit of God, for they are foolishness to him; nor can he know them, because they are spiritually discerned. But he who is spiritual judges all things, yet he himself is rightly judged by no one. For 'who has known the mind of the Lord that he may instruct Him?' But we have the mind of Christ." As we feed our minds with truth, particularly as found in Scripture, our thinking radically changes. You have a new mind in Christ.

6. New Love

If we're born-again, we'll love as Jesus loved. First John 4:7 says, "Beloved, let us love one another, for love is of God, and everyone who loves is born of God and knows God." Because God is love, when he makes us new, we're connected to the source of all true love—the Trinity. As a result, we have the capacity, if we walk in obedience, to love God, our spouses, our children, our friends, our neighbors, and even our enemies. You have new love in Christ.

7. New Desires

A new person has new desires that are akin to a new appetite for the things of God. Paul spoke of this in Galatians 5:16–17, saying, "I say then: Walk in the Spirit, and you shall not fulfill the lust of the flesh. For the flesh lusts against the Spirit, and the Spirit against the flesh; and these are contrary to one another, so that you do not do the things that *you wish*" (emphasis added). That last phrase is incredibly important. As Christians, we desire God's will instead of our will because of the indwelling, transforming presence and power of God the Holy Spirit.

In this life, as we grow to be more and more like Jesus, we still wrestle with sinful desires and temptations. When we do give in to those sinful desires, we become miserable until we repent and live in obedience to God.

Have you ever experienced the anguish of sin? Paul described his own experience with this: "For I do not understand my own actions. For I do not do what I want, but I do the very thing I hate."[ac] The Christian life is to be in passionate pursuit of our regenerated hearts' deepest desires without settling for the lesser, sinful desires of our former self. Psalm 37:4 admonishes, "Delight yourself also in the LORD, and He shall give you the desires of your heart."

As Christians, we're free to pursue with great passion our deepest, God-given desires. When we do, we worship God by not just obeying what he commands in duty, but rather, in delighting in his commands, as our will and God's will become one and the same.

Religion doesn't understand the new desires of a regenerated heart and wrongly assumes that Christians, at their deepest level, primarily have an appetite for sin. As a result, religion deadens our desires with guilt and man-made, legalistic rules, assuming that passion leads to sin. The biblical understanding of regenerated desires overturns this thinking, teaching that we don't overcome sin by religion and rules and by deadening our passion, but rather we overcome sin by becoming more passionate for new desires that are the things of God.

C. S. Lewis says it aptly: "It would seem that Our Lord finds our desires not too strong, but too weak. We are half-hearted creatures, fooling about with drink and sex and ambition when infinite joy is offered us, like an ignorant child who wants to go on making mud pies in a slum because he cannot imagine what is meant by the offer of a holiday at the sea. We are far too easily pleased."[3] You have new desires in Christ.

8. New Community

As regenerated people, we are forgiven of our sins and we're reconciled both to God as Christians and to fellow Christians as the church.

---

ac. Rom. 7:15 (ESV).

Subsequently, we desire and pursue community with other Christians in the church. This community is given multiple names in the New Testament, including citizens of God's kingdom, members of God's family, a temple for God's presence,[ad] and parts of one body.[ae] By living in community with fellow Christians as the church, we learn more about God and how to live a life that glorifies him and help others do the same. You have a new community in Christ.

9. New Power

God gives us new, supernatural power to live new lives. This new power is the indwelling power of God the Holy Spirit in the regenerated Christian. This is why Jesus called the Holy Spirit "the Helper"[af] and our teacher.[ag] The new power of God the Holy Spirit is unleashed to help us continually repent of sin, turn from it and toward God, and be "filled with the Spirit."[ah]

To be filled with the Holy Spirit is like being a sail filled with wind. Just as a ship opens its sail, that it may be powerfully driven toward a destination, as Spirit-filled Christians, we open our minds, hearts, and wills to the things of God and welcome his powerful direction.

Through the power of the Holy Spirit, God helps us live holy lives and enables us to obey him. In this way, regeneration is the opposite of religion, which tragically teaches that if you obey God, he will then love you. The exact opposite is true. Regeneration reveals that because God loves us, we can obey him by the power of the Holy Spirit. You have new power in Christ.

10. New Freedom

Accompanying your new power is a new freedom—the ability to say no to sin and yes to God. In this life, we either will have our faces toward

---

ad. Eph. 2:19–22.
ae. Rom. 12:5.
af. John 14:26; 16:7.
ag. John 16:13.
ah. Eph. 5:18.

sin and our backs toward God or our faces toward God and our backs toward sin. One of the freedoms of regeneration is the ability to repent, turn our backs on sin, and turn our faces toward God to live new lives in holiness. Theologians are fond of calling this living "*coram Deo*," which means living "in the face of God." You don't have to hide your sin, excuse your sin, blame others for your sin, or deny your sin. In Christ, your sin can be put to death because Jesus died for it. In Christ, you can live a new life because Jesus rose in newness of life. You have a new freedom in Christ.

11. New Life

The culmination of regeneration is a new life that is vastly different from our old lives. The New Testament is fond of contrasting our old, sinful life with our Spirit-regenerated new life to clearly distinguish what our life is and is not.[ai]

Ephesians 4:17–19 speaks of our old life apart from Christ, saying, "You should no longer walk as the rest of the Gentiles walk, in the futility of their mind, having their understanding darkened, being alienated from the life of God, because of the ignorance that is in them, because of the blindness of their heart; who, being past feeling, have given themselves over to lewdness, to work all uncleanness with greediness."

Ephesians 4:20–24 then contrasts our old life apart from Christ with our new life in Christ: "But you have not so learned Christ, if indeed you have heard Him and have been taught by Him, as the truth is in Jesus: that you put off, concerning your former conduct, the old man which grows corrupt according to the deceitful lusts, and be renewed in the spirit of your mind, and that you put on the new man which was created according to God, in true righteousness and holiness." You have a new life in Christ.

Eternally New: Glorification

As mentioned earlier, it's sometimes said that a Christian is a combination of both "old man" (sometimes called old nature) and "new

---

ai. Rom. 6:19–22; 1 Cor. 6:9–11; 1 John 2:15–29.

man" (sometimes called new nature). Some people like to explain sin and temptation in terms of constant war between our two natures. The new man rules when we choose holiness, and the old man wins when we choose sinfulness. While it's understandable that someone would think this way based on the experiences of everyday life, biblically it's not true.

A Christian is not simultaneously saved and lost, a child of God and an enemy of God, both forgiven and unforgiven by Jesus Christ. As Christians we're altogether new in Christ.

While we're *genuinely* new in Christ, we're not yet *completely* new in Christ. There is still a seed of rebellion from Adam in us, the temptations of the world around us, and the snares of the devil set for us. In this life we continually grow to live out of our new identity as new people in Christ through a process called *sanctification*. In this process we learn more about Jesus and become more like him by the power of the Holy Spirit as we believe the Bible truths outlined in this chapter and act upon them in faith.

One day, we will die. If we die in Christ, we're made fully, completely, unchangingly, and eternally new—what theologians call *glorification*. On that day, your faith will be sight as you see the risen and reigning Jesus face to face. On that day, everyone in Christ will be made completely perfect as together we rise like Jesus to be like him forever. In Christ, you are new.

And Christ is not done with you.

12

I AM FORGIVEN

Therefore, putting away lying, "Let each one of you speak truth with his neighbor," for we are members of one another. "Be angry, and do not sin": do not let the sun go down on your wrath, nor give place to the devil. Let him who stole steal no longer, but rather let him labor, working with his hands what is good, that he may have something to give him who has need. Let no corrupt word proceed out of your mouth, but what is good for necessary edification, that it may impart grace to the hearers. And do not grieve the Holy Spirit of God, by whom you were sealed for the day of redemption. Let all bitterness, wrath, anger, clamor, and evil speaking be put away from you, with all malice. And be kind to one another, tenderhearted, forgiving one another, even as God in Christ forgave you.

—EPHESIANS 4:25–32

Rose grew up in a Christian home and from an early age was surrounded by Christians. She attended a conservative church every Sunday; went to a private Christian school run by the church, from preschool through her freshman year; and participated in church activities, such as Awana. "I was basically immersed in Jesus," she says. "I was on campus six days a week, played all my sports there, had youth group there . . . I grew up in a holy bubble, so to speak, and never had any reason to interact with anyone outside of it. I knew Bible verses like the back of my hand. By junior high I had already read the whole Bible straight through and knew every answer to every question concerning the Bible or Christianity." Rose was a "good kid." She never did anything "rebellious" and always followed all the rules. But she "had no relationship with God whatsoever."

Rose's devotion to the church was high, but her devotion to Jesus was nonexistent. As a result, she became legalistic (replaced a relationship with God with rules that God didn't make) and dealt with people harshly. "Looking back on my life," she said, "I did not witness to people with love but with condemnation and out of a sense of duty. Just like everything I did to be a 'good' Christian, it was to fulfill some unspoken list of requirements, and not to really know God better."

In her teen years, everything changed for Rose. She became convicted about her lack of relationship with God. "I remember very distinctly the day I realized I wasn't a Christian, that my whole life I had been living a lie," shared Rose. "I went straight to a trusted teacher and explained my new enlightenment. He prayed for me and talked with me, but really, I already knew all the answers. I knew how to fix it. So, I prayed for probably the thousandth time for salvation."

Though Rose now knew she needed Jesus and began to love him relationally, not just legalistically, she soon discovered she had a long road of growth ahead of her. "I still didn't have a grasp on how deep into legalism I was until a few years later," she says.

Rose's process of discovery regarding her legalism began when her family left the church in which she grew up. "After attending church there for over ten years," she told me, "my mother began to feel the depression . . . no grace, no mercy, no encouragement, only condemnation. Over the course of the next year, my father also became aware through my mother and God opening his eyes, and we finally left the church and school after my freshman year of high school."

Rose said that she was bitter for over a year, as she and her family looked for and found a new church. There, God began peeling back Rose's layers of legalism, helping her to understand the weight of her sin against him and her need to view others with the same grace that Jesus viewed her. "It took some time for me to really see how tainted I had become by legalism," she said. "To change those habits and thoughts and how I treat people, especially non-Christians. The Lord is still working on my heart every day, and even now [five years later], I still struggle with my old ways of judging others harshly and 'dealing' with others' sin without grace, rather than loving them through it the way Jesus did for me."

Rose revealed that her legalism resulted in years of doubting her salvation, as she worked hard to please God and felt the guilt of judging others when she was sinful herself. "I cannot express the overwhelming difference Jesus has made on my life," she says. "He has brought me out of legalism and self-righteousness, religion and hate. I no longer have to doubt my salvation, and I have a lot more faith in Jesus and a lot less faith in myself. He sustains me now, not my unspoken list of Christian duties."

Rose's story is easily one that could have resulted in bitterness and a falling away of faith. Or it could have been a story of trying harder to please God and continually feeling the weight of falling short. Instead, it's a story of deep knowledge of grace and forgiveness. "I know legalism well," she says, "and I never want to go back there. Jesus has given me a sympathy for people that I didn't have before, and I'm so thankful to experience his mercy and grace."

Rose is forgiven and can also now forgive.

THE POWER OF FORGIVENESS

The apostle Paul, who also was a legalist prior to meeting Jesus, experienced the radical power of forgiveness. In Acts 7, Stephen, a deacon in the early church, preached an amazing sermon. To silence his preaching, an angry mob "cast him out of the city and stoned him." Paul oversaw this mob who stoned Stephen and approved of their actions. As Acts relates, "The witnesses laid down their clothes at the feet of a young man named Saul [Paul]. And they stoned Stephen as he was calling on God and saying, 'Lord Jesus, receive my spirit.' Then he knelt down and cried out with a loud voice, 'Lord, do not charge them with this sin.' And when he had said this, he fell asleep."[a]

In his moment of death, Stephen forgave Saul for murdering him and

---

a. Acts 7:58–60.

prayed that God would also forgive Saul. God answered Stephen's prayer. Saul became a Christian, experienced forgiveness of all his sins, including the murder of Stephen, and changed his name to Paul. More than most, Paul knew the power of forgiveness.

Have you ever considered how sinful you are? Imagine writing down every wrong thing you've done and everything you should've done but didn't—including every person you should've helped, every injustice you should've fought, and every dollar you should've given to help others. Add to that all the sinful thoughts you've had, every sinful word you've communicated, and every sinful motive that's compelled you to do anything, even seemingly good things.

Now, consider that each of the sins on your list is a direct assault on God and his rightful place as ruler of creation. As R. C. Sproul says, "Every sin is an act of cosmic treason, a futile attempt to dethrone God in his sovereign authority."[1] God feels anger over sin, and he hates it.[b] And the Scriptures tell us that he even hates some sinners.[c] In response to sin, God justly pours out his wrath on unrepentant sinners—those who continually oppose him with their actions, inaction, and thoughts.

The doctrine of God's wrath isn't popular in our day, but the fact is that in the Old Testament alone, nearly twenty words are used for God's wrath, which is spoken of roughly six hundred times. In the New Testament the wrath of God appears roughly twenty-five times, including Ephesians 5:6, which plainly says, "The wrath of God comes upon the sons of disobedience."

Regarding God's anger and hatred, it's commonly protested that God can't hate because he is love. But you may be surprised to learn that the Bible speaks of God's anger, wrath, and fury more than his love, grace, and mercy. That is not to say that God hates as we hate. As sinners, we often carry grudges and wish harm on our enemies. Every expression of God's emotions, including anger and hatred, are perfect and without sin. God tells us to love our enemies and models this by inviting his enemies

---

b. Prov. 6:16–19; Zech. 8:17.
c. Ps. 5:5, 11:4–5; Hos. 9:15; Mal. 1:2–3; cf. Rom. 9:13.

to repent and wishing that none would perish.[d] This is possible because God's hate is not vindictive, as human hate is, but rather a holy rejection, and ultimately, if they're unrepentant, a just condemnation of sinners and sin, as he is a holy God and can't be in the presence of unholy sinners unrepentant of their sin.

For unrepentant sinners, the place of God's unending, active wrath is hell, which Jesus spoke of more than anyone in the Bible.[2] Hell is an eternal place of painful torment, akin to taking a beating, getting butchered, and being burned.[e]

The Bible uses strong and scary language for hell because the deserved consequences for our sins—our cosmic treason against God—should scare us. Also consider that we can't save ourselves from the conscious, eternal torments of God's wrath in hell. If any of us really took this to heart, we'd each sleep with a helmet on and one eye open. Thankfully, there is good news for us in the work of Jesus on the cross and the power of forgiveness.

You Are Forgiven in Christ

In love, Jesus substituted himself for our sins and took God's wrath for us on the cross.[f] Scripture uses a word to describe this: *propitiation.* This means God's wrath against sin is satisfied.[g]

Understanding the truth of God's wrath allows us to appreciate more deeply the truth of his grace, and to understand the happiest words a sinner could ever hear, "God in Christ forgave you."[h]

Are you in Christ? Then God has forgiven you for all of your sins—past, present, and future. Jesus Christ shouted from the cross as his final words in triumphant victory, "It is finished!"[i] At that moment, sin was atoned for and sinners were forgiven.

---

d. 2 Peter 3:9.
e. Matt. 8:11–12, 29; 13:49–50; 18:8–9; 24:50–51; 25:41, 46; Mark 1:24; 5:7; 9:43–48; Luke 12:46–48; 16:19–31; Rev. 14:10.
f. Rom. 5:9; 1 Thess. 1:9–10.
g. Rom. 3:23–25; Heb. 2:17; 1 John 2:2; 1 John 4:10.
h. Eph. 4:32.
i. John 19:30.

Do you accept your forgiveness in Christ? Do you *appreciate* it? If so, then you should extend forgiveness as Christ did. As Rose learned by God's grace, to accept forgiveness while refusing to extend it is hypocritical and wrong. It's in effect saying that others' sins are more grievous than the sins you've committed against God and others. And ultimately, it leads to bitterness.

You Can Forgive in Christ

I hate doing yard work. But as the oldest of five kids, I was given this chore. One day, my parents asked me to go out and pull the weeds. That seemed like a lot of work. So I concocted what I thought was an ingenious and simple plan. Rather than taking hours to pull the weeds, I instead took minutes to hit them with a powerful, electric Weed Eater and used the rest of my day to ride my bike. I remember feeling quite proud of myself for such a brilliant solution . . . until a few days later, when it seemed as though the weeds had not only returned but also multiplied, taking over the entire yard. I overlooked the fact that weeds have roots.

God, through Paul, says that we only have two possible responses when it comes to those who've sinned against us: forgiveness or bitterness. And like weeds, the Bible tells us, bitterness has roots.[j] Consequently, when others sin against us, we can whack away at the surface—our frustrations, disappointments, angers, hurts, and sadness—or we can pull up our bitterness before it takes root. If you don't pull up the root of bitterness, it invariably returns, bigger than ever. It's like a taproot: the longer you wait, the harder it is to pull it up.

As a general rule, bitter people have good reasons to be angry—they've been sinned against. The sin may have been something catastrophic, such as adultery, abuse, or damaging gossip. Or the sin may not have seemed like a big deal from the outside, but the pain it caused is severe because the person who caused it was loved, trusted, and given privileged access to our souls. Sometimes the worst pain is betrayal.

Bitterness is often related to how much you love the offender. If a

j. Heb. 12:15.

stranger sins against you, you're unlikely to become bitter. But if a beloved family member or friend sins against you, you're likelier to become bitter because you have higher expectations for the relationship. Those you love most are the likeliest candidates for causing bitterness—and that includes bitterness against God.

In dealing with our potential bitterness, Paul exhorted us to "put away lying" and to "speak the truth."[k] To do that, we must be honest about some of our most painful memories. We must ask soul-searching questions and get beyond simply saying we're fine.

THE CYCLE OF BITTERNESS

Paul was clear that if bitterness isn't exchanged for forgiveness, it escalates and becomes increasingly devastating to both you and others. He listed a pattern that proceeds from bitterness: wrath, anger, clamor, slander, and malice.[l]

When we're bitter, we refuse to forgive. Wrath develops when we become irritated, agitated, and can feel our blood pressure rising. Unrighteous anger proceeds not from injustice but rather our bitterness and causes us to be furious with someone and motivated to harm him or her in some way. "Clamor" means that our anger can no longer be contained and we engage in a conflict with others for the purpose of harming them either emotionally or physically. Slander occurs when, in an effort to vindicate ourselves and vilify others, we gossip about them and seek to ruin their reputations. Malice manifests when we invent ways of doing evil to punish those against whom we're bitter, regardless of personal cost. The entire goal is to make those individuals lose, even if that should mean that we lose as well. At the point of malice, people are capable of horrific evil and out-of-character conduct that is oftentimes hard to even imagine.

Sometimes the cycle of bitterness can move very quickly, like a raging

k. Eph. 4:25.
l. Eph. 4:31.

fire, over the course of minutes or days. Other times, bitterness smolders slowly over the course of months or years.

If we're honest, we're all bitter at various times in our lives. In those seasons, we tend to blame others for our bitterness. The truth is that people, even the worst of them, don't embitter us. Rather, they provide us an opportunity to choose to either forgive or be bitter, for which we remain morally responsible.

"Be Angry and Do Not Sin"

A common word of advice to those who are bitter is that they shouldn't be angry about the wrongs they've suffered. That counsel is both unbiblical and unhelpful. God himself got angry throughout the Bible in response to sin, though we're repeatedly told that his wick is long and he is "slow to anger."[3] Furthermore, Jesus got angry on various occasions in Scripture.[4]

Righteous anger is the right response to sin and far more consistent with the character of God than faking happiness, approval, or acceptance. The Bible, on many occasions, gives us examples of human anger as justified.[m] This is why Paul *didn't* say, "Don't get angry," but rather said, "Be angry, and do not sin."[n] He accepted anger as a legitimate emotional response to being sinned against. But he also warned us to be careful not to accept or empower anger that comes from sin. Instead, he told us to harness the energy of our anger toward righteousness rather than letting it fuel our descent into clamor, slander, and malice—to "not let the sun go down on [our] wrath." We are not to let anger rule us and set up camp in our souls but rather take our anger to God, and by the power of the Holy Spirit, seek to deal in a just way with the wrongs committed against us.

When our anger, rather than the Holy Spirit, rules us, we become the kind of quick-tempered, hotheaded fool the Bible warns against in the book of Proverbs: "A quick-tempered man acts foolishly. . . . He who is slow to wrath has great understanding, but he who is impulsive exalts

---

m. Ex.32:19; see also Ex. 11:8; 16:20; Num. 16:15; Lev. 10:16; 1 Sam. 11:6; 20:34; 2 Sam. 12:5; Neh. 5:6; Mark 3:5; Luke 14:21.
n. Eph. 4:26.

folly." Conversely, "the discretion of a man makes him slow to anger, and his glory is to overlook a transgression."[o]

Describing unrighteous anger in contrast to righteous anger, one Christian counselor says, "There is an anger that is only concerned with our self-absorbed, self-centered issues and really doesn't care about the other person. There is also self-directed anger, which is anger directed at oneself and is an expression of our not caring anything about ourselves. Healthy anger involves a concern with justice, with protecting both you and me, and is disciplined in its actions."[5]

Anger, when rightly harnessed and directed at true injustices (not our perceived injustices), can be a powerful force for justice, goodness, and love. A tragic example helps illuminate the positive power of righteous anger.

On May 3, 1980, a repeat drunk driver climbed into his car after a three-day bender and ran over fourteen-year-old Cari Lightner as she walked to church. The impact threw her 125 feet, and once the driver awoke from his passed-out state, he sped away. He was later caught, and Cari's mother, Candace, said she felt "rage" that her daughter's murderer wouldn't even get jail time, despite the fact that he had four other drunk-driving arrests in the past five years (he was already out on bail for one of them).

Rather than seek revenge, Candace channeled her anger toward justice and good works. She founded Mothers Against Drunk Driving (MADD), whose grassroots efforts have resulted in legislation that has saved thousands of lives.[6] Indeed, our anger can be a great force for good if it compels us toward justice rather than malice.

Paul exhorted us to urgently deal with our anger and not wait even a day to address it, lest it consume us. Failure to do so, he said, grieves the Holy Spirit, who desires and is able to help us work through our anger and bitterness so Satan doesn't have a foothold in our soul. Practically speaking, this doesn't mean we can't take an hour or two to pray, clear our heads, calm down, seek wise counsel, and jot down a few thoughts so

---

o. Prov. 14:17; Prov. 14:29; Prov. 19:11.

we can engage those who've angered us constructively. But it does mean the longer we wait, the more ground we give to the enemy in our life.

The only helpful answer to our bitterness and anger is the gospel. Paul put it this way: "Be kind to one another, tenderhearted, forgiving one another, even as God in Christ forgave you."[p] Admittedly, when we are bitter and angry, words like this can sound like a hyper-spiritual platitude, which pushes us to defend our bitterness by recalling the valid reasons for our pain. When we defend our angry bitterness, we appeal to a sense of justice—that to simply forgive someone who has not apologized, changed, or made amends is tantamount to condoning evil.

How do I know? I've done it myself. Many times.

In those moments, I find myself able to recall intricate details of exact circumstances surrounding the sins that contributed to my hurt and anger. I can remember where I was when sinned against, exactly what was said, and other, similar details, such as what the offenders were wearing and their tone of voice and facial expressions. Regarding these moments, my memory is keen because I've recounted the events over and over in my mind, digging up the past to emotionally relive it in the present, which, said Paul, is an unloving record-keeping of wrongs.[q]

As someone who is prone to angry bitterness, I hope Paul's words to the Ephesians minister to you as much as they have to me. With some people, I hadn't done what Paul exhorted: "get rid of *all* bitterness."[r] This was due in large part to the fact that I didn't deem their grief, suffering, or repentance commensurate to the pain they'd caused me. But God, in his kindness, reminded me that we're to "forgiv[e] one another, even as God in Christ forgave [us]."[s] How did God forgive us in Christ? We caused Jesus to suffer unjustly, and he received it without bitterness, forgave us, pursued us, and wants good for us. We are to do the same to those who sin against us and cause us harm.

Biblical forgiveness is a revolutionary idea and a gospel issue. In our

p. Eph. 4:32.
q. 1 Cor. 13:6.
r. Eph. 4:31 (NIV; emphasis added).
s. Eph. 4:32.

hurt, we can easily lose sight of the truth that no one has been sinned against more than God. Furthermore, we've each contributed to the pain God experiences, as all sin is ultimately against God.[t] This means that God could've been the most embittered person of all, but instead he came as Jesus and took our place to suffer for our sins. He speaks to us through the bloody lips of Jesus from the cross, "It is finished," pronouncing that we are forgiven.

Therefore, when we forgive others, it has very little, if anything, to do with them. Instead, it has everything to do with God. As an act of worship, we must respond to sinners as God responds to us sinners—with forgiveness. Of course, whether or not they experience ultimate forgiveness with God depends upon whether or not they accept Jesus' work on the cross in their place for their sins. If they reject Jesus, then the Father will reject them. So, in forgiving them we are leaving them to God, praying that they come to repentance, and freeing ourselves of bitterness. In the end, we simply cannot accept forgiveness from God without extending it to others.

This leads to the question, what does forgiveness look like?

SEVEN THINGS FORGIVENESS IS

Forgiveness is both a decision and a process. The decision to forgive is usually preceded by intense emotions, such as grief, sadness, and anger. Because forgiveness is emotionally taxing, it's usually best formalized by declaring it in word and deed. This might include meeting face to face with your offender in a safe setting, with a mediator or witness; speaking to him or her on the phone; or writing that individual a letter expressing the facts of his or her sin, your feelings about that sin, and forgiveness for the sin, which you can either send to your offender or burn as a symbolic means of letting it go. The process of forgiveness, however, can take days to years, depending on the offense committed, how it harmed you, how the offender responded, and a myriad of other variables. The following aspects of forgiveness may help you understand what it actually is:

---

t. Ps. 51:4.

1. Forgiveness is cancelling a debt owed to you. When someone sins against you, a wrong is committed and a debt is accrued. In forgiving others, you relinquish your right to make them repay that debt.
2. Forgiveness is removing the control your offender has over you. So long as your offenders remain unforgiven, they continue to loom large in your life by maintaining an emotional presence. Through forgiveness, you not only free them from their debt to you but also emotionally free yourself from them.
3. Forgiveness is giving a gift to your offender and yourself. Forgiveness includes the physical benefits of reduced anxiety, stress, and blood pressure; and the mental benefits of no longer obsessing over a person or act, freeing you up to move on with your life. Forgiveness also allows you to move from a life centered on pain to one centered on God and others as you regain emotional health, empathy, and perspective. This improves all of your relationships and is a gift to you, your friends, and your family.
4. Forgiveness is forsaking revenge. Romans 12:19 says, "Beloved, do not avenge yourselves, but rather give place to wrath; for it is written, 'Vengeance is Mine, I will repay,' says the Lord." When we seek revenge, we place ourselves morally alongside our offenders. When we forgive, we rise above them by grace and leave them to a perfect and holy God. Revenge may temporarily placate our rage, but it can never undo a wrong. By feeding rage, we become like the person who hurt us—self-interested and dangerous. This is why one ancient Chinese proverb says, "He who seeks revenge should dig two graves."
5. Forgiveness is leaving ultimate justice in God's hands. Sometimes forgiveness is difficult because it violates our sense of fairness and justice. But the Bible promises that God will deal with everyone's sins justly. For those who repent of sin and come to faith in Jesus Christ, justice came at the cross of Jesus, when our Savior suffered and died in our place for our sins. Those who don't repent of sin and come to faith in Jesus Christ will have justice in the punishment of conscious eternal torments of hell. In forgiving, we don't

neglect justice, but rather, we trust God for perfect justice and get out from between the sinner and God.

6. Forgiveness is often an ongoing process. In Jesus' time, a rabbinic teaching said that you only had to forgive someone three times, and after that no more. In Matthew 18:21–22 we read, "Then Peter came to [Jesus] and said, 'Lord, how often shall my brother sin against me, and I forgive him? Up to seven times?' Jesus said to him, 'I do not say to you, up to seven times, but up to seventy times seven.'" A noted Bible commentator says of this, "It is a way of saying that for Jesus' followers forgiveness is to be unlimited."[7]

7. Forgiveness is wanting good for your offender. In forgiving our offenders, we change from wanting them to suffer and pay to wanting them to repent and change by God's grace.

SEVEN THINGS FORGIVENESS IS NOT

Forgiveness is a word that is often uttered but not often understood. As important as it is to understand what forgiveness is, it's equally important to understand what forgiveness is not.

1. Forgiveness is not denying that sin occurred or diminishing its evil. In forgiving someone, we don't say, "Nothing happened," or that something was "no big deal." Instead, we say sin happened and that it was such a big deal that Jesus died for it.

2. Forgiveness is not enabling sin. To forgive is not to allow offenders to remain stuck in their cycle of sin, thus being complicit and enabling their continued transgression. We can forgive while still being truthful about someone's behavior.

3. Forgiveness is not necessarily a response to a repentant apology. Sometimes sinners will acknowledge their wrong and ask for forgiveness. Sometimes they won't. Sometimes we don't even know who the offender is or how to locate him or her; other times the person is deceased. Either way, we're to forgive whether there is an admission of guilt or not. Christianity is unique in this way, as

other major world religions teach that you cannot forgive someone who hasn't apologized.

4. Forgiveness is not covering up sin committed against us. In fact, if a crime is committed, we can simultaneously forgive someone and seek legal action.[u]

5. Forgiveness is not forgetting. It's commonly believed that we should "forgive and forget," which is impossible. When God said, "I will forgive their iniquity, and their sin I will remember no more,"[v] he didn't mean he has no recollection, as that is impossible, because God is all-knowing. Instead, it means that God doesn't begrudgingly hold our sin against us and keep it as the basis of our identity and interaction with him. Furthermore, when we forgive someone, we're remembering the sin so that we can forgive it. To demand that someone completely forgive without remembering that he or she was beaten, raped, betrayed, or any other array of sinful actions is to demand the impossible and add burden.

6. Forgiveness is not trust. Forgiveness takes a moment, but trust is built over time. And once trust is lost through sin, it can take much time to be rebuilt.

7. Forgiveness is not reconciliation. It takes one sinner to repent and one victim to forgive, but it takes both to reconcile. Therefore, unless there is both repentance by the sinner and forgiveness by the victim, reconciliation can't occur, which means the relationship remains continually broken until reconciliation does occur. Your forgiveness is the beginning of potential reconciliation but not in and of itself reconciliation.

LIFE AND DEATH IN THE TONGUE

Proverbs 18:21 says, "Death and life are in the power of the tongue." The true test of whether or not we're bitter is our tongues. What do we say

u. Rom. 13:1–7.
v. Jer. 31:34; cf. Heb. 8:12; 10:17.

about our offenders? Do we pray for them? We should. Paul said, "Let no corrupting talk come out of your mouths, but only such as is good for building up, as fits the occasion, that it may give grace to those who hear. And do not grieve the Holy Spirit of God, by whom you were sealed for the day of redemption."w Even when the person against whom we're bitter isn't present, the Holy Spirit is, and he grieves when we speak ill of others.

As a pastor, I have noticed two common trends in the speech of those who are bitter. First, they are prone to nickname people against whom they're bitter, imposing a demeaning and contemptuous new identity on the offender. Second, they can't constrain their tongues, but rather, the "'root of bitterness' springs up and causes trouble, and by it many become defiled."x Practically, this means that children are impacted by their parents' bitterness, generations are affected, circles of friends are poisoned, and entire churches can be consumed with the demonic drama that proceeds from one tongue speaking on behalf of a bitter heart. Making matters even worse in our day are the innumerable opportunities that technology affords us to type up our bitterness and send it off in haste to the world.

In closing, how have you felt reading this chapter? I pray you've been served, informed, and freed. Still, that is not enough, and I long for more on your behalf. Bitter people can sometimes be blind or indifferent to those they have themselves embittered. Who, if they read this chapter, would be thinking about you and your sin against them? Who would read this not as the sinner, but rather as the victim of your sin? What does repentance from you look like for them?

As Paul exhorted us, I exhort you: "Do not let the sun go down on your wrath." Make things right today by forgiving others who've harmed you and, by God's grace, seeking forgiveness from those whom you've harmed. You are forgiven. Walk in forgiveness.

---

w. Eph. 4:29–30 (esv).
x. Heb. 12:15 (esv).

13

I AM ADOPTED

Therefore be imitators of God as dear children. And walk in love, as Christ also has loved us and given Himself for us, an offering and a sacrifice to God for a sweet-smelling aroma.

But fornication and all uncleanness or covetousness, let it not even be named among you, as is fitting for saints; neither filthiness, nor foolish talking, nor coarse jesting, which are not fitting, but rather giving of thanks. For this you know, that no fornicator, unclean person, nor covetous man, who is an idolater, has any inheritance in the kingdom of Christ and God. Let no one deceive you with empty words, for because of these things the wrath of God comes upon the sons of disobedience. Therefore do not be partakers with them.

For you were once darkness, but now you are light in the Lord. Walk as children of light (for the fruit of the Spirit is in all goodness, righteousness, and truth), finding out what is acceptable to the Lord. And have no fellowship with the unfruitful works of darkness, but rather expose them. For it is shameful even to speak of those things which are done by them in secret. But all things that are exposed are made manifest by the light, for whatever makes manifest is light. Therefore He says:

"Awake, you who sleep,

Arise from the dead,

And Christ will give you light."

See then that you walk circumspectly, not as fools but as wise, redeeming the time, because the days are evil.

Therefore do not be unwise, but understand what the will of the Lord is. And do not be drunk with wine, in which is dissipation; but be filled with the Spirit, speaking to one another in psalms and hymns and spiritual songs, singing and making melody in your heart to the Lord, giving thanks always for all things to God the Father in the name of our Lord Jesus Christ, submitting to one another in the fear of God.

—EPHESIANS 5:1–21

ittle Benjamin was packed into a small orphanage room filled with cribs and fatherless children. He rarely got to go outside and play, and he called the only man working at the orphanage—a security guard—father.

One of six million orphans in his nation, Benjamin has a story that is tragically common in a country ravaged by famine and poverty. His mother, a poor peasant and most likely raped by her boyfriend's brother, gave birth to Benjamin in a culture that views him as worthless because he has no father and will not inherit land. The superstition is that boys such as Benjamin will grow up to be murderers and criminals. They are considered a blight on the family and often abandoned.

That Benjamin even ended up in an orphanage is an act of God's grace. His mother, faced with pressure from the family and no way to provide for the boy, wished to take Benjamin to the forest, lay him down, and simply leave him there to die—a common occurrence in his culture. By God's grace, the tribal elders of her village prevented her actions for fear that the government would find out and they would get in trouble. Rather than leave him in the forest, they took Benjamin to an orphanage, not to have a better life but to remove the shame from their family.

A friend recently took a trip to Benjamin's village. He and his wife finalized their adoption of Benjamin and excitedly brought him home to meet his two older sisters.

My friend explains how this all began, "The poverty was tough—ugly. I had never seen aggressive begging before by children my kids' age. It really affected me, and Matthew 25:40 came alive—the way we treat the least of these is how we treat Jesus," he shared. "These children were the heart of Jesus. Next to my salvation experience in Africa in 2005, which also opened my heart to Africa, this adoption process has been the most impactful event in my life."

As part of his travels, my friend learned about the horrible plight of many of the country's orphans. "The orphans that are on the streets are partly a result of parents who've died from HIV, but the rest are from families that send these kids to the street to literally die. Most either end up dead or turn to child prostitution."

Though not able to save everyone, my friend and his wife decided to adopt at least one of these boys to do what they could to redeem him from such a horrific life. That is how they came to meet and love baby Benjamin, now a part of their loving family. My friend shares how the adoption process has helped him more fully understand the gospel of Jesus.

"Benjamin was doomed, and nothing of his own doing," he said. "And he could not save himself. Someone needed to save him. The picture of adoption is the story of Jesus. We are all sinners, but by the grace of God we have a savior and salvation through Jesus. Nothing that we did earned this. Pure grace. A hundred percent. There are over six million orphans in that nation, and Benjamin is one of only a few that will make it out. He will live a life of blessing that he does not deserve and he did not pay for (grace). He will have a church family that loves him, and he will learn about Jesus in a way that would not be possible otherwise."

Just as Benjamin is adopted by his new earthly father, we're also adopted by our spiritual Father in Christ.

ADOPTED BY GOD

Benjamin's story was common to many children in New Testament times.[1] Throughout the Roman Empire children were often severely beaten and even tossed out into the garbage or on a dung heap to either die or be taken by someone and used as a slave, prostitute, gladiator, or worse.

Infant mortality was so high that only half of the children born lived to their fifth birthdays, and fewer than 40 percent lived until their twentieth birthdays. Consequently, a family would need to birth five children to have two that lived to adulthood, and most families usually waited until between eight and nine days after a birth to name the child because it wasn't worth the effort until they knew it would live.

Infanticide was also common, particularly with disabled children and girls. Methods included abandonment in the desert, tying babies to a rock and throwing them in a river, and even suffocation.

Within this culture of abandonment and infanticide, adoptions happened on the part of the wealthy upper class, but their motivations weren't generally noble and were mostly self-serving. "In this ancient Roman context, adoption was generally not about babies and childless couples finding a way to have children. Instead, the adoptees were usually adults, and adoption was first of all a legal arrangement to provide an heir who would receive an inheritance and enter into a new household with all its privileges and responsibilities."[2]

Simply put, political leaders in need of protecting massive empires occasionally chose an adult heir to adopt in an effort to extend the greatness of their legacy beyond their lifetime. "In fact, all of the Julio-Claudian emperors adopted 'sons.' Although Claudius had a biological son by Julia Agrippina, he adopted Nero at age twelve and made him heir to the dynasty."[3]

In the midst of this, Christians started doing something countercultural by adopting children for reasons quite different from those in more affluent classes. Christians, many of them poor, began adopting throwaway children as family. Why would Christians do this?

The answer lies in Paul's comparison of the gospel to adoption. We were once "sons of disobedience,"[a] but now we're "heirs with Christ."[b] Paul connected adoption as a major theme of the Bible to the center of all Scripture—Jesus (who was himself adopted by his earthly father, Joseph) and his work on the cross for us. Adoption is an amazing concept to trace biblically.

In the Old Testament, God described his relationship with the liberated nation of Israel as a Father to a firstborn, favored son.[c] The truth is that all whom God calls his children are adopted into his family. Even Abraham, the father of the Jews, was a Gentile before God adopted him.[d] None of us is a natural-born child with rights to the Father's grace.

In the New Testament, Paul picked up on these Old Testament themes and expanded them, explaining that those who are not physically descended from Israel are spiritually adopted into the family of God through faith

---

a. Eph. 2:2.
b. Rom. 8:17.
c. Ex. 4:22; Hos. 11:1.
d. Deut. 32:10; Ezek. 16:3; Rom. 9:4.

in their big brother Jesus Christ.ᵉ It's challenging for us, as modern-day readers, to imagine the significance of Paul's words. As Russell Moore has written, "It's hard for us to get the force of the 'brothers' language since almost none of us think of ourselves as 'Gentiles.' That's a boring 'Bible word.'"⁴ But it's helpful for us to ponder this revolutionary idea.

Imagine being a new Gentile Christian coming out of paganism only to discover that "every time people like you are mentioned in the book you believe is the Word of your God, it seems to always be pointing out that you're 'the other.' Sure, sometimes people like you are spoken of as 'strangers and aliens' to be treated well. But most of the time you're one of the villains of the story, with names like Goliath, Nebuchadnezzar, or Jezebel. People like you keep getting their heads cut off by the good guys in the story, or else drowned by God himself. You're what they call a 'Gentile.'"⁵ When viewed from that perspective, you can imagine how encouraging it would be to hear Paul's words that "there is neither Jew nor Greek . . . for you are all one in Christ Jesus."ᶠ

ADOPTED BY A FATHER

A father is one of the most significant influences in a person's life. So much of our life is determined by who our father is and how he behaves. For example, little Benjamin has on his birth certificate the words "Father disown." But now he has a new father who has adopted him with all the resources and willingness to transform his entire life and destiny. His life will be vastly different than it could have been.

Benjamin could never have declared himself part of my friend's family. Adoption is a legal matter, and as a father, my friend had to decide to legally adopt Benjamin into his family—which he gladly and lovingly did. The point is that just like little Benjamin, we can't force our way into God's family. Rather, God the Father lovingly adopts us as his sons and daughters through the work of our big brother Jesus.

---

e. See especially Rom. 8–9 and Gal. 4.
f. Gal. 3:28.

In most English translations of Ephesians, Paul refers to God eight times as a "Father." In fact, the book opens speaking of "God our Father" (1:2) and closes referencing "God the Father" (6:23). If you're a Christian, God the Father has freely chosen to spiritually adopt, love, live with, and bless you. Consider that for a moment. God has no obligation toward you, but he has affection for you. If you didn't have a good earthly father, you now have a perfect heavenly Father. And if you did have a good earthly father, you now have the additional blessing of your perfect heavenly Father.

ADOPTED THROUGH A BROTHER

In Ephesians 1:5, Paul introduced this concept of adoption, saying we're "adopt[ed] as sons by Jesus Christ."[6] In an age when some wonder if there are other paths, saviors, and plans to find salvation, we must never forget that our spiritual adoption is solely "by Jesus Christ." There is no other path, savior, or plan by which we can be adopted. The Father has chosen to only adopt those who are in Christ. It has rightly been said, "The God of the Bible has no 'natural' or 'begotten' children apart from Jesus the Son; all the rest of us need to be adopted."[7] Jesus knew this and promised that he would accomplish our adoption, saying in John 14:18, "I will not leave you orphans; I will come to you."

Jesus is both the Son of God and our big brother.[g] He is the heir of all that is the Father's.[h] In Christ alone we're adopted and receive all the benefits and blessings that are his because he has graciously chosen to share them with us.[i]

In the Old Testament, the oldest brother was often the heir of the estate. In the New Testament, Jesus is the Elder Brother of all the children of God, and the children of God, by being "in Christ," are heirs of Christ's estate. This is why Paul called Christians "joint heirs" with Christ.[j]

---

g. Matt. 3:17; John 20:17.
h. Ps. 2:7–8.
i. Gal. 3:16, 26–27; 4:4–5; Rom. 6:5.
j. Rom. 8:17.

Our inheritance and our status as heirs are solely because of the person and work of Jesus. Martin Luther elaborates:

> A son is an heir, not by virtue of high accomplishments, but by virtue of his birth. He is a mere recipient. His birth makes him an heir, not his labors. In exactly the same way we obtain the eternal gifts of righteousness, resurrection, and everlasting life. We obtain them not as agents, but as beneficiaries. We are the children and heirs of God through faith in Christ. We have Christ to thank for everything.[8]

Practically, just as an adopted child receives a new identity through a new family name, so it is with us spiritually. This is why we're called "Christians." Our adoption and identity are only because of our big brother Jesus Christ. He became a substitute orphan for us on the cross that we might be adopted in him.

ADOPTED WITH BROTHERS AND SISTERS

There are really only two families in this world: one under Adam and one under Christ.[k] The family of Adam, sinners by nature and choice, are called in Ephesians 2:2 and 5:6 "sons of disobedience," and in Ephesians 2:3 "children of wrath." Once God the Father adopts us, we move from being "sons of disobedience" and "children of wrath" to "sons of God." As Paul wrote in Ephesians 2:19, "You are no longer strangers and foreigners, but fellow citizens with the saints and members of the household of God."

Little Benjamin is now safe at home with his new family in the United States, and he has the joy of meeting and living with his two sisters. Similarly, when the Father adopts us spiritually, we're adopted into a family with other brothers and sisters. As Christians, we're part of an extended family that carries God's name.[l]

Perhaps most curious about the biblical language of family in Christ

---

k. Rom. 5:12–21; 1 Cor. 15:23, 45.
l. Eph. 3:15.

is that, in Paul's time, it may have been illegal to call someone a close relative, such as brother or sister, if one was not legally related. Doing so risked confusing the inheritance rights that were only to be distributed to close family members upon someone's death. For the Christian, however, sometimes our relationships in the family of God are even closer than those of blood relatives. Many early Christians saw their brothers and sisters in Christ as the primary designation for their identity and risked losing the inheritance from their biological families. This was a cataclysmic shift in thinking and identity.

Today, the words *brother* and *sister* are often used casually and are emptied of meaning. But in Paul's time, family was important, and your position in your family was paramount. As Christians, we're equal joint heirs as brothers and sisters in Christ. Imagine the radical implications of taking our family ties seriously. As Russell Moore has written, "What would it mean, though, if we took the radical notion of being brothers and sisters seriously? What would happen if your church saw an elderly woman no one would ever confuse with 'cool' on her knees at the front of the church praying with a body-pierced fifteen-year-old anorexic girl? What would happen if your church saw a white millionaire corporate vice president being mentored by a Latino minimum wage–earning janitor because both know the janitor is more mature in the things of Christ?"[9]

ADOPTED WITH AN INHERITANCE

As a legally adopted son of his adoptive father, Benjamin will share in the joys and blessings of being a part of his family. One of the many benefits he receives is a right to an eventual inheritance. This is also true for those who are adopted by the Father in Christ. Ephesians 3:6 says that Gentiles are fellow heirs. Ephesians 1:11, 1:14, 1:18, and 5:5 also speak of our "inheritance," which is both spiritual and material.

Spiritually, the greatest gift we receive is God himself. Revelation 21:3–4 gives us wonderful imagery of the day when God will dwell fully among us, "And I heard a loud voice from heaven saying, 'Behold, the tabernacle of God is with men, and He will dwell with them, and they shall be His people. God Himself will be with them and be their God. And God will wipe away every tear from their eyes; there shall be no more death, nor sorrow, nor crying. There shall be no more pain, for the former things have passed away.'"

Jesus is the heir of all that is the Father's and has chosen to share his inheritance with us. When the kingdom of God is fully established, this will include a resurrected glorified body, entrance to the kingdom,[m] and the new heavens and the new earth,[n] which will be a huge family reunion filled with worshipful feasting and celebrating at the table of our Father.[o]

Today, Benjamin has an incredible inheritance that now includes a new nation, family, home, and church. There is rich, nutritious food in the fridge like he has never seen and fun to be had that he's never known during his life in the orphanage. It's not an overstatement to say that he now lives in an entirely new world that he's never imagined.

But before he was brought home, Benjamin was still adopted, and though the inheritance was his, he hadn't received it fully. The blessings of his adoption had begun as his adoptive parents held and loved him in his birth nation. His adoption had already commenced, but wasn't yet complete until he arrived at his new home. It's the same with us spiritually.

In many ways, our world is simply a massive orphanage. The Father has adopted us, but he hasn't yet taken us home. But he promises he will, and, as the perfect Father, he always keeps his promises. As Ephesians 1:13–14 says, we are "sealed with the Holy Spirit of promise, who is the guarantee of our inheritance until the redemption of the purchased possession, to the praise of His glory."

ADOPTED WITH A NEW IDENTITY

Perhaps most important, through adoption our identity is forever changed from rejected to a reborn, redeemed, and remade child in Christ. The

m. 1 Cor. 15:12–28.
n. Rev. 21:1.
o. Rev. 19:9–10.

story of a woman at our church, named Sarah, illustrates this clearly and powerfully.

Before Sarah was born, her birth father disappeared from her life. Her mother often used her father's abandonment as a weapon against her, reminding her that she was "such worthless garbage" that her own father didn't want her as a daughter.

Sarah's stepfather, an evil man, took pleasure in physically tormenting her, often forcing her to eat food from the dog bowl and sleep outside. As Sarah relates, "I spent my childhood covered in bruises, nursing broken bones, and cowering in a corner. He raped me daily. My stepfather, fueled by my mother's hatred of me, prostituted my body to thousands of men. I knew how to please a man sexually before I knew how to spell my own name."

The abandonment by her natural father and horrific abuse by her stepfather left Sarah numb and disgusted by the idea of fatherhood. "Every time I heard God referred to as a father, I fought the urge to vomit," she says. "To me, 'daddy' was a word that began with abandonment and ended in sick sexual perversion."

As a result of the sins against her, Sarah didn't see herself as a human being, much less as a daughter of God. "I was completely convinced that I was less than human—some vile and worthless animal. I believed for a long time I was a prostitute. I was disgusted by what had been done to me and ashamed of the dirt on my soul that no number of showers could wash away."

God, through his grace, dragged Sarah "kicking and screaming" into a youth group meeting as a teenager. It was there that God called her to himself and turned a light on in her heart. Though she was saved, she had a long way to go in understanding who she was in Christ. "I spent the next few years knowing that what had happened that night was real and that I was a Christian and belonged to God but had no idea what that actually meant," she shares. "I read through the Bible a few times and didn't understand any of it. I felt a huge disconnect between this God I was reading about in the Bible and all of the pain I'd gone through. I wondered how God could possibly be good when he'd allowed so much to happen to me."

Eventually, Sarah and her husband, facing massive relationship problems, began attending our church. There, they got plugged into a community group, and their group leader recommended they meet with a pastor for counseling. Around the same time, Sarah also went through a redemption group,[10] which is an intensive care group that digs deep into past issues to apply the hope of the gospel to find healing. "I can only describe what happened as a miracle," says Sarah. "The last night of redemption group, as I was praying, I heard these words: 'God is good, I am his precious daughter, and that is enough.' God dropped the truth of his goodness in my heart, held me close, and called me his precious daughter. Everything in my life changed.

"God's love is bigger and more powerful than most people realize," Sarah says. "God rescued me from my hellish childhood, moved me to a safe place, gave me a godly husband, a beautiful daughter (and another baby on the way!), a church family to walk through life with, and transformed my heart and identity with his love. I did nothing to deserve God's grace or his love. He chose me and redeemed me. I am not a dirty prostitute or a worthless animal. I am God's precious daughter." That is the power of finding our new identity as adopted children in Christ.

Acting as Sons and Daughters

Our identity as adopted children of God also means transformation in our behavior—obeying our Father and living a life imitating our big brother Jesus by following in his footsteps. We put off the things of the past life (the old man) and turn wholeheartedly to those things that reflect the life and character of God (the new man). God doesn't bring us into his family only to turn around and punish us with constricting rules. Rather he sets up family rules for our *good*. Our flesh wars against our spirit, telling us that true life only comes when we indulge our fallen desires. God knows better. True life is only found in the holy joy, love, and peace that flow through us by the work of his Spirit. In this life, we must continually choose the things of God, obeying our Father, the source of lasting joy and life.

In Paul's teaching on adoption, the believer both enjoys the blessings of adoption and fights to walk in the obligations of adoption. Which brings us to Ephesians 5:1–21, a long list of things we should and should not do. If we were merely moralists, we would make a list of dos and do nots that would look something like this:

Do

- ⭕ imitate God (5:1)
- ⭕ walk in love (5:2)
- ⭕ walk as in the light (5:8b)
- ⭕ discern what pleases God (5:10)
- ⭕ walk as wise (5:15)
- ⭕ make the best use of time (5:16)
- ⭕ be filled with the Spirit (5:18b)
- ⭕ sing in passionate worship to God (5:19)
- ⭕ give thanks (5:4, 20)
- ⭕ submit to one another (5:21)

Do Not

- ⭕ engage in sexual immorality, impurity, or covetousness (5:3)
- ⭕ participate in filthiness, foolish talk, and crude humor (5:4)
- ⭕ associate with practitioners of the above (5:7)
- ⭕ take part in works of darkness, but expose them (5:11)
- ⭕ get drunk (5:18)

Have you done some of the things on the "don't" list? How about avoided things on the "do" list? If we're honest, we've all sinned and fallen short. So, what is the answer? The key to changing our behavior is knowing our Father. In Ephesians 5:1, Paul prefaced his list of dos and don'ts saying, "Therefore be imitators of God as dear children." And, he closed this unit of thought in 5:20 reminding us of "God the Father."

Bryan Chapell, a professor of practical theology and president at Covenant Seminary, shared that for a while his son was having behavioral issues. Bryan tried a number of tactics to change his son's behavior, but to no avail. Then it dawned on Bryan that he wasn't applying the truths of the gospel that he knew and taught in class about our relationship with the Father as sons and daughters to his relationship with his son: that understanding who we are determines what we do.

In response to his son's disobedience, Bryan started saying to him, "Son, I want you to know that I'm your father and I love you. No matter what you do or say, I'll always love you as a son. The way you're acting now isn't how a son acts. I want you to start acting like a loved son."

As an understanding of his identity as a loved son began to take hold, Bryan noticed a marked change in his son's behavior and response to discipline. Rather than try to make his son earn love by being good, he saw his son become good by knowing he was loved. So it is with us as children of God.

Your Father is perfect, loving, gracious, merciful, patient, holy, helpful, and generous. The more you get to know him through Scripture, prayer, song, service, and time with your brothers and sisters in Christ, the more you will come to love and enjoy him. Your desires will change from sin to holiness, and you'll increasingly want to be like your Dad. You'll love what he loves and hate what he hates.

As Christians, our goal is not to merely experience behavior modification by changing how we act and react. Our primary goal is getting to know, love, and trust God as our Father. In the end, we become like those whom we love the most. As we grow in love for our Father, the Holy Spirit helps us become more like him. The result is that we stop sinning and start worshipping, not so the Father will love us, but because He already does. Our big brother Jesus taught this very principle, saying of himself while on the earth, "Most assuredly, I say to you, the Son can do nothing of Himself, but what He sees the Father do; for whatever He does, the Son also does in like manner" (John 5:19).

How can we live like our big brother Jesus, doing what we see the Father doing? The same way Jesus did, by being "filled with the Spirit."[p]

---

p. Eph. 5:18.

In humbling himself to take upon a human body, the second member of the Trinity entered human history as the God-Man Jesus Christ. Jesus' life was lived as fully human, relying on the power of the Holy Spirit. This point is perhaps best witnessed in the writings of Luke.

The empowerment of Jesus through the Holy Spirit is repeatedly stressed in Luke's gospel. In it, we learn that Jesus was conceived by the Holy Spirit and given the title "Christ," which means "anointed by the Holy Spirit."q Jesus baptized people with the Holy Spirit,r and the Holy Spirit descended upon Jesus at his own baptism.s Furthermore, Jesus was "filled with the Holy Spirit," "led by the Spirit,"t came "in the power of the Spirit,"u and declared regarding himself, "The Spirit of the Lord is upon Me."v He also "rejoiced in the Spirit,"w and promised that God the Father would "give the Holy Spirit to those who ask Him,"x and that the Holy Spirit would teach us.y

In Luke's sequel to his gospel, the book of Acts, Jesus tells his disciples to wait to begin their ministry until the Holy Spirit comes and empowers them.z Later in the book, the Holy Spirit descends on the early Christians just as he descended on Jesus.aa In this way, God reveals that we're given the ability to live a life like Jesus through the power of the Holy Spirit (though imperfectly, since we remain sinners).

Throughout the book of Acts, God's people were empowered by the Holy Spirit to missionally engage people and in cultures, just as Jesus did. People were saved, churches were planted, cultures were redeemed, and God's kingdom was advanced by the power of God the Holy Spirit working through human beings. The same Holy Spirit who empowered Jesus also empowers us to live like Jesus.

---

q. Luke 1–2.
r. Luke 3:16.
s. Luke 3:21–22.
t. Luke 4:1–2.
u. Luke 4:14.
v. Luke 4:18; cf. Isa. 61:1.
w. Luke 10:21.
x. Luke 11:13.
y. Luke 12:12.
z. Acts 1.
aa. Acts 2.

In closing, the biblical revelation that God is a Father, and that we're adopted children of God, is a truth perhaps more desperately needed now than ever.[11] Sociologist Christian Smith has conducted mammoth research projects to study culture and spirituality. The first study was the largest ever undertaken on the spirituality of teenagers. It culminated in his book *Soul Searching: The Religious and Spiritual Lives of American Teenagers.* He followed that up with a study of the spirituality of post–high school young adults, culminating in *Souls in Transition: The Religious and Spiritual Lives of Emerging Adults.* His research concludes that most teens and young adults hold to what he calls Moralistic Therapeutic Deism (MTD). The basic idea is as follows:

1. There is a god who made the world but lives far away. He watches life on earth but isn't involved in any meaningful way, and we won't meet this nameless, faceless god unless we live a good life so that we can go to heaven (Deism).
2. We're not sinners who need a savior, but rather, basically good people. We're each supposed to live a moral life by being good, fair, and nice to people as taught in the Bible and most world religions and ideologies. All religions teach basically the same moral message (Moralistic).
3. The central goal of life is to be happy and feel good. So, we should take the encouraging and empowering information we find in disciplines such as psychology and spirituality, and integrate it together in ways that work for us. Then we can make good decisions and live good lives that we are proud of and happy with (Therapeutic).

This widespread view of God by young people tragically resembles so many of their earthly fathers. In their view, God is basically a dad who left the family when we were too young to even remember him. Still, he's a decent enough guy, and though we don't know him and he doesn't visit, he nevertheless wants us to be good people and live good lives.

God the Father revealed in the Scriptures is so much better than the false god invented by us confused orphans. Praise God! We have been adopted by a Father who loves us, lives with us, cares for us, and as needed, disciplines us for our good.[ab] We are heirs of all that is Christ's, fully privileged sons and daughters of God, and adopted fully in Christ, with the best Dad ever!

---

ab. Prov. 3:12; Heb. 12:6.

14

I AM LOVED

Wives, submit to your own husbands, as to the Lord. For the husband is head of the wife, as also Christ is head of the church; and He is the Savior of the body. Therefore, just as the church is subject to Christ, so let the wives be to their own husbands in everything.

Husbands, love your wives, just as Christ also loved the church and gave Himself for her, that He might sanctify and cleanse her with the washing of water by the word, that He might present her to Himself a glorious church, not having spot or wrinkle or any such thing, but that she should be holy and without blemish. So husbands ought to love their own wives as their own bodies; he who loves his wife loves himself. For no one ever hated his own flesh, but nourishes and cherishes it, just as the Lord does the church. For we are members of His body, of His flesh and of His bones. "For this reason a man shall leave his father and mother and be joined to his wife, and the two shall become one flesh." This is a great mystery, but I speak concerning Christ and the church. Nevertheless let each one of you in particular so love his own wife as himself, and let the wife see that she respects her husband.

—EPHESIANS 5:22–33

Kimberly was born into a family where her mom and dad abused alcohol and each other, constantly yelling at each other and physically hurting one another. "I thought love was when you beat on each other and yelled all the time," says Kimberly. Eventually Kimberly's parents both had affairs and divorced, leaving Kimberly's mother to raise her and her four young siblings.

After the divorce, Kimberly's mom changed the kids' names to hide them from their dad, and Kimberly watched as her mother went through eight husbands and numerous other men. "Some even took their turns at my sisters and me," Kimberly shared. "Incest followed closely behind. Mom had multiple personalities, and we were beat often or left for weeks at a time while she ran off with men. I remember thinking at a young age that I would like to grow up and be a stripper or a prostitute. I think I was only seven or eight at the time."

As a young girl, Kimberly dreamt of a heroic knight who would come and rescue her from her mom's abusive husbands and boyfriends. "I would never have to hear I was worthless again," says Kimberly. But when Kimberly was fifteen, her mother kicked her out of the house. Shy, scared, and alone, Kimberly fell in love with the first boy who paid attention to her, and, at age sixteen, she found herself homeless and pregnant.

Kimberly shared with me how she felt at that time. "I was a loser. I had nothing and would amount to nothing, just like my mother said. I proceeded to find solace in many arms, losing hope of ever finding my knight. I had never known love, or had anyone say they loved me. For a year I was a young mother who was raped, homeless, worthless, and without hope."

Then Kimberly's life was radically changed. A girl from her past invited her to stay the night and told her about Jesus. "She told me all about this Christ who died for me and wanted more for me," says Kimberly. "She told me I was his princess, his little girl, and he wanted to take care of me. I could hardly believe it. She was introducing me to my Knight. He rescued me on the floor with my baby asleep at my side that very night."

Over the years since giving her life to Jesus and trusting in his love, Kimberly had her ups and downs. It wasn't an easy road. But the love of Jesus gave Kimberly hope, and by his grace, she's moved from under-standing love as abuse, rape, incest, and sex to knowing the fullness of Jesus' love for her. "I am not worthless," she declares. "I am of great value to him. I didn't need to shop around for love. I had love. I felt a peace, and love I had never known. I knew he had a purpose for everything."

Today, Kimberly still loves her Knight Jesus, and Jesus still loves her and has blessed her with a wonderful husband and a beautiful family. "I grew stronger in Christ, and I met a great Christian man, married him, and we have six kids," she shares. "I have parented very differently than my mother did. I love my children, and they love the Lord. He has given this family a new beginning. I hope for future generations."

Kimberly is loved by Jesus. And so are you.

LONGING FOR LOVE

Everyone longs to be loved. In popular culture, love is celebrated like a god. Nearly every movie, book, and television show has a love story. Generally these love stories are faced with some difficulty and then resolved in a happy ending. This tension and resolution are important in that we're wired as humans to avoid tension and long for peace. But as we all know, life isn't like the stories that are spun on the screen and in pages of books.

In this life, we're loved by only a handful of people, and for some, by no one at all. And even those who do love us don't do so completely unselfishly, continually, and perfectly. Yet, there is one person who loves us in this way. In Christ, we're perfectly loved.

When most people think about love, they think about marriage. Frank Sinatra even immortalized the two words together in a song, which was then ruined by the television show *Married with Children*. In Ephesians 5:22–33, Paul spoke of Jesus as a groom who loves his bride the church so much that he died for her. Paul used this love as a pattern for Christian marriage, which ultimately exists to share and show Christ's love. This is what is meant by Ephesians 5:25: "Christ also loved the church."

The noun *love* occurs more often in Ephesians than in any other Pauline epistle, with the exception of 1 Corinthians, which is much longer and contains the famous love passage read at many weddings. The word *love* appears six times in Ephesians 5:25–33 alone. Anytime someone says the same thing six times in a few sentences, be it in a conversation or in a letter, it means that it's very important.

The Greek word used in Ephesians 5:22–33 for "love" is *agapé*, which, if you grow up in the church, you've heard about a lot, as pastors and church ladies *agapé* the word *agapé*. This word is central to the message of the section[1] because it expresses an unconditional and irrevocable love. But *agapé* is more than just feeling; this kind of love is displayed perfectly in *action*, sometimes even *despite* feeling.

In our culture this is a lost concept. We're ruled by our feelings when it comes to love and rarely think of it as unconditional and irrevocable. People often speak of falling out of love or losing that loving feeling, and these lost feelings are then used as excuses to move on to the next partner, so the high of feeling in love can be once again felt. Thankfully, Paul and others in the Bible taught that Jesus loves us not with a shallow love predicated on feelings but with the deep *agapé* love of action.

JESUS LOVES

In the 1960s, a very prominent but not always evangelical German theologian named Karl Barth, who's famous for standing up to Adolf Hitler, visited the United States to lecture at Yale, Princeton, and the University of Chicago. Crowds came out in droves to hear him speak. During his tour, a reporter asked Barth what was the single most important theological discovery he'd made. After stopping to consider his answer carefully, Barth said, "Jesus loves me. This I know, for the Bible tells me so." Indeed, we can never outgrow that one great, majestic, and simple transforming truth.

Jesus loves me. That's the bedrock of the Christian faith.

Jesus' love for us, the church, is called "a great mystery."[a] Bible scholar Peter T. O'Brien summarizes the important "mystery" theme in Ephesians: "Ephesians has been called the 'epistle of the mystery.' Paul uses the term six times in the letter (Eph. 1:9; 3:3, 4, 9; 5:32; 6:19)."[2] By "mystery," the Bible means that something previously unknown has now been made known in Jesus Christ.

The Old Testament speaks often about God's love, but that love was not fully known, or even widely known, beyond the nation of Israel, until the greatest act of love the world will ever see was accomplished—the death and resurrection of Jesus Christ in our place, for our sins, as our

---

a. Eph. 3:3–4; 5:32.

loving Savior. The Bible takes the concept of God's love and connects it to the cross of Jesus Christ because that is where the mystery of God's love was most clearly revealed. This is what Paul said in Ephesians 5:25, "Christ also loved the church and gave Himself for her." Other Scriptures echo this fact and clearly demonstrate that the love of God simply cannot be understood apart from the cross of Christ:

- John 15:13: "Greater love has no one than this, than to lay down one's life for his friends."
- John 3:16: "For God so loved the world that He gave His only begotten Son."
- Romans 5:8: "God demonstrates His own love toward us, in that while we were still sinners, Christ died for us."
- 1 John 4:9–10: "In this the love of God was manifested toward us, that God has sent His only begotten Son into the world, that we might live through Him. In this is love, not that we loved God, but that He loved us and sent His Son to be the propitiation for our sins."

Sometimes, we're so weighed down by our sin, losing sight of our identity in Christ, that we struggle to believe that God actually and personally loves us. We may believe that God loves the world, or individual people in it, but we're less likely to truly believe that God loves us. This is because we struggle to accept that God's love is pure, unmerited, and free grace. Into this doubt Paul repeatedly brought a freeing truth: Jesus loves you. He cannot love you any more. He will not love you any less!

Other times, we're so unfamiliar with our sin, often because we really don't consider it honestly or feel it personally, that we don't appreciate God's love. We neglect to remember that God's love is not for the undeserving but for the ill deserving. We're all sinners who instead of our deserved death, hell, and wrath get life, heaven, and love through Jesus. The truth is that we deserve love less than we could ever imagine, yet Jesus loves us more than we could ever dream.

Indeed, the love of Jesus is something we can know truly but never know fully. My poetic, youngest daughter likes to tell me that she loves me "bigger than the sky and deeper than the ocean." Jesus' love is something like that—seen and appreciated but never fully explored. As Paul wrote, "For this reason I bow my knees to the Father of our Lord Jesus Christ . . . that you, being rooted and grounded in love, may be able to comprehend with all the saints what is the width and length and depth and height—to know the love of Christ which passes knowledge; that you may be filled with all the fullness of God."[b]

I've been a Christian since I was nineteen, more than half of my life, and I can honestly say that I continue to learn more and more about the love of Jesus every day. Other Christians I've known that have been loved by and have loved Jesus for upwards of ninety years report the same thing. Indeed, the love of Christ is so deep and so wide that as Christians we'll spend all of eternity continually swimming in the ocean of it.

How Jesus Loves

Simply but profoundly, Jesus loves the church as a groom loves his bride. Of all the images and metaphors that Paul could've chosen, this one connects at the heart level of affection and emotion perhaps most effectively.

Next time you're at a wedding, pass a bridal magazine, or see a couple in love, take it as a divine appointment to remember that Christ loves the church, which includes you, like a bride.

I can still recall my wedding day and often view the photos from that day. Every time I see my wife's face in them, I smile as I warmly and fondly remember the day our covenant relationship started and every day since. I love my wife. I don't love her as perfectly as Jesus does, but knowing that he feels devoted to me as I do to her, only infinitely and perfectly, taking the best of my love and perfecting it, is life changing.

This imagery of God's people being like a bride and God loving them like a groom finds its origins in the Old Testament. There, Hosea's marriage to the adulterous Gomer serves as a prophetic portrait of God's

---

b. Eph. 3:14, 17–19.

faithful devotion to his people even when we're unfaithful. The bride-groom imagery appears in multiple other places in the Old Testament as well,[c] and continues all the way to the end of the Bible.[d] In fact, history is promised to end with an unprecedented wedding, better than the scene from any movie, where Jesus, wearing white, rides in on a white horse to marry his bride, also adorned in white, and they feast and celebrate their new life together forever ever after.[e] Indeed every wedding feast and white bridal gown is a prophetic reminder of the Wedding Supper of the Lamb.

For most women, the image of Jesus as a groom who tenderly loves them, pursues them, forgives them, serves them, and is faithful to them is helpful. It was for Kimberly, who desperately hoped for a knight to rescue and love her, which she found in Jesus. For most men, however, this image is difficult to conceive of personally, as men are understandably not fond of considering themselves as a bride in a white gown. I would remind the men that the Bible never speaks of individuals as Christ's bride, but always the corporate people of God: the church. So, we aren't to relate to Jesus in a personally romantic sense but rather as part of the church, submitting, trusting, and respecting his leadership.

Five Ways Jesus Loves the Church

Paul taught us five ways that Jesus demonstrates his love for his church.

1. As *head*, Jesus took the sin that was our fault and made it his responsibility. By dying in our place for our sins, Jesus took our punishment. Practically, this means that God will never punish those who are in Christ. To be sure, we will reap the consequences of our sin in this life, and like any loving Father, God may discipline us for our good and growth, but never for retribution. The price for our sin was paid once and for all by Jesus because as our leader and head, he has made us his responsibility and loved us unconditionally.

c. Isa. 54:5; 58:8; 61:10; 62:5; Jer. 2:2; 3:6; and Ezek. 16.
d. Rev. 18:23 and 22:17.
e. Rev. 19:1–16.

2. As *savior*, Jesus delivers us from the horrendous fates that our sin causes. Sin brings death in every conceivable way. Health, joy, friendships, families, and fruitfulness all die because of sin, and one day we will physically die because of sin. As savior, Jesus delivers us from countless miseries and tragedies that our sin would cause in us and for others, and he promises us new and everlasting life in him in the life to come. Because Jesus is our Savior, we don't need to foolishly trust in false and functional saviors or lose hope, even in the worst of seasons.

3. As *giver*, Jesus gave himself for his bride. His comfort, safety, and well-being were not his highest priority. In humility, he set aside his rights and life in service to his bride, the church. Today, Jesus remains the same and continues to give lavishly of himself for our good.

4. As *sanctifier* and *cleanser*, Jesus is patient with us, never gives up on us, and always seeks to make us more holy. Jesus is not sick of you, done with you, or overwhelmed by you. He is sanctifying you, cleansing you, and has hope for you. He is not finished with you and will not be until you see him face to face as a friend.

5. As *nourisher* and *cherisher*, Jesus loves you and the rest of his people enthusiastically, not begrudgingly or regrettably. And he continually reveals to us through Scripture the areas where he longs to help us grow and change. He does this not by standing back and making demands of us but rather lovingly placing his life in us through the Holy Spirit.

Jesus loves the church, and he loves you as part of the church. As a pastor, I'm keenly aware that the church and its leaders are imperfect sinners in need of the grace of God for everything every day. I also know that the church can sometimes feel like the least loving place on earth. But Jesus loves the church, and gave himself for her. We must also love the church and give ourselves for her if we want to love whom Jesus loves. As we do, we'll see the love of Jesus not only for us but also for others. Amazingly, in the church, among God's sinful and often bad bride, the great mystery of Jesus' love is most clearly seen. So, please don't give up on the church, but rather give to the church, as Jesus gave himself up for the church.

Sometimes the simplest things are the most profound. So it is with the love of Jesus Christ. His love is freeing, liberating, and transforming. There is a deep desire in each of us to be loved, and Jesus alone provides perfect love. Perhaps the best way to understand Jesus' love for the church is to insert his name in place of the word *love* in each of the declarations in 1 Corinthians 13:4–8:

> *Jesus suffers long and is kind.*
> *Jesus does not envy.*
> *Jesus does not parade himself.*
> *Jesus is not puffed up.*
> *Jesus does not behave rudely.*
> *Jesus does not seek his own.*
> *Jesus is not provoked.*
> *Jesus thinks no evil.*
> *Jesus does not rejoice in iniquity, but rejoices in the truth.*
> *Jesus bears all things, believes all things, hopes all things, endures all things.*
> *Jesus never fails.*

HUSBANDS AND WIVES

Those who believe they are unloved often become so desperate and needy for love that they use others to meet their longing. Such people enable others, put up with abuse, and must constantly be in some romantic relationship or best friendship, or risk becoming emotionally undone. Psychologists have diagnosed this condition as *love hunger, love addiction*, and *relationship addiction*.

In a spiritual sense, this addiction to relationships is really an idol. Rather than have Jesus be their all, those addicted to relationships make an idol out of someone's love. The problem is that our idols always fail us, and eventually we end up demonizing the people we idolize. In the end, the love of Jesus is the only perfect love to meet our deep longing. Once we know his love, we can stop using people for their love and simply start loving them as Jesus loves us. This was Paul's big idea in Ephesians as he transitioned from the love of Jesus for his bride, the church, to husbands loving their wives as Christ loves the church.

Ephesians 5:22–33 speaks of the duties of a Christian wife to respectfully submit to her husband as the church does to Christ, and the duties of a husband to love his wife as Christ loves the church. It's important to note that Paul wasn't talking about men and women in general when it comes to submission but rather focusing narrowly on one man and one woman in the context of covenant marriage. Additionally, when Paul spoke of submission, he wasn't talking about the obliteration of self but rather deference to the head. For example, Jesus showed us perfect submission in the Garden of Gethsemane when he prayed to the Father and shared his feelings and desires ("Take this cup away from Me"), yet still deferred to the Father's will ("nevertheless, not what I will, but what You will").[f]

Numerous articles, sermons, blogs, books, conferences, and organizations have arisen to interpret and debate what Paul and other scriptures meant by this concept of submission. My purpose in this chapter, however, isn't to wade into the debate too deeply, as it is too important and complex for such a brief treatment.[3] For those curious about my beliefs on gender roles, I do have a host of free sermons, articles, and blogs you are welcome to access.[4]

What I do want to stress is quite simple. Jesus is the head of the church and takes responsibility for her well-being by sacrificially loving and serving her. A husband is the head of his wife and should likewise take responsibility for her well-being by sacrificially loving and serving her. In this way, the wife is like a garden, and the husband is like a gardener. The question is not whether or not a husband should be the head of his home, as the Bible simply and repeatedly says he is, just as Jesus is the head of the church. The only real question is whether or not he is a

---

f. Mark 14:36.

good head whose wife is flourishing because of Jesus' love to her through her husband. In the context of marriage, the wife is the one who gets to decide whether or not her husband is loving her well, and a husband gets to decide if he is being well respected. Ultimately, however, God is the final judge, so our determinations of these things must be in alignment with his Word. This is what Paul meant in Ephesians 5:21 when he wrote, "Submit to one another out of reverence for Christ" (NIV).

For those who are single, as are the majority of adults in America, this principle applies to you as well. Single man, are you currently loving your potential future wife by how you conduct yourself spiritually, financially, emotionally, mentally, and sexually? Are you growing in love for Jesus and conducting yourself in such a way that when you do meet your wife, she'll know that you loved her before you even met her? Rather than dating, relating, and fornicating, you could be praying, serving, and worshipping.

Single woman, is your current life a demonstration of love for Jesus and respect for your future spouse? When you meet your husband one day, will he think that the clothes you wear, the company you keep, and the life you live right now were respectful to Jesus and in turn to him? Indeed, loving Jesus helps us love our spouses before we even know them.

A friend of mine demonstrated this perhaps most clearly to me. As a young man in his late teens, he wanted to be married but knew he could easily get into sin and trouble. He intentionally became active in a church, joined a small group with some older married couples he could learn from, and worked hard at his job to set money aside for marriage. Meanwhile, he didn't date casually, but remained sexually pure and started journaling prayers, Scripture, and thoughts for his wife, in faith that one day God would give him a wife to love as Christ loved the church.

He eventually met a girl, dated her, and proposed. She said yes. My friend and his fiancée went through premarital counseling at the church, got input from their community of family and godly friends, and eventually married. As a wedding present, he gave her the journal he'd kept for a few years. Not surprisingly, she felt incredibly loved and wept a great deal reading page after page of the ways he loved Jesus and loved her before they'd ever met.

For a husband to love his wife in many regards means he is to be a friend to her as Jesus is a friend to him. My wife, Grace, and I wrote an entire book on marriage called *Real Marriage*, and the big idea that dominates the book is that of friendship. When a wife reads that a husband is to love her like Jesus, she hears God desiring her husband to be her loving friend. And she is correct.

This idea of friendship in marriage, modeled after Jesus' friendship for and with us, was revolutionary for Grace and me, along with those who've read the book. It's not a new idea, but it's a powerfully popular idea because it's God's idea.

To get the book's content out to others, Grace and I went on tour to multiple cities, teaching weekend conferences for both singles and married couples at Bible-believing, Jesus-loving churches. At each event we saw people come to Jesus, couples reconciled, sin forgiven, and divorces avoided because of the love of Jesus. It was awesome.

As I write this chapter, I'm in Fort Lauderdale, Florida, having just completed a Real Marriage event. Last night, I turned on the news at the hotel, only to be devastated by a story that has gone global.[5] The news reported that a young man named Mike and his wife, Alanna, who was seven months pregnant, were on vacation in the area. After each went into a poolside cabana, tragedy struck. A car veered out of control, plowed into the restroom Alanna was in, and killed her and the baby instantly. I prayed for the couple before heading to bed last night.

This morning, as I awoke to write this chapter, I was unsure how to end it. Then, I received an e-mail telling me the rest of Mike and Alanna's story.

More than three thousand people joined us for the Real Marriage event, and the most emotional moment of our time together was when the men stood to take this vow:

I vow that:

my church will be served by me;
my wife will be loved by me;
my wife will be served by me;
my family will be led by me;
my wife will be prayed over by me;
the Bible will be opened in our home by me;
and my grandchildren will worship the same God as me, because
my children will worship the same God as me.

After saying this vow, the husbands then spent time praying over their wives in love as the sound of weeping women could be heard. It was powerful, as many women saw their husbands become Christians and pray over them for the first time. Jesus' love and their husband's love came together in a sacred moment.

One of those men who stood to vow and pray was Mike. He and Alanna had come down from Boston. Their pastor, who is part of our Acts 29 Church Planting Network, sent them to the event. He had been preaching a sermon series called "I Do" in conjunction with the *Real Marriage* book. As part of the series, the church generously gave away two fully paid trips for couples to attend the Real Marriage tour event in Fort Lauderdale.

Alanna really wanted to attend, and out of love for his wife, Mike agreed. Alanna was a maturing Christian, active in her church, leading a small group, and by all accounts a loving, gracious, and wonderful woman. Mike was on his journey of faith, but when he stood to vow and pray, his lovely wife told him it was the happiest day of her life.

They left the conference and returned back to their hotel very much in love and excited about their future together. They both went into a restroom, but only Mike exited alive. I had an opportunity to speak with both the pastor and the grieving widower, and to pray for him.

Mike's entire life had just gone upside down. In an instant, he went from what his bride called the best day of her life to the worst day of his life. It was an honor to speak to Mike and hear how his family and friends have supported him.

Mike and Alanna's tragic story is a good reminder for us all. We never know when our last day will be. When it comes to marriage, we spend money and make plans to have the perfect first day. But the truth is that the last day of marriage is the most important. None of us knows the last day of our lives or the life of someone we know and love. While I deeply grieve with and for Mike, I'm so glad that the last day for his wife was the best day of her life. She was loved well by her husband and welcomed home by her Jesus.

Today, in the providence of God, I feel compelled by the Holy Spirit to encourage you to have a sense of urgency to grow in friendship with your spouse—if you're married—and with Jesus. If you're not yet a Christian, today is the day to give your life to Jesus. And today is the day to start loving your spouse, by God's grace, as Jesus loves the church.

15

I AM REWARDED

Children, obey your parents in the Lord, for this is right. "Honor your father and mother," which is the first commandment with promise: "that it may be well with you and you may live long on the earth."

And you, fathers, do not provoke your children to wrath, but bring them up in the training and admonition of the Lord.

Bondservants, be obedient to those who are your masters according to the flesh, with fear and trembling, in sincerity of heart, as to Christ; not with eyeservice, as men-pleasers, but as bondservants of Christ, doing the will of God from the heart, with goodwill doing service, as to the Lord, and not to men, knowing that whatever good anyone does, he will receive the same from the Lord, whether he is a slave or free.

And you, masters, do the same things to them, giving up threatening, knowing that your own Master also is in heaven, and there is no partiality with Him.

—EPHESIANS 6:1–9

In his book *The 360° Leader*, John Maxwell shares the story of General George Marshall, who was instrumental in the Allied victory of World War II. While men such as Winston Churchill and Franklin D. Roosevelt generally come to mind as leaders in the Second World War, it was Marshall, working behind the scenes under Roosevelt's authority, who orchestrated many of the strategies for victory.

Marshall's career was distinguished in the Army. As Maxwell points out, he was generally considered to have a "record of achievement rarely equaled by any other."[1] Marshall's achievements were impressive and resulted in his appointment to U.S. Army chief of staff under President Roosevelt, making him responsible for leading the armed forces.

During his appointment, Marshall oversaw the expansion of the armed forces from 200,000 soldiers to more than 8,300,000, and was credited with being "the organizer of victory" by Winston Churchill. As Maxwell says, "President Roosevelt found his advice invaluable and said that he could not sleep unless he knew Marshall was in the country. And Roosevelt requested Marshall's presence at every major war conference, from Argentia, Newfoundland, in 1941, to Potsdam in 1945."[2]

Though initially viewed as a smart soldier and organizer, Marshall also proved himself a skilled politician and strategic thinker, helping to develop successful battle plans, including the battle of Normandy, and often going head-to-head with other generals, including the more famous General MacArthur. In the end, working tirelessly in the background, Marshall won over his doubters and gained the respect of some of the most powerful leaders in the world.

By war's end, Churchill said of Marshall that he was "a statesman with a penetrating and commanding view of the whole scene," and General Dwight D. Eisenhower said, "In every problem and in every test I have faced during the war years, your example has been an inspiration and your support has been my greatest strength. My sense of obligation to you is equaled only by the depth of pride and satisfaction as I salute you as the greatest soldier of your time and a true leader of democracy."[3]

After the war, when Europe required rebuilding, it was once again Marshall who stepped up to the plate, formulating the now-famous Marshall Plan. It was originally named the Truman Plan, after President Harry Truman, but at Truman's insistence, the name was changed to honor Marshall.

Chances are, most people don't immediately know who General George Marshall is or his significant accomplishments when he's mentioned apart from the Marshall Plan. Like many people, he spent his life tirelessly working under authority, committed to his work rather than to gain fame for himself. As a member of the military, Marshall had a deep understanding of authority and submission to it. He also understood that he was serving a greater cause than himself. His faithful service was rewarded time and time again, however, by those in authority over him, with promotions and praise. And later in life, Marshall was awarded the Nobel Peace Prize, the only professional soldier to ever receive such an award.

Though a name generally only known by history buffs, General Marshall was rewarded for his commitment to his country, the world, and those in authority over him.

Likewise, as we labor under authority, Paul promised us that both in this world and the world to come, we will receive just rewards for our faithfulness and effort.

A NOTE ON EPHESIANS AND SLAVERY

In Ephesians 6:9, Paul addressed the relationships between those in power and the powerless. For many, this is a tough passage because Paul was discussing a topic that understandably hits a raw nerve for modern readers: slavery. As a result, many miss the intent of this part of Paul's letter. Paul didn't mean to comment on social structures but rather to give important instructions on how to live like Christ within those social structures, both for those in authority and those under authority, which also contributes to changing unjust social structures.

Given that, it will be beneficial to spend a little time discussing the differences between slavery in Paul's time and the modern, American understanding of slavery so we can then talk about his commands to believers concerning their conduct within difficult social structures.

American Slavery

Slavery as practiced in the United States was almost entirely racial, with whites owning blacks. It was also a lifetime of service. Once slaves were owned, they and any children they bore belonged to the master. Particularly shocking are the wills of some of America's founding fathers, which listed slaves and their children, in addition to livestock and land, as property to be passed on to one's family. From the Founders' perspective, there was little, if any, difference between blacks and animals.

American slavery was grossly sinful, and one of the greatest tragedies of the faith is that men and women who claimed Christ also owned slaves. Frederick Douglass, a former slave and nineteenth-century African-American, Methodist, abolitionist leader, wrote the following indictment upon those American Christian slaveholders in his autobiography:

> What I have said respecting and against religion, I mean strictly to apply to the slaveholding religion of this land . . . I love the pure, peaceable, and impartial Christianity of Christ; I therefore hate the corrupt, slaveholding, women-whipping, cradle-plundering, partial and hypocritical Christianity of this land . . . We have men-stealers for ministers, women-whippers for missionaries, and cradle-plunderers for church members.[4]

It's important to understand that Paul denounced the kind of slavery (slave trading) practiced in the United States as evil, listing it among the most horrific sins in 1 Timothy 1:9–10: "We also know that the law is made not for the righteous but for lawbreakers and rebels, the ungodly and sinful, the unholy and irreligious, for those who kill their fathers or mothers, for murderers, for the sexually immoral, for those practicing homosexuality, for *slave traders* and liars and perjurers" (UPDATED NIV; emphasis added).

Additionally, God demonstrated righteous anger toward the oppression of people groups in his response to Pharaoh's evil, cruel, and racist enslavement of the Jews in Egypt. Pharaoh's cruelty prompted God to intercede by killing many Egyptians and freeing his enslaved people as an act of justice. This history as told in Exodus and related scriptures, such as the stories of Daniel and Joseph, is a clear demonstration of the fact that unjust and racially motivated slavery is deplorable in the sight of God.

Slavery in the New Testament

Given this, it's important to contrast the significant differences between slavery as it was practiced in Paul's time versus later slavery in America. In Paul's time, slavery was not primarily a racial issue, as all races were slaves and all races had slaves, and rather than a lifelong social status, as it was in early American history, it was economically motivated.

New Testament–era slavery was often an arrangement made to pay off a defaulted debt. Unlike our day, in which people can declare bankruptcy and default on their debts, in the ancient world people would work for their lender until they repaid their debt. In other cases, people in extreme poverty sold themselves into slavery with a kind and benevolent master in order to enjoy a higher quality of life, not unlike a modern-day nanny who lives in the home as part of the family.

Generally, most slaves were free by age thirty, either by purchasing their freedom or through governmental emancipation. And during their time as slaves, many people were given formal education and specialized job training that would greatly benefit them if they were ever emancipated. Often, freed slaves became Roman citizens and developed a client relationship with their former masters. And within the church, one's status in society was not necessarily related to his or her status in the church. It was possible for someone to be a slave outside of the church and an elder or deacon in spiritual authority over slave masters in the church.

In other, less-ideal cases, people were enslaved because they were taken in war, a common practice for many nations, and sometimes children were taken in as slaves because their parents had abandoned them or could no longer provide for them.

Admittedly, the nuanced forms of ancient slavery are diverse and complicated (and sometimes unjust), which explains why Scripture never expressly forbade slavery as practiced in the New Testament, but did encourage those who were able to obtain their freedom to do so.[a] As Clinton Arnold has written, "In spite of these substantive differences between Roman-era slavery and New World slavery, it is important not to construe this ancient form as more humane or as a morally justifiable economic system. Although we can point to some features that make it appear better than slavery in the Antebellum South of the United States, it still involved the coercive ownership of another person."[5]

---

a. 1 Corinthians 7:21.

Additionally, we must be careful to not read into the text that Paul condoned ancient forms of slavery. Ephesians simply does not tell us what Paul thought of the system, because his letter was not a treatment of current societal ills with which he took issue. His purpose for writing was to address how believers in the world should behave within the institutions in which they found themselves. Further, while "there is no explicit criticism of slavery [in Ephesians] . . . the level of mutuality and reciprocity that is assumed to exist between master and slave creates an atmosphere in which it would have been difficult for slavery to survive if the advice of the passage had been rigorously followed."[6]

Nevertheless, understanding ancient slavery versus the cultural, American perception of slavery better equips us to understand Paul's instruction for those both in and under authority.

God Rewards

Through Paul, God encourages both those in and under authority to live in such a way that he can reward them both in this life and the life to come. This is precisely what is meant by Ephesians 6:8, which says, "Whatever good anyone does, he will receive the same from the Lord."

It often seems as if those who lie, steal, and cheat are the winners in our world, whereas the honest, trustworthy, and hardworking are the losers. This causes some people to stop trying to do right altogether, skate by with minimal effort, or actually start sinning and acting unethically.

How about you? Are you discouraged or even angry because of how you have been treated by those in authority over you or those under your authority? Do they not really appreciate you, thank you, or compensate you as you see fit? Have you failed to receive your due reward?

Many Christian leaders and teachers are reticent to speak much about God rewarding faithfulness because they fear that people will become self-righteous, proud, and religiously competitive, trying to outperform one another. While this is a legitimate concern, the Bible teaches repeatedly that God does in fact reward the works of faithful believers as a way of encouraging them to persevere in holiness and faithfulness, knowing that the God who loves them sees and knows all and will reward every act of obedience.[7] Consider the following words as an encouragement to you and whatever trials you're facing (emphasis is added to each):

> Blessed are you when others revile you and persecute you and utter all kinds of evil against you falsely on my account. Rejoice and be glad, for *your reward is great in heaven*.[b]

> Do not lay up for yourselves treasures on earth, where moth and rust destroy and where thieves break in and steal, but *lay up for yourselves treasures in heaven*, where neither moth nor rust destroys and where thieves do not break in and steal. For where your treasure is, there your heart will be also.[c]

> His master said to him, "Well done, good and faithful servant. You have been faithful over a little; *I will set you over much. Enter into the joy of your master*."[d]

> But love your enemies, and do good, and lend, expecting nothing in return, and *your reward will be great*.[e]

> *He will render to each one according to his works*: to those who by patience in well-doing seek for glory and honor and immortality, he will give eternal life; but for those who are self-seeking and do not obey the truth, but obey unrighteousness, there will be wrath and fury.[f]

> *We will all stand before the judgment seat of God; for it is written,*
> *"As I live, says the Lord, every knee shall bow to me,*
> *and every tongue shall confess to God."*
> *So then each of us will give an account of himself to God.*[g]

b. Matt. 5:11–12 (ESV).
c. Matt. 6:19–21 (ESV).
d. Matt. 25:23 (ESV).
e. Luke 6:35 (ESV).
f. Rom. 2:6–8 (ESV).
g. Rom. 14:10–12 (ESV).

Each one's work will become manifest, for the Day will disclose it, because it will be revealed by fire, and the fire will test what sort of work each one has done. If the work that anyone has built on the foundation survives, *he will receive a reward.*[h]

Whatever you do, work heartily, as for the Lord and not for men, knowing that *from the Lord you will receive the inheritance as your reward.* You are serving the Lord Christ.[i]

Therefore do not throw away your confidence, *which has a great reward.* For you have need of endurance, so that when you have done the will of God *you may receive what is promised.*[j]

He [Moses] considered the reproach of Christ greater wealth than the treasures of Egypt, for *he was looking to the reward.*[k]

Watch yourselves, so that you may not lose what we have worked for, but may *win a full reward.*[l]

"The nations raged, but your wrath came, and the time for the dead to be judged, and for *rewarding your servants.*"[m]

And *the dead were judged by what was written in the books, according to what they had done.*[n]

"Behold, I am coming soon, *bringing my recompense* with me, to *repay everyone* for what he has done."[o]

---

h. 1 Cor. 3:13–14 (esv).
i. Col. 3:23–24 (esv).
j. Heb. 10:35–36 (esv).
k. Heb. 11:26 (esv).
l. 2 John 8 (esv).
m. Rev. 11:18 (esv).
n. Rev. 20:12 (esv).
o. Rev. 22:12 (esv).

In speaking of rewards from God, the Bible is not saying that we earn salvation as a reward for our works. Early in the book of Ephesians, Paul clearly established that we are saved solely by grace through faith in Jesus Christ and not by the contribution of any human works.[p] He also impressed upon his readers that we're not saved *by* our good works but rather *to* our good works.[q] Yet, he also expounded upon this theme, saying that the good works are known and rewarded by God.

When Paul said, "Knowing that whatever good anyone does, this he will receive back from the Lord," the Greek verb he used for "receive back" is *komizō*, which goes beyond merely "receiving" to the idea of "recompense or reward."[8] Paul also used the word in Colossians 3:25 and in 2 Corinthians 5:10, which discusses reward at the final judgment: "For we must all appear before the judgment seat of Christ, so that each of us may receive [*komizō*] what is due us for the things done while in the body, whether good or bad"(UPDATED NIV).

It's important to realize that the judgment of believers is intended to evaluate and bestow various degrees of reward, not to determine our eternal fates. As Jesus said, "He who hears My word and believes in Him who sent Me has everlasting life, and *shall not come into judgment*, but has passed from death to life."[r]

Positively, our day of testing can be a day of great rejoicing. If we're faithful stewards in this life, we'll hear Jesus declare, "Well done, good and faithful servant." Negatively, there will be Christians who will be grieved by the lack of reward given to them for the lives they lived. In 1 Corinthians 3:15, Paul said, "If anyone's work is burned, he will suffer loss; but he himself will be saved, yet so as through fire."

The idea of different levels of rewards upsets many, but the Bible is clear that there are eternal consequences for believers doing both good and evil.[s] Many feel offended that Jesus doesn't equally reward everyone, but to do so would be unjust and would encourage Christians to waste

---

p. Eph. 2:8–9.
q. Eph. 2:10.
r. John 5:24.
s. 2 Cor. 5:10.

their lives by serving and giving as little as possible. Like any parent, God the Father loves all of his children and will disown none of them, but he doesn't equally reward the obedient, generous, and hardworking children the same as he does the disobedient, stingy, and lazy ones.

God's Rewards

What do God's rewards look like, and what do they involve? Because the biblical descriptions of rewards, such as money and crowns, is likely figurative, it's hard to be sure what is meant. Most important, rewards are greater opportunity and responsibility in the kingdom.[t] We will be able to fulfill our original purpose to rule God's creation in partnership with him.[u]

Paul hinted that a reward will be seeing the full impact we've had on other people, resulting in a deep, internal joy rather than external riches. Perhaps our deepened relations with others we've served in Christ will also be a reward.[v]

For all believers, a rich reward will be our capacity to know and experience God himself, to see Jesus face to face, as he is our ultimate reward.[w] I personally wonder if God in all his creativity will not reward each of his faithful servants with some special reward that is most meaningful to them, such as a big hug from Jesus, a meal alone with him, or just a good laugh reflecting back on life with him. Whatever the reward, the important idea is that life matters and God is watching.

Rather than making us competitive with one another, knowing that Jesus rewards faithfulness should cause us to spur one another on to love and good deeds. In this way, Christians are to be somewhat like athletes on a team who push one another to do their very best. Similarly, Christians should lovingly push one another to become more like Jesus and build up his church. Since God has infinite rewards to bestow, there is no need for jealousy. We aren't competing with one another for limited

---

t. Luke 16:10–12; 19:17–19.
u. Gen. 1:26–28.
v. 1 Thess. 2:19–20; 2 Cor. 1:14.
w. 1 Cor. 13:12; 1 John 3:2.

rewards but rather pursuing the fullness of Jesus and sharing that fullness with others. Importantly, even the works we perform are possible only because of God's empowering grace through the Holy Spirit at work in and through the believer. And God's rewards are for those both under and in authority.

God Rewards Those Under Authority

Curiously, when speaking of God's rewards, Paul wrote first to those who are under authority—children and slaves.

Children are commanded to "obey" and "honor" their parents, "that it may be well with you and you may live long on the earth."[x] The two rewards are remarkable and highly motivating. It's important not to over-spiritualize the promises, as if Paul were speaking only of eternal life. If that were the case, Paul wouldn't have included the phrase "upon the earth." God promises every believing child that obeying one's parents will lead to their well-being and long life on earth. This cannot, of course, be applied in a meticulous way to every single case. Like any proverb, this is to be understood as a general pattern.[9]

To slaves, Paul said, "Be obedient to those who are your masters . . . in sincerity of heart . . . doing the will of God from the heart."[y] In that day, slaves did not have rights. So in our culture, where there's considerable emphasis placed on individual rights, Paul's words to slaves seem odd. Yet, if God would command those under authority without any legal rights to conduct themselves in a godly way, knowing that God would reward them in this life and the life to come, how much more should we with legal protections and rights pursue the same kind of good works?

This doesn't mean we shouldn't fight for justice and just laws, but it does mean that just as Jesus was mistreated and didn't sin, we can and should glorify God by refraining from sin when we are mistreated, to both honor him and be honored by him.

How about you? Who is in authority over you, and how are you

---

x. Eph. 6:3.
y. Eph. 6:5–8.

responding? Do you sense any conviction of sin in light of what Paul said and to whom he said it?

God Rewards Those in Authority

Having addressed those under authority, Paul then addressed those in authority by using parents (especially fathers) and then slave masters as examples of how God commands those in authority, with the power to bless, to act in a godly way and reward those under authority with love and provision. Fathers are told, "Do not provoke your children to wrath, but bring them up in the training and admonition of the Lord" (6:4). A father is not to act harshly in word or deed toward his children, goad them to frustration and anger, discourage or demean them, neglect them, or harm them in any way. He is instead to be a blessing from the Lord to his children by taking responsibility to raise them rather than leaving it to the mother and various institutions, such as schools, churches, foster care systems, adoption agencies, and prisons. In short, fathers are supposed to be Pastor Dad, actively involved in the development of every aspect of their children's growth with love, humility, and wisdom.

Slave masters are told to use their authority as Jesus uses his. In Ephesians 6:9, Paul wrote, "And you, masters, do the same things to them, giving up threatening, knowing that your own Master also is in heaven, and there is no partiality with Him." In this way, masters were to see Jesus as their Master, to whom they would be accountable and were called to love those under their authority.

Perhaps the best biblical illustration of this is Paul's letter to Philemon, which is addressed to the wealthy master of a servant named Onesimus, who became very dear to Paul. Onesimus may have been a fugitive slave who stole money from Philemon and fled to Rome. While in Rome, he converted to Jesus under Paul's ministry and became a personal friend to Paul and a worker in his ministry. Paul's letter appeals to Philemon to receive Onesimus as a brother instead of a slave.[z] It's a testimony to Jesus' transforming grace in relationships, and demonstrates how Paul

z. Phil. 1:16.

subverted the cultural views of authority of that day in slave-master relationships.

Over whom are you in authority at work, home, church, or any other context? How would those under your authority say that you treat them? Would they say you treat them as Jesus treats them? Would they say that you bless and reward them as Jesus does?

Fear of God Versus Fear of Man

What keeps us from obeying God and living a life of good works, that he might reward us? The answer is fear. Knowing this, Paul wrote of "fear and trembling."[aa] We live either with fear of God or fear of someone else, and we can never live fearing both God and someone else at the same time. Who we fear determines what we do and how we live.

Who are you afraid of?

Proverbs 29:25 says, "The fear of man brings a snare, but whoever trusts in the LORD shall be safe." Biblical counselor Ed Welch says,

> Fear in the biblical sense . . . includes being afraid of someone, but it extends to holding someone in awe, being controlled or mastered by people, worshipping other people, putting your trust in people, or needing people. . . . The fear of man can be summarized this way: We replace God with people. Instead of a biblically guided fear of the Lord, we fear others. . . . When we are in our teens, it is called "peer pressure." When we are older, it is called "people-pleasing." Recently, it has been called "codependency."[10]

Which person comes to mind first when you think of this type of fear? Whose opinion matters far too much to you? Is your appetite for praise unhealthy? Are you overly devastated by criticism? Are you overcommitted to doing things God never asked you to do, but someone else did? Do you pretend to be someone you are not when certain people are looking? Do you fear their rejection, criticism, disappointment, hatred, or conflict?

---

aa. Eph. 6:5.

Does the fear in your mind manifest itself in anxiety in your body? Does it show up in mood swings, a nervous twitch, weight changes, suicidal thoughts, sleeplessness, depression, aggressive driving, panic attacks, high blood pressure, or something equally unhealthy? Are you prone to act out or to self-medicate with such things as food, alcohol, or drugs?

Fear is vision without hope, and it turns us into false prophets seeing only a bleak and dreaded future. Fear is about not getting what we want, getting what we want and losing it, or getting what we don't want.

The answer to fear of man is fear of God. The number-one command in the Bible is "Fear not," appearing more than 150 times.[ab] Rather than having unhealthy fear of man, the Bible commands us to have a healthy fear of Jesus, meaning we care more about what he says than what others say and we endure whatever we have to, knowing that he will reward us for being faithful. Paul affirmed this, commanding us to work "not with eyeservice, as men-pleasers, but as bondservants of Christ, doing the will of God from the heart, with goodwill doing service, as to the Lord, and not to men" (Eph. 6:6–7).

Admittedly, I don't know about the circumstances of your life. I don't know who is in authority over you, or the difficulties you face in exercising authority over others. But I do know that it's very unlikely that anyone reading this book will be under more difficult circumstances than those whom Paul used as our example—children and slaves in the ancient world. Therefore, what applies to them, applies to us—both the responsibilities and rewards.

Every Christian ultimately works for Jesus. Jesus' estimation of your life and works is all that will count in the end. Given that, we're to work hard and honestly for Jesus, not just when others are looking, but all the time because Jesus is always looking. And we can rest assured that if we work in this way for the Lord, he will reward us in this life and the life to come, so we are not wasting our lives, but rather investing them for a reward. That's a promise!

---

ab. Gen. 15:1; 26:24; 28:15; Ex. 33:14; 2 Kings 1:15; Ps. 23:4; 2 Chron. 20:17; Isa. 41:14; Jer. 1:8; Dan. 10:12; Hag. 2:4–5; Luke 12:32.

16

I AM VICTORIOUS

Finally, my brethren, be strong in the Lord and in the power of His might. Put on the whole armor of God, that you may be able to stand against the wiles of the devil. For we do not wrestle against flesh and blood, but against principalities, against powers, against the rulers of the darkness of this age, against spiritual hosts of wickedness in the heavenly places. Therefore take up the whole armor of God, that you may be able to withstand in the evil day, and having done all, to stand.

Stand therefore, having girded your waist with truth, having put on the breastplate of righteousness, and having shod your feet with the preparation of the gospel of peace; above all, taking the shield of faith with which you will be able to quench all the fiery darts of the wicked one. And take the helmet of salvation, and the sword of the Spirit, which is the word of God; praying always with all prayer and supplication in the Spirit, being watchful to this end with all perseverance and supplication for all the saints—and for me, that utterance may be given to me, that I may open my mouth boldly to make known the mystery of the gospel, for which I am an ambassador in chains; that in it I may speak boldly, as I ought to speak.

But that you also may know my affairs and how I am doing, Tychicus, a beloved brother and faithful minister in the Lord, will make all things known to you; whom I have sent to you for this very purpose, that you may know our affairs, and that he may comfort your hearts. Peace to the brethren, and love with faith, from God the Father and the Lord Jesus Christ. Grace be with all those who love our Lord Jesus Christ in sincerity. Amen.

—EPHESIANS 6:10–24

His whole life, Travis felt he didn't measure up to his father's expectations. "I find that to this day his influences echo through my soul," he says, "fighting my efforts to find my identity in Christ alone at every turn."

Travis's father is a self-made man. Travis shares that his father came from very little and accomplished great things by the world's standards, both in terms of business and the ministry. In contrast to his father, Travis was raised with great resources available to him and investment in him. Undermining these investments was a continual feeling that Travis could never measure up to his father's expected return on those investments, stemming from constant criticism.

"Since I respected my dad and had always seen him as a godly man I should go to for counsel, guidance, and wisdom," Travis told me, "I struggled as I wondered if he was right and I should be ashamed of myself. This created a deep-rooted insecurity in me as I constantly questioned if I was being a good steward or if I was fooling myself and wasting my talents in a way that I should be ashamed of. This created an incredible degree of frustration and a cycle of failure and shame."

As a result, Travis built a whole life around trying to please his earthly father through his accomplishments, always feeling that he came up short. "In an effort to challenge me," says Travis, "he would say things like, 'Aren't you ashamed of yourself? I know I would be! You should be accomplishing so much more. Doesn't your character mean anything to you?'" Consequently, Travis became incapacitated by the overwhelming sense of inadequacy in the face of his father's expectations.

Travis describes the feelings of inadequacy that he faces as a "constant war" raging within his heart and mind. "I have to constantly battle lies!" he says. "I have to constantly bathe my experiences in prayer—asking God to give me eyes to see things clearly and rightly so I can rest in him and not be discouraged by lies, a false perspective, and distorted identity." He rightly identifies his struggles and hardships in life and with his father as a spiritual battle led by an enemy who hates him. "I am aware that the enemy wants me to attach my identity to my accomplishments and my failures instead of Christ alone," he shares. "The enemy tries to draw my focus to my accomplishments to fill me with pride when things go well, and discouragement and shame when things don't go well. I know that these are all pitfalls and lies that I have to be on guard against."

Thankfully, Travis knows he doesn't fight this battle alone. "God has been gracious to place me in an environment where the true gospel is spoken boldly and regularly." God has blessed Travis with fellow Christians who war alongside him against the attacks of an enemy seeking to destroy him in a constantly raging spiritual war. "I'm grateful that God has given me men who are diligent to constantly speak the gospel into my life, drawing my attention off of myself and onto the Lord. I pray that God would continue to press upon my heart the truth and that he would continue to renew me day by day that I would know the love of God in a way that would overcome the fears and doubts that have been so engrained within me."

Travis knows the enemy hates him, but he finds strength in knowing that Christ and his brothers and sisters in Christ love him, and that ultimately he will be victorious against his enemy because Christ is victorious. In Christ, Travis is victorious. And so are you.

THIS MEANS WAR

Have you ever wondered why life is so hard, suffering is so painful, agony is always near, and God seems far away? It's because there's an enemy who hates God, hates you, and has set his army against you because you're in Christ. God loves you. But Satan hates you. God plans good for you. But Satan plots to destroy you.

Every Christian is a soldier in a war—including little kids praying to Jesus at night and old ladies who wear head coverings as they carry their King James Bibles into church. When we don't know that life is a war and Satan is an enemy, or forget when we need to know it most, we can't make sense of our struggles, suffering, and strife. When this happens, we wrongly interpret everything negative in our lives as judgment from God when in reality it is most often an attack from our enemy or a result of our own bad choices. The good news is that rather than God judging us, he poured out his wrath on Jesus, who secured victory over Satan, sin, and death for us on the cross.

When life gets hard, we can easily forget that we're victorious in Christ and lose hope. Some people practice self-centered contempt and blame themselves when things go wrong. Some practice others-centered contempt and blame other people. And some practice God-centered contempt and blame God. The trouble in our life is sometimes partially the fault of our sin or someone else's sin, but it's never the fault of God, as he is good and does not cause sin. Behind all sin, however, is Satan. While we remain morally responsible for our sin, Satan sometimes also bears some degree of responsibility, as he is the deceiver who delights when we join him in his rebellion against God.

Throughout Ephesians, Paul discusses Satan and demonic powers frequently. In so doing, he wants us to know that we're in a spiritual battle. If we really believe this, we view life differently. We no longer expect comfort and ease in this life any more than an exhausted soldier on the front lines of battle. This begs the question, why do we so often act surprised when trouble comes into our lives as Christians?

Perhaps the trouble begins with how we're invited to become Christians. In varying ways we're told, "Confess your sins to Jesus, and he will take you to heaven." While true, what's often left out is the time between our commitment to Christ and the day we see him face to face—also called life. And it's probably also because we often suffer from spiritual amnesia—or delusions, much as Leonard did in the movie *Memento*, which I talked about at the very start of this book. But the reality is that in this life there's a war between two kings, Jesus and Satan; two kingdoms, light and darkness; and two armies, Jesus' and Satan's. And while the Bible promises us that King Jesus is victorious, we're on a pilgrimage to get to Jesus' eternal kingdom while preaching the gospel by the power of the Holy Spirit in hopes of setting some war captives free from their bondage to Satan, sin, and death.

KNOWING YOUR ENEMY

The Nazi regime commissioned the famed *Bismarck* battleship in 1940. Stretching 825 feet, it was the largest battleship in the world. It boasted eight guns that held shells fifteen inches across, as well as some five dozen other armaments. The *Bismarck*'s onboard targeting computer was so precise that it blew away the HMS *Hood*, which had been the pride of the Royal Navy, with a single shot. As grand as the *Bismarck* was, it had one small but fatal weakness. A vulnerable rudder was located right beneath its thermal exhaust port. In the darkness of night on May 24, 1941, the Royal Navy attacked the ship with little success—until one torpedo hit this rudder. The boat was severely disabled, attacked fiercely, and defeated.[2]

The key to victory in war is knowing your enemy.[a] If you don't know your enemy, you can't know how to attack them or defend yourself. The Royal Navy found the *Bismarck*'s weakness, but it took many battles and heavy losses. Imagine how many lives and ships would have been saved had they known the ship's weakness before it was even launched. In this life, we have to know our enemy's weakness so we can both defend ourselves and attack to be victorious.[3]

The Scriptures consistently present Satan as an enemy of God and his people. He's named in a variety of ways, including the devil, the dragon, the Serpent, the enemy, the tempter, a murderer, the father of lies, our adversary, the accuser, the destroyer, and the evil one. Unlike human beings, for whom Jesus died and rose, Satan and demons have no possibility of salvation. Only hell and just, eternal torment await them.[b]

The Scriptures, from Genesis 3 to Revelation 21, make it clear that Satan and his demons are real. This truth wasn't widely questioned by professing Christians until the last couple hundred years. Largely influenced by the atheistic philosopher David Hume and the subsequent era of modernity, liberal Bible "scholars" dismissed the supernatural, from miracles to demons, as mythical, outdated, and primitive. Such things didn't fit into their modern view of the world as a closed, natural system.

Christianity isn't opposed to science, and many great scientists have been and are also Christians. But the spiritual realm is beyond science's ability to test and know. Rather than accept that there are some things science can't explain, many instead choose to only believe in the natural, physical world, which Satan counts as a victory in his war. As the line

---

a. 2 Cor. 2:11.
b. 2 Peter 2:4.

from the movie *The Usual Suspects* rightly says, "the greatest trick the Devil ever pulled was convincing the world he doesn't exist."

To believe the Bible, belief in Satan, demons, the supernatural, and miracles is required. We can't take the parts of the Bible we like and discard the rest. Before we delve too deeply into studying what the Bible says about these things, I want to ease some concerns.

It's not uncommon for people to make either too much or too little of Satan. As C. S. Lewis said, "There are two equal and opposite errors into which our race can fall about the devils. One is to disbelieve in their existence. The other is to believe, and to feel an excessive and unhealthy interest in them."[1] Some people want to blame everyone and everything but Satan and themselves for the ills in the world. Others want to shirk responsibility and blame Satan and demons for everything, as if we're only victims and never perpetrators. Though it's far more important to know Jesus and his power over our enemy, Satan is real, and as Christians, it's important to know as much about our enemy as possible.

For starters, Satan is a created being, and therefore is in no way equal to God. His knowledge, presence, and power are limited because he is an angelic being created by God for the purpose of glorifying and serving him. However, Satan became proud in his heart and desired to be worshipped and exalted as God. So, he declared war upon God, and one-third of the angels joined his army to oppose God.[c] Judged by God for his sin, the Serpent and his servants were then cast down to the earth.[d] According to the repeated language of the Bible, fallen angels are like a military unit and have organized battle plans against God's people. Subsequently, throughout this chapter, when I discuss Satan, it's not always in reference to him personally but rather to the entire demonic realm that he oversees like a military commander in chief.

The motivation for all of Satan's work is pride and self-glory instead of humility and God-glory.[e] And one of his most powerful allies in opposing us is our own pride. Some have speculated as to why the Serpent

c. Rev. 12.
d. Isa. 14:12–23; Ezek. 28:1–19.
e. Ezek. 28:2; James 4:6–7.

continues in his war against God even though Scripture is clear that Jesus has already won the war and the Serpent will be ultimately defeated and painfully judged. It may be that the Serpent is indeed so proud that he has deceived himself and now believes that God is a liar who can be beaten. It is this deception that he whispers into our ears every day, telling us we aren't victorious in Christ and also telling us lies about ourselves and about God.

In his war against God, the Serpent not only has demons but also people who are allies in his army, either by demonic possession, demonic influence, or simply by living according to their sinful nature and flesh. Such people include false prophets,[f] counterfeit apostles,[g] phony Christians,[h] and deceptive teachers who teach heretical doctrine for the Serpent.[i]

Satan's ultimate goal for those of us in Christ is a compromised and fruitless life beset by heresy and sin[j]—and ultimately, death.[k] If the enemy can't tempt us with sin and error, he will simply try to exhaust us into surrender. This demonic opposition is increasingly pronounced for those who serve God most faithfully. As the Puritan William Gurnall said, "Where God is on one side, you may be sure to find the devil on the other."[4]

How Satan Fights Us

The Bible speaks of Satan's work in what can commonly be understood as ordinary and extraordinary. Ordinary demonic work entices us to sexual sin,[l] marriage between Christians and non-Christians,[m] false religion based on false teaching about a false Jesus,[n] unforgiveness and bitterness,[o]

---

f. 2 Peter 2:1.
g. 2 Cor.11:13.
h. Gal. 2:4.
i. 2 Peter 2:1.
j. 1 Tim. 4:1–2; 1 John 3:7–10.
k. John 8:44; 1 Peter 5:8.
l. 1 Cor. 7:5.
m. 2 Cor. 6:15.
n. 1 Cor. 10:14–22; 1 Tim. 4:1–2; 2 Cor. 11:1–4.
o. Eph. 4:17–32.

foolishness and drunkenness,[p] idle gossiping and "busy-bodying,"[q] lying,[r] attacking our identity through false and condemning thoughts,[s] demonic dreams and night terrors,[t] and idolatry.[u] Extraordinary demonic work includes torment,[v] physical injury,[w] counterfeit miracles,[x] accusation,[y] death,[z] and interaction with demons.[aa]

Many Christians wonder, and even worry, about whether someone can be demon possessed. For those who aren't Christian, it's possible through such things as occult involvement, witchcraft (including Wicca and non-Christian spiritual practices), drug and alcohol abuse, and habitual severe sin, when practiced to an extreme measure, to be significantly influenced by evil forces.[ab]

Dr. Gerry Breshears has helped me understand that whether or not Christians can be demon possessed is a question many people answer too quickly. The problem is that the word *possess* has several meanings. According to the *Merriam-Webster's 11th Collegiate Dictionary*, it can mean several things, including: (1) to "own," so that a Christian essentially belongs to Satan; (2) to bring or cause to fall under "influence," so that the life of a Christian is marked by the influences of Satan; (3) to "dominate," so that a Christian is controlled by Satan. Obviously, what you mean when you say *possessed* is important.

In the first sense, the devil never *owns* a Christian. We have been rescued from the dominion of darkness and transferred into the kingdom of the Son.[ac]

In the second sense, the devil can *influence* a Christian. This was

---

p. Eph. 5:8–21.
q. 1 Tim. 5:11–15.
r. John 8:44.
s. 1 Chron. 21:1; Matt. 4:8–10; Luke 4:5–8.
t. Job 4:13–16; Ps. 9:5.
u. 1 John 5:18–21.
v. Acts 5:16.
w. Matt. 9:32–33; 12:22–23; Acts 8:4–8.
x. Acts 8:9–23; Acts 16:16; 2 Thess. 2:9–10.
y. Rev. 12:10.
z. Prov. 8:36; John 8:44.
aa. 1 John 4:1–6.
ab. 1 Sam. 16:14–23; Mark 5:1–15; Mark 9:17–29; Luke 8:27–39.
ac. Col. 1:13.

the case with Peter, to whom Jesus said, "Get behind Me, Satan!"[ad] and Ananias and Sapphira, of whom Peter asked, "Why has Satan filled your heart to lie to the Holy Spirit?"[ae]

The third sense is where there's much debate among Christians. Can demons dominate a Christian through demonic *possession*? Christians may be deceived, accused, or tempted by Satan, and may yield to those attacks (though they do not have to). If we wrongly respond to such attacks, we may give demons influence in our lives. Evil spirits can empower, energize, encourage, and exploit a believer's own sinful desires. But as children of God, regenerated and indwelt by the Holy Spirit, we're empowered by God and commanded to resist Satan. If we do, we need not suffer from the influence of our enemy.[af] While some teach that through personal sin, generational sin, or even curses, demons can dominate believers through possession, Scripture is clear that Christians are never under the ruling authority of darkness.[ag] The devil can never take authority over a Christian.[ah] Because of Jesus' victory secured for us on the cross, in Christ, we have the ability to resist our enemy, and when we do, he must flee.[ai]

How We Fight Satan

Every Christian soldier needs to learn how to "be strong in the Lord and in the power of His might" (Eph. 6:10). Thankfully, this is something God wants to do for us and in us. As Dr. D. A. Carson says, Paul's command "*Be strong* perhaps fails to bring out the force of the passive verb ('be strengthened')."[5] In order for us to be strong, God must strengthen us. This is accomplished in Christ and "in the power of His might" (Eph. 6:10).

The Lord Jesus Christ is strong. While on the earth, Jesus resisted every temptation from the enemy. In Jesus, the debt we owed to Satan

ad. Matt. 16:23.
ae. Acts 5:3.
af. Eph. 6:10–18; James 4:7; 1 Peter 5:7–9; 1 John 4:1–4; 5:1–5, 18–19.
ag. Eph. 5:8; Col. 1:13; 1 Thess. 5:5.
ah. John 10:27–30; Rom. 8:38–39; 1 John 4:4; 5:18.
ai. James 4:7.

through sin is cancelled, thereby setting us free from enslavement to the kingdom of darkness and welcoming us as citizens of the kingdom of light. Today, Jesus rules and reigns as King of kings and Lord of lords over all things. By being in Christ, we, too, can live by the power of the Holy Spirit, as Jesus did on the earth, honoring his kingdom and living in victory over our enemy.

In Christ, we're strengthened by his strength and become strong. If we try to "be strong" in our own strength, we fall victim to the enemy's tactic of pride. But since we can "be strengthened . . . in the Lord," we can have both humility and victory. Life is a war against a spiritual enemy we cannot see. We can't win on our own, but the God who sees all gives us courage, perseverance, and wisdom to win an otherwise unwinnable war.

"Be strong in the Lord" is among Paul's final commands to us. When you read it, think of a general giving final orders to his troops before a big offensive. These are Paul's marching orders for the war that is our life in Christ. His language is of "a hand-to-hand fight" (as the Spanish say, *mano a mano*). The root idea here is swaying back and forth while locked in mortal battle. An exchange of arrows or artillery is not pictured here, but sweat against sweat, breath against breath.[6]

There are times when it feels as if Satan has us locked in a battle that it seems will never end as we fight for the gospel in our lives, families, and churches. One Bible commentator says, "Although Paul borrows his language from the Old Testament, the image Paul's words in this paragraph would have evoked for most of his readers is that of a Roman soldier ready to do battle. Most adults who heard his letter read would have seen Roman soldiers and could relate this image to their spiritual warfare against the demonic powers at work in the world; God who fought for them had supplied them his armor."[7]

The Weapons of Our Warfare

In this battle, Paul spoke of weapons for our war.[8] Some are *offensive*, for the forward progress of the kingdom of God through the advance of the gospel and church of Jesus Christ. Some are *defensive*, for protection from our enemy and his attacks on us.

As a victorious warrior of Christ, your life is about being on kingdom mission with Jesus to help set other captives free. People are not ultimately your enemy; rather, they're held in captivity by your enemy, and they need to be set free. Jesus doesn't leave us to our own devices to fight this war. He leads the charge through his defeat of Satan, sin, and death and equips us with powerful weapons.

1. Truth: The enemy is a liar and the "father of lies." All he ever does is lie. If you believe his lies, you will disbelieve the truth God gives. The truth is found in the Bible, and it always leads to the glory of Jesus Christ. You must know the truth, believe the truth, and share the truth, even when it costs you dearly. When dealing with people, always get both sides of the story to ensure you know the truth before you render a verdict. If you struggle with believing Satan's lies, get a journal, write a line down the middle of the pages, and write, "Lies" at the top of one column and "Truth" in the other column. Every time you hear a lie, write it down in the "Lies" column, and next to it, in the "Truth" column, record a refuting truth from Scripture. As you do, you are engaging in spiritual warfare.

2. Righteousness: The Puritan Thomas Brooks says that our enemy baits our hooks, as he did our first parents', with anything that we find desirable.[9] This means he gladly gives us such things as sex, money, power, pleasure, fame, fortune, comfort, and relationships to draw us away from God. Satan's goal is for you to take his bait without seeing the hook. Once the hook is in your mouth, he'll reel you in to take you as his captive. Jesus was tempted, and you will be too. When you say no to sin and yes to righteousness, you win a spiritual battle. When you say yes to sin and no to righteousness, you lose a spiritual battle and need to quickly repent to Jesus, renounce your sin, get the hook out of your mouth, and press onward in Christ's righteousness.

3. The gospel: The good news of the person and work of Jesus Christ is the most powerful weapon we have. Use it for yourself, and share

it with everyone. You're part of God's ground war, and Jesus sends you every day to tell others about your King and his kingdom so they may be freed from captivity.

4. Faith: Faith is an internal conviction that leads to an external action. For example, if you believe that Jesus rose from death, you'll not die gripped by the fear of death but rather holding on to faith that you'll be with him on the other side of death. It's this very faith that took a coward like Peter, who denied Jesus three times before Christ died on the cross, and turned him into a courageous warrior who died for Jesus, hanging upside down on a cross. He saw the living Jesus and in faith no longer feared death. It should be the same for us.

In this life, the enemy sends "fiery darts" (Eph. 6:16). In antiquity, without a large, protective shield, a soldier was defenseless against such attacks. Satan's fiery darts come in the form of haunting memories, condemning thoughts, temptations, accusations, vain regrets, disturbing dreams, and the like. Faith is your shield. Repent of your sin, trust God and his promises, command your enemies to leave in the power of Jesus' name, and you'll be safe.

5. Salvation: Paul says that salvation is like a helmet. A helmet guards our minds so we're not damaged in such a way that we can no longer think clearly and cogently. You must never forget that you're saved and assured victory in Christ. Remind yourself daily. You're saved from Satan, sin, death, hell, and God's wrath. Never forgetting or doubting your salvation will protect you in all spiritual battles.

6. Scripture: The Bible is like a sword for defending ourselves against the attacks of the liar and his false teachers. It's also an offensive weapon for spreading the truth and setting captives free. What the church needs is fewer war historians and more warriors like the great preacher John Knox. Since his life was in danger, Knox often traveled carrying a two-handed battle sword and a Bible. When preaching, he would pound the pulpit so forcefully that it would splinter. Don't simply share the Word—proclaim it with thunder!

Don't timidly suggest how to live—passionately model what the Bible commands! Don't just provide interesting lectures about the Bible being a sword—wield it with great effectiveness to set captives free. The last thing the church needs is cowards that treat the Bible like an artifact more fit for a museum than a weapon for the battlefield.

7. Prayer: In every field of combat, communication is key. King Jesus is always available to hear from you and speak to you. Pray offensively about everything and anything. Pray before trouble comes. Pray to God both in your personal prayer time and corporately regarding the enemy's attacks, as is common in the Psalms. And when attacked by demons pray something like this:

Lord Jesus Christ, I acknowledge that this [name the specific area of sin] may be empowered by demons and evil spirits. If it is, I want nothing to do with them. I confess that you triumphed over these demons and evil spirits by the power of your shed blood that purchased forgiveness for all my sins and by your death, burial, and resurrection that provided my new life in Christ. I ask that you send any demons and evil spirits away from me. Demon, in the name and authority of Jesus, I command you to get away from me now.

Lord Jesus, I thank you for hearing and answering my prayer. Please fill me anew with your Holy Spirit so I will be empowered to live in obedience to you and in freedom from sin and harassment.

8. The Strength to Stand: No fewer than four times in the closing of his epic letter, the Holy Spirit, through Paul, commanded us to "stand."[10] This is a military term for holding the line. One way we do this is, as Jesus did in Matthew 4 when resisting the temptations of Satan, is to quote the truths of Scripture in the face of spiritual attack, rebuking the devil and commanding him to go away. In this spiritual battle, don't retreat; run to Jesus. Don't surrender; move forward in the assurance of Jesus' victory. Hold the line for Jesus, empowered by his Holy Spirit, in your life, family, church, and community until you die and see Jesus face to face and hear, "Well done, good and faithful servant," or see him return in glory.

PEACE AND GRACE THROUGH JESUS

Just as he began his letters, Paul closed them with two words that are pregnant with meaning: "peace" and "grace." He wrote, "*Peace* to the brethren, and love with faith, from God the Father and the Lord Jesus Christ. *Grace* be with all those who love our Lord Jesus Christ in sincerity. Amen."[aj]

The question is not whether or not you live amid a spiritual war. The only question is what side you're on. For those who have peace with God through Jesus Christ, we're not only saved by grace; we're also empowered by grace to victoriously live out our new identity in Christ.

In Adam, a war was lost. In Jesus, a war is won. Satan tempted our first parents to sin, and they did. In so doing, they implicated all of us in their tragedy and misery. We're all born sinners by nature and live as sinners by choice.

As a Christian, you were once a captive in this war until Jesus gave you grace from him and peace with him, which is exactly what he promised he would do at the beginning of his public ministry,

> "*The Spirit of the* LORD *is upon Me,*
> *Because He has anointed Me*
> *To preach the gospel to the poor;*
> *He has sent Me to heal the brokenhearted,*
> *To proclaim liberty to the captives*
> *And recovery of sight to the blind,*
> *To set at liberty those who are oppressed.*"[ak]

The theme of freedom from captivity to Satan and sin is woven throughout the tapestry of Scripture. The first promise of Jesus freeing us from captivity is found shortly after the first humans sin in Genesis 3:15. God preached the first good news (or gospel) of Jesus to Adam and Eve,

---

aj. Eph. 6:23–24 (emphasis added).
ak. Luke 4:18.

promising to Eve that Jesus would be born of a woman and would grow to be a man who would battle with Satan, boot stomp his head, defeat him, and set captives free. And this theme of redemption runs throughout the Old Testament in the stories of Noah, Abraham, and Moses, in the Psalms and the Prophets, and more. Its fulfillment is seen in the Gospels through Jesus and taught deeply in the Epistles.

Jesus was born to his mother, Mary, as promised in Genesis 3, and the battle for our souls began in earnest.[11] Satan's attack on Jesus commenced when Jesus was only a boy. King Herod, who was a descendant of a demonically influenced family line of evil dictators, decreed that all male children under the age of two be put to death in an effort to murder Jesus as an infant. Satan worked this plot because he rightly knew that Jesus had come to conquer him and liberate his captives. God warned Jesus' parents of the plot, and they fled to Egypt as refugees, so Jesus' life was spared.

Satan attacked Jesus as a young man by offering him a much easier life than the one planned out for him by God the Father. God sent Jesus to earth on a mission of sinless living to go to the cross to die for sinners. In contrast, Satan offered a kingdom without a cross and promised that Jesus could rule in glory and power without any opposition or crucifixion—as long as he bowed down in honor to Satan. Satan set forth this proposal through a simple friendship offering to break bread while Jesus was near starved after forty days of fasting. Jesus resisted these temptations, as he did all temptations.

Jesus then went to the cross and died the death we should have died. Every single sin you have committed or will ever commit was forgiven at the cross, and every sin that was or ever will be committed against you was cleansed in full without exception at the cross. You are free from captivity, redeemed by Christ to live in him. In Christ, you are victorious.

In Colossians 2:13–15 we read, "And you, being dead in your trespasses and the uncircumcision of your flesh, He has made alive together with Him, having forgiven you all trespasses, having wiped out the handwriting of requirements that was against us, which was contrary to us.

And He has taken it out of the way, having nailed it to the cross. Having disarmed principalities and powers, He made a public spectacle of them, triumphing over them in it."

The imagery from Colossians is taken from the great battle victories celebrated in antiquity. In those days, wars were common between kings and kingdoms. Through sin, we all surrendered to Satan and were taken as captives in war. So God came as our Warrior King, Jesus Christ. We were legally Satan's possession because of our debt to him through our sin, but Jesus redeemed us through his victory on the cross. Jesus' final words from the cross, "It is finished," are his heralding of your liberation. And his resurrection to life signifies his complete victory over Satan, sin, and death in the life of all believers.

In Christ, you are forgiven. In Christ, you are clean. In Christ, your captivity has been replaced with a new identity. For those not in Christ, this life is the closest to heaven they will ever get, and defeat is ultimately theirs. But for those of us in Christ, this life is the closest to hell we will ever get, and victory is ultimately ours. And as Winston Churchill once famously said, "If you're going through hell, keep going."

So who do you think you are? If you love Jesus, serve him, follow him, and call him your Lord and Savior. There's good news: in Christ you have a new identity. And the *great* news about this good news is that once you really know and believe that, your life will be changed forever.

Grace and peace to you *in Christ*.

NOTES

Chapter 1

1. In particular I want to thank Mars Hill Pastor Bill Clem for teaching me and the rest of Mars Hill Church so much on this issue, which has made a great difference in our preaching, teaching, and counseling. Clem's book *Disciple* is a good summary of his insights.

2. Commenting on Danish philosopher Søren Kierkegaard's 1849 book, *The Sickness Unto Death*, Dr. Tim Keller says, "Sin is the despairing refusal to find your deepest identity in your relationship and service to God. Sin is seeking to become oneself, to get an identity apart from him. . . . Most people think of sin primarily as 'breaking divine rules,' but Kierkegaard knows that the very first of the Ten Commandments is to 'have no other gods before me.' So, according to the Bible, the primary way to define sin is not just the doing of bad things, but the making of good things into *ultimate* things. It is seeking to establish a sense of self by making something else more central to your significance, purpose, and happiness than your relationship to God." (Timothy Keller, *The Reason for God: Belief in an Age of Skepticism* [New York: Penguin Group, 2008], 162, emphasis in original).

3. Harold M. Best, *Unceasing Worship: Biblical Perspectives on Worship and the Arts* (Downers Grove, IL: InterVarsity Press, 2003), 21.

4. Ibid. 23, emphasis in original.

5. Ibid. 18, italics in original.

6. Ibid. 17–18.

7. David Powlison, "Idols of the Heart and 'Vanity Fair,'" *Journal of Biblical Counseling* 13, no. 2 (Winter 1995): 35. Also available at http://www.ccef.org/sites/default/files/pdf/IdolsOfTheHeart&VanityFair.DP.pdf.

8. http://www.amazon.com/Conspicuous-Consumption-Penguin-Great-Ideas/dp/0143037595/ref=sr_1_4?s=books&ie=UTF8&qid=1341197536&sr=1-4&keywords=thorstein+veblen.

Chapter 2

1. Joseph Lelyveld, *Great Soul: Mahatma Gandhi and His Struggle with India*, Kindle ed. (New York: Knopf, 2011).

2. See my session on ministry marriages at the 2011 NewSpring Leadership Conference, http://unleash.cc/previous/2011/.

3. "William Wilberforce: Antislavery Politician," *Christianity Today*, August 8, 2008, http://www.christianitytoday.com/ch/131christians/activists/wilberforce.html?start=2.

4. Clinton Arnold, *Ephesians*: *Zondervan Exegetical Commentary on the New Testament* (Grand Rapids: Zondervan, 2010), 10:45.

5. P. T. O'Brien, *The Letter to the Ephesians*: *The Pillar New Testament commentary* (Grand Rapids: W. B. Eerdmans Publishing Co., 1999), 57.

6. Peter Williamson, *Ephesians, Catholic Commentary on Sacred Scripture*, (Grand Rapids, MI: Baker Academic, 2009), 20–21.

7. Robert Letham, *Union With Christ: In Scripture, Theology, and History* (Phillipsburg, New Jersey: R & R Publishing, 2011), 2.

8. John Calvin, *Sermons on the Epistle to the Ephesians*, trans. Arthur Golding (1577) (Edinburgh: Banner of Truth, 1973), viii.

9. John Chrysostom, *Homilies of St. John Chrysostom, Archbishop of Constantinople, on the Epistle of St. Paul the Apostle to the Ephesians* (NPNF1-13), Christian Classics Ethereal Library, http://www.ccel.org/ccel/schaff/npnf113.iii.iv.i.html.

10. O'Brien, *The Letter to the Ephesians*, 1–2.

11. John A. MacKay, *God's Order: The Ephesian Letter and This Present Time* (New York: Macmillan, 1959), 17.

12. J. Armitage Robinson, *St. Paul's Epistle to the Ephesians* (London: Macmillan, 1903), vii.

13. Samuel Taylor Coleridge, *Specimens of the Table Talk* (London: John Murray, 1858), 82.

14. Max Turner, "Ephesians," in *Theological Interpretation of the New Testament*, ed. Kevin J. Vanhoozer (Grand Rapids: Baker, 2008), 124.

15. William Owen Carver, *The Glory of God in the Christian Calling* (Nashville: Broadman, 1949), 3.

16. David Powlison, *Seeing with New Eyes: Counseling and the Human Condition Through the Lens of Scripture* (Phillipsburg, New Jersey: P & R Publishing, 2003), 17.

17. Martin Luther, *What Luther Says: An Anthology*, comp. Ewald M. Plass (St. Louis: Concordia Publishing House, 1959), entry no. 3258, p. 1026.

18. Paul Barnett, *Paul: Missionary of Jesus* (Grand Rapids: Eerdmans, 2008), 7.

19. Ibid., 198.

20. D.A. Carson and Douglas J. Moo, *An Introduction to the New Testament*, 2nd edition (Grand Rapids: Zondervan, 1992, 2005), 354.

21. Evidence also points to the veneration of the following deities in Ephesus: Agathe Tyche, Aphrodite, Apollo, Asclepius, Athena, the Cabiri, Concord, Cybele (the Mother Goddess), Demeter, Dionysus, Enedra, Hecate, Hephaestus, Heracles, Hestia Boulaia, Kore, Nemesis, Pan, Pion (a mountain god), Pluto, Poseidon, Theos Hypsistos, Tyche Soteira, Zeus, and several river deities. Modern-day religious and spiritual pluralism has nothing on ancient Ephesus.

22. Strab's Geography (14.1.24).

23. C. J. Hemer, "Ephesus" in *New Bible Dictionary*, 3rd ed., eds. D. R. W. Wood and I. Howard Marshall, (Leicester, UK; Downers Grove, IL: InterVarsity Press, 1996), 326.

24. E.g., E. D. Martin, *Colossians, Philemon, Believers Church Bible Commentary* (Scottdale, PA: Herald Press, 1993), 25; R. J. D. Utley, *New Testament Survey: Matthew–Revelation* (Marshall, TX: Bible Lessons International, 2001), 91; A.

C. Myers, *The Eerdmans Bible Dictionary* (Grand Rapids: Eerdmans, 1987), 851; J. W. Drane, *Introducing the New Testament*, rev. and upd. (Oxford: Lion Publishing PLC, 2000), 365; D. R. W. Wood and I. H. Marshall, *New Bible Dictionary*, 3rd ed. (Leicester, UK; Downers Grove, IL: InterVarsity Press, 1996), 216; P. T. O'Brien, *The Epistle to the Philippians: A Commentary on the Greek Text* (Grand Rapids: Eerdmans, 1991), 21.

25. Lewis B. Smedes, *Union with Christ: A Biblical View of the New Life in Jesus Christ*, rev. ed. (Grand Rapids: Eerdmans, 1983), 55.

26. Frank Thielman, *Ephesians: Baker Exegetical Commentary on the New Testament* (Grand Rapids: Baker Academic, 2010), 37; Andrew T. Lincoln, *Ephesians, Word Biblical Commentary* (Dallas: Word, 1990), 10.

27. As an illustration of how often the phrase is used, a search on the exact phrase "in Christ" in Greek turns up the following: Rom. 3:24; 6:11, 23; 8:1, 2, 39; 9:1; 12:5; 15:17; 16:3, 7, 9, 10; 1 Cor. 1:2, 4 (ESV), 30; 3:1; 4:10, 15, 17; 15:18, 19, 31; 16:24; 2 Cor. 2:17; 3:14; 5:17, 19; 12:2, 19; Gal. 1:22; 2:4, 17 (ESV); 3:14, 26, 28; Eph. 1:1, 3; 2:6, 7, 10, 13; 3:6, 21 (ESV); 4:32; Phil. 1:1, 13, 26 (ESV); 2:1, 5; 3:3, 14; 4:7 (ESV), 19 (ESV), 21; Col 1:2, 4, 28; 1 Thess. 2:14; 4:16; 5:18; 1 Tim. 1:14; 3:13; 2 Tim. 1:1, 9, 13; 2:1, 10; 3:12, 15; Philem. 1:8, 20 (ESV), 23. This does not include variations such as "in Him," or phrases that are worded differently but have the same idea. Additionally, not all of those above are used in a way to describe believers being "in Christ," though many are.

28. Bruce Demarest, *The Cross and Salvation: The Doctrine of Salvation* (Wheaton, IL: Crossway, 1997), 313.

29. R. K. Hughes, *Ephesians: The Mystery of the Body of Christ, Preaching the Word* (Wheaton: Crossway, 1990), 42.

30. Ibid, 42.

Chapter 3

1. Kate Pickert, "A Brief History of Sainthood," *Time*, October 13, 2008.

2. James Martin, "How to Become a Saint in Ten Steps," January 2012, http://www.beliefnet.com/Faiths/Catholic/2010/01/How-to-Become-a-Saint.aspx.

3. Ibid.

4. Jean-Paul Sartre, *The Flies*, available for viewing at http://www.scribd.com/doc/72494205/h-Jean-Pau-Satre-the-Flies.

5. Anthony Hoekema, "The Reformed Perspective," in Melvin E. Dieter, et al., *Five Views on Sanctification* (Grand Rapids: Zondervan, 1987), 74.

6. C. H. Spurgeon, *The Saint and His Saviour: The Progress of the Soul in the Knowledge of Jesus* (Bellingham, WA: Logos Research Systems, Inc., 2009), 12.

7. For more on humility, see C. J. Mahaney, *Humility: True Greatness* (Sisters, OR: Multnomah, 2005).

Chapter 4

1. For more on this topic, see Clinton Arnold, *Powers of Darkness: Principalities & Powers in Paul's Letters* (Downers Grove, IL: InterVarsity Press, 1992).

2. Walter Bauer, et al., eds., *A Greek-English Lexicon of the New Testament and Other*

Early Christian Literature, 3rd ed. [BDAG] (Chicago: University of Chicago Press, 2000), 408.

3. Thomas R. Schreiner, *Paul, Apostle of God's Glory in Christ: A Pauline Theology* (Downers Grove, IL: InterVarsity Press, 2001), 156.

4. Charles H. Spurgeon, "Adoption." No. 360, *The Charles H. Spurgeon Library, Version 1* (AGES Digital Library, CD-ROM), 183.

5. Demarest, *The Cross and Salvation*, 72. (See chap. 2, n. 29.)

6. Thielman, *Ephesians*, 37. (See chap. 2, n. 27.)

Chapter 5

1. Patrick Stump, "We Liked You Better Fat: Confessions of a Pariah" (entry, *Patrick Stump* blog), February 28, 2012, http://www.patrickstump.com/.

2. J. Ligon Duncan III, "Ephesians 1:1–2: Revelation and Benediction," June 26, 2005, http://www.fpcjackson.org/resources/sermons/Ephesians/01a_ephesians_1.1to2.htm.

3. J. M. Boice, *Ephesians: An Expositional Commentary* (Grand Rapids: Ministry Resources Library, 1998), 35–36.

Chapter 6

1. Klyne Snodgrass, *Ephesians: The NIV Application Commentary* (Grand Rapids: Zondervan, 1996), 93.

2. A. W. Pink, *The Redeemer's Return* (Bellingham, WA: Logos Research Systems, Inc., 2005).

3. See Thielman, *Ephesians*, 121. (See chap. 2, n. 27.)

4. Andrew T. Lincoln, *Ephesians: Word Biblical Commentary* (Dallas: Word, 1990), 97.

5. Ernest Best, *Ephesians: International Critical Commentary* (Edinburgh: T. & T. Clark, 1998), 206.

6. Lincoln, *Ephesians*, 97.

7. BDAG, 1069.

8. O'Brien, *The Letter to the Ephesians*, 166–67. (See chap. 2, n. 6.)

9. Thielman, *Ephesians*, 139–40.

10. F. F. Bruce, *The Epistle to the Ephesians* (London: Pickering & Inglis, 1973), 52.

11. Abraham Kuyper, "Not a Square Inch," February 1, 2006, http://kuypersociety.blogspot.com/2006/02/not-square-inch.html.

12. Martin Luther, "The Estate of Marriage," in Timothy F. Lull. ed., *Martin Luther's Basic Theological Writings*, 2nd ed. (Minneapolis: Augsburg Fortress, 2005), 158–59.

Chapter 7

1. All quotes and details from Perkins's story in this chapter are from Roberta Rand's "The Amazing Journey of John Perkins," parts 1–3, http://www.thrivingpastor.org/aa/A000001790.cfm; http://www.thrivingpastor.org/articles/A000001791.cfm; http://www.thrivingpastor.org/articles/A000001792.cfm.

2. Rand, "The Amazing Journey of John Perkins." (see chap. 7, n. 1.)

3. Ibid.
4. http://www.jmpf.org/content/about/mission/.
5. Flavius Josephus, *Antiquities of the Jews*, XV, 11.5, http://gutenberg.org/ebooks/2848.
6. Flavius Josephus, *The Wars of the Jews*, trans. William Whiston, bk. 5, chap. 5, par. 2.
7. Some translations use the term "the Cushite woman" for Moses' wife. From the ESV Study Bible: "Nothing is known about 'the Cushite woman' beyond this brief mention. She may be the same person as Zipporah (Ex. 2:16–22), though she is usually described as a Midianite. Some texts, however, suggest Midian and Cushan are the same (see Hab. 3:7). Since Cush normally refers to ancient Ethiopia, most interpreters think that 'the Cushite woman' probably was Moses' second wife, and that she came from Ethiopia."
8. O'Brien, *Ephesians*, 182. (See chap. 2, n. 6.)
9. Craig S. Keener, *The IVP Bible Background Commentary* (Downers Grove, IL: InterVarsity Press, 1993), comment on Eph. 2:11–13.
10. William Barclay, in John Stott, *The Message of Ephesians* (Downers Grove, IL: InterVarsity Press, 1979), 91.
11. Keener, *The IVP Bible Background Commentary*, comment on Eph. 2:19–22.
12. Keener, *The IVP Bible Background Commentary*, comment on Eph. 2:14–16.
13. Martin Luther King Jr., "Letter from a Birmingham Jail," April 16, 1963, African Studies Center–University of Pennsylvania, http://www.africa.upenn.edu/Articles_Gen/Letter_Birmingham.html.

Chapter 9

1. O'Brien, *The Letter to the Ephesians*, 266. (See chap. 2, n. 6.)
2. Martyn Lloyd-Jones, *Studies in the Sermon on the Mount*, 2 vols. (Grand Rapids: Eerdmans, 1979), 2:45.
3. John R. W. Stott, *God's New Society: The Message of Ephesians* (Downers Grove, IL: InterVarsity Press, 1979), 137.
4. O'Brien, *The Letter to the Ephesians*, 258–59.
5. Jonathan Edwards, "Concerning the End for Which God Created the World," in *Ethical Writings: The Works of Jonathan Edwards*, vol. 8, ed. Paul Ramsey (New Haven: Yale University Press, 1989), 405–15.
6. Westminster Shorter Catechism, Q. 1., http://www.reformed.org/documents/WSC.html.
7. John Piper, *Desiring God* (Sisters, OR: Multnomah, 2003), 18.

Chapter 10

1. For a theological treatment of spiritual gifts, D. A. Carson, *Showing the Spirit: A Theological Exposition of 1 Corinthians 12–14* (Baker Publishing House, Ada, MI, 2000); and Wayne Grudem, *Systematic Theology* (Leicester, UK: InterVarsity Press; Grand Rapids: Zondervan, 1994), are helpful. For a more practical examination of the gifts to help you discover yours, read Sam Storms, *The Beginners Guide to Spiritual Gifts* (Regal, Ventura, CA, 2002).

2. The following are some common errors regarding the gift of healing: Some say that the more supernatural gifts, such as healing, ceased to operate at the end of the first century, but the church fathers from the second and third century report that such things as healing continued to occur in their day. Some extreme groups teach that since God can heal, Christians should not use a doctor, but the Bible does not speak against doctors, and doctors like Luke used their medical ability as part of their pastoral ministry to help people (Col. 4:14; 2 Tim. 4:11; Philem. 1:24). Some say that by walking in faith and not sinning, no Christian needs to ever be sick, but Epaphroditus (Phil. 2:25–27), Timothy (1 Tim. 5:23), Trophimus (2 Tim. 4:20), and Paul (1 Cor. 2:3; 2 Cor. 11:30; 12:5, 7–10; Gal. 4:13) all had some sickness that was not healed despite the fact that they deeply loved God and walked with Jesus faithfully.

3. Common errors regarding miracles: (1) Some people who claim to have this gift use it to exalt themselves, but the gift exists to exalt God and spread the name of Jesus. (2) Some say that the most godly people will have this gift, but even John the Baptizer never performed a miracle (John 10:41). (3) Some Christians are prone to chase signs and wonders, but Jesus said that it is a wicked and evil thing to seek a sign (Luke 11:29). (4) Some people think that a sign or miracle is guaranteed to prove to a non-Christian that Jesus is real, but even Jesus said that some people would never believe in Him even if they saw a miracle (John 4:48).

4. Common errors regarding apostles: Cult leaders and erroneous teachers say that they have authority that is, in effect, equal to Scripture because they are apostles just like those who wrote the Bible. But such people are false apostles (2 Cor. 11:13; Rev. 2:2) and delusional "super-apostles" (2 Cor. 11:5, 13; 12:11).

5. Common errors: The Bible is clear that not everyone can or will have the gift of tongues, and so it is not a sign of whether or not someone has the Holy Spirit (Rom. 12:6; 1 Cor. 12:10–11, 29–30). Those who pray or sing in tongues should also ask God to enable them to have the gift of interpretation so their minds as well as their hearts are engaged in their worship (1 Cor. 14:13–17). When the whole church gathers, there are rules for tongues speaking to provide orderliness to the service (1 Cor. 14:18–19). Sometimes tongues were also used as a sign of God's judgment on the disobedient (1 Cor. 14:20–22; cf. Isa. 28:11–12; Deut. 28:49–50).

6. Common Errors: Jesus (Matt. 7:15; 24:11, 24), Paul (Acts 20:29–31), and John (1 John 4:1) all promised that false prophets would come. False prophets deceitfully claim to speak for God (1 Kings 22) and may also perform false miracles (Deut. 13:1–3; 2 Thess. 2:9; Rev. 13:13–15). A true prophet had outstanding moral character (Ezek. 13:10–16), while false prophets did not (Isa. 28:7). The prophecy of a true prophet came true every time (Deut. 18; Jer. 28; 1 Kings 22). False prophets were for hire and preached what they were paid to preach (Mic. 3:11). False prophets prophesied only peace (Jer. 6:13–14; 8:10–11). The message of a false prophet conflicted with God's prior revelation, led to the worship of false gods, and was punishable by death (Deut. 13). Perhaps the most thorough descriptions of false prophets are given in Deuteronomy 18:14–22 and Jeremiah 23:9–40. Today, Christians can also help discern between true and false prophets by their inward testimony of the Spirit (Deut. 18:14–22; John 7:17).

Chapter 11

1. R. R. Melick, *Philippians, Colossians, Philemon, The New American Commentary*, vol. 32, electronic ed., Logos Library System (Nashville: Broadman & Holman Publishers, 2001), 130.
2. Daniel B. Wallace, "A Brief Word Study on: Skuvbalon," http://bible.org/article/brief-word-study-font-facegreekskuvbalonfont.
3. C. S. Lewis, "The Weight of Glory," *The Weight of Glory and Other Addresses*, ed. W. Hooper (New York: Simon and Schuster, 1996), 25–26.

Chapter 12

1. R. C. Sproul, *Essential Truths of the Christian Faith* (Carol Stream, IL: Tyndale, 1992), 144.
2. John Piper, *What Jesus Demands from the World* (Wheaton: Crossway, 2006), 92.
3. Ex. 34:6 esv. According to Martin H. Manser, the causes of God's anger include idolatry and unbelief (Num. 25:3; see also Ex. 32:8–10; Deut. 8:19; Judg. 2:10–14; 1 Kings 14:9; 16:32–33; 22:53; 2 Kings 23:19); idolatrous shrines and offerings (2 Chron. 28:25; 34:25; Jer. 8:19; 32:29; 44:3); the unbelief of rejecting the Son of God (John 3:36; Rom. 1:18–23; 2:8); disobedience and disloyalty (Josh. 7:1; see also Deut. 9:7; 2 Kings 22:13; 1 Chron. 13:10; Ps. 106:29; Jer. 32:32; Zech. 7:13; Eph. 5:6); ungodly living, as God's judgment against the ungodly is a sign of his anger against actions that contradict his righteous character and purposes (2 Tim. 3:1–9; Jude 14–16); pride, arrogance, and hypocrisy (Matt. 23:27–28; see also 2 Chron. 32:25; Prov. 3:34; 8:13; Isa. 13:11; Hos. 12:14; Mal. 4:1); complaints against, and opposition to, God's purposes (Num. 11:1; see also Num. 14:27; 21:5); injustice (Zech. 7:9–12; see also 2 Chron. 19:7; Jer. 22:13; Ezek. 9:9; Mal. 3:5; Matt. 23:23); and the rejection of God's servants (Heb. 10:29–31; see also Deut. 32:35–36; Ps. 135:14; Neh. 9:26; Zech. 7:12; Matt. 21:33–41; Acts 7:35–37). Martin H. Manser, *Zondervan Dictionary of Bible Themes: The Accessible and Comprehensive Tool for Topical Studies* (Grand Rapids: Zondervan, 1999).
4. Manser identifies various examples and causes of Jesus Christ's anger, including petty legalism in religious observance (Matt. 15:3; 23:1–4; Mark 3:4–5); attempts to prevent access to him (Mark 10:14); and people leading others into sin (Matt. 18:6–7; Mark 9:42; Luke 17:1–2). Jesus demonstrated his anger when he purged the temple (Matt. 21:12–13; Mark 11:15–17; Luke 19:45–46; John 2:14–16) and when he cursed the fig tree (Mark 11:14; Matt. 21:19). Jesus also spoke words in anger against demons (Matt. 17:18; Mark 9:25; Luke 9:42; see also Mark 1:25–26; Luke 4:35); against his disciples (Luke 9:55–56; see also Matt. 16:23; Mark 8:33); against Pharisees (Matt. 23:13; see also Matt. 12:34; 15:7–9; cf. Mark 7:6–8; Matt. 23:15–16, 23–33; Luke 11:42–44; 13:15; John 8:44); against unbelief (Matt. 17:17; Mark 9:19; Luke 9:41; see also Matt. 12:39–45; cf. Luke 11:29–32; Mark 8:38; Luke 11:50–51); against false prophets (Matt. 7:15); against the rich (Luke 6:24–26); and against unrepentant cities (Matt. 11:20; see also Matt. 11:21–24; Luke 10:13–15). Jesus expresses the anger of God the Father (John 3:36; see also Matt. 5:21–22, 29; 22:7, 13; 25:30, 46; Luke 21:23). We also read of the anger of the glorified Christ against the unbelieving world (Rev. 6:16)

and against the wayward church (Rev. 2:16; see also Rev. 2:5, 22–23; 3:3, 16). Manser, *Zondervan Dictionary of Bible Themes.*

5. David Stoop, *Forgiving the Unforgivable,* (New York: Wiley, 1992), 97.

6. "MADD has saved 27,000 young lives through passage of groundbreaking public health laws." (http://www.madd.org/statistics/)

7. L. Morris, *The Gospel According to Matthew* (Grand Rapids; Leicester, UK: W. B. Eerdmans; InterVarsity Press, 1992), 472.

Chapter 13

1. For more, see W. A. Strange, *Children in the Early Church: Children in the Ancient World, The New Testament and the Early Church* (Wipf & Stock Publishers; Eugene, OR, 2004).

2. J. Todd Billings, *Union with Christ: Reframing Theology and Ministry for the Church* (Grand Rapids: Baker Publishing Group, 2011), 18. For more information, see Trevor J. Burke, *Adopted into God's Family* (IVP Academic, 2006), 60–63.

3. Jeanne Stevenson Moessner, "One Family, Under God, Indivisible," *Journal of Pastoral Theology* 13 (2003): 52–53.

4. Russell Moore, *Adopted for Life: The Priority of Adoption for Christian Families & Churches* (Wheaton, IL: Crossway, 2009), 25–26.

5. Ibid.

6. In calling both Christian men and women *sons*, the Bible is saying that we enjoy the same privileged legal status and benefits as sons did in the time of Paul's writing. This doesn't exclude women in any way. Rather, in New Testament days the family life and inheritance were passed on through the sons, not the daughters, and by calling men and women "sons," the Bible bestows on both the highest honor and most privileged familial position in that culture. Men and women are equally adopted with equal legal standing and an equal inheritance from God the Father.

7. Billings, *Union with Christ,* 16.

8. Theodore Graebner, ed., *Commentary on St. Paul's Epistle to the Galatians,* Christian Classics Ethereal Library, http://www.ccel.org/ccel/luther/galatians .vii.html, chap. 4, 160.

9. Moore, *Adopted for Life,* 38–39.

10. For more on Redemption Groups, see Mike Wilkerson, *Redemption: Freed by Jesus from the Idols We Worship and the Wounds We Carry* (Crossway; Wheaton, IL, 2011). For more on healing from sexual abuse, see Justin and Lindsey Holcomb, *Rid of My Disgrace: Hope and Healing for Victims of Sexual Assault.*

11. Billings, *Union with Christ,* 21–25.

Chapter 14

1. Harold Hoehner, *Ephesians* (Grand Rapids: Baker, 2002), 749.

2. Peter T. O'Brien, "Mystery," in Gerald F. Hawthorne, Ralph P. Martin, and Daniel G. Reid, *Dictionary of Paul and His Letters,* (Downers Grove, IL: InterVarsity Press, 1993), 622.

3. The debate is between what is called complentarianism and egalitarianism. I

believe the complementarian view is most faithful to Scripture and find John Piper and Wayne Grudem's *Recovering Biblical Manhood and Womanhood*, along with Andreas Kostenberger's *God, Marriage, and Family*, to be quite helpful books on the subject. For those wanting to study further, see also www.cbmw .org, which is filled with helpful articles on gender roles in marriage.

4. For examples, see Real Marriage sermons, "Men and Marriage" and "The Respectful Wife," http://marshill.com/media/real-marriage/sermons. See also "FAQ: Women and Ministry," http://pastormark.tv/2011/09/20/faq-women-and-ministry; my February 29, 2012, *Washington Post* article titled "Let's Have a Baby," at http://www.washingtonpost.com/blogs/guest-voices/post/sad-statistics-on-sex-and-marriage-lets-have-a-baby/2012/02/29/gIQAb8sZiR_blog.html; and my January 11, 2012, essay "Why Men Need Marriage," at the *Washington Post*, http://www.washingtonpost.com/blogs/guest-voices/post/why-men-need-marriage/2012/01/11/gIQALubyqP_blog.html.

5. Mike Clary, "Tragedy strikes Fort Lauderdale visitors preparing for son's birth," *Sun-Sentinel*, March 19, 2012, http://www.sun-sentinel.com/news/broward/fort-lauderdale/fl-alanna-demella-cabana-death-20120319,0,5397749.story.

Chapter 15

1. John Maxwell, *The 360° Leader: Developing Your Influence from Anywhere in the Organization* (Nashville: Thomas Nelson, 2005), 293.

2. Ibid., 293.

3. Ibid., 294.

4. *Narrative of the Life of Frederick Douglass, An American Slave* (Boston: Anti-Slavery Office, no. 25 Cornhill, 1845), 93–94. To read online, see http://ucblibrary3.berkeley.edu/Literature/Douglass/Autobiography/.

5. Clinton E. Arnold, *Ephesians*, (Grand Rapids, MI: Zondervan) 2010.

6. Thielman, *Ephesians*, 404 (see chap. 2, n. 27). See also W. N. Kerr, "Slavery," in *Evangelical Dictionary of Theology*, 2nd ed., ed. Walter A. Elwell (Grand Rapids: Baker, 2001), 1113: "The early church did not attack slavery as an institution. It did, however, reorder the relationship of slave and masters (Philem.), indicate that in God's sight there was neither 'slave nor free' (Gal. 3:28), and state that both were accountable to God (Eph. 6:5–9). The interpersonal relationship was recast in terms of the character of Christ and his kingdom."

7. Wayne Grudem offers the following list of passages that "teach or imply degrees of reward for believers at the final judgment": Dan. 12:2; Matt. 6:20–21; 19:21; Luke 6:22–23; 12:18–21, 32, 42–48; 14:13–14; 1 Cor. 3:8; 9:18; 13:3; 15:19, 29–32, 58; Gal. 6:9–10; Eph. 6:7–8; Col. 3:23–24; 1 Tim. 6:18; Heb. 10:34, 35; 11:10, 14–16, 26, 35; 1 Peter 1:4; 2 John 8; Rev. 11:18; 22:12; cf. also Matt. 5:46; 6:2–6, 16–18, 24; Luke 6:35 (*Systematic Theology*, 1144n 4; see chap. 10 n. 6).

8. Ibid, 425. Clinton Arnold, *Ephesians*. See also Walter Bauer, Frederick William Danker, William F. Arndt, and F. Wilber Gingrich, eds., *A Greek-English Lexicon of the New Testament and Other Early Christian Literature*, 3rd ed. [BDAG] (Chicago: University of Chicago Press, 2000), 557.

9. Arnold, *Ephesians*, 417. (See chap. 2, n. 5.)

10. Edward T. Welch, *When People Are Big and God Is Small: Overcoming Peer Pressure, Codependency, and the Fear of Man* (Phillipsburg, NJ: P & R Publishing, 1997), 14.

Chapter 16

1. C. S. Lewis, *The Screwtape Letters* (New York: HarperCollins, 2001), ix.
2. Tony Long, "May 27, 1941: Sink the Bismark," *Wired*, www.wired.com/thisdayintech/2009/05/dayintech_0527.
3. Ibid.
4. William Gurnall, *The Christian in Complete Armour* (London: William Tegg, 1862), 781.
5. Carson et al., *New Bible Commentary* (Downers Grove, IL: IVP Academic, 1994), 1242.
6. R. K. Hughes, *Ephesians: The Mystery of the Body of Christ, Preaching the Word* (Wheaton, IL: Crossway Books, 1990), 214.
7. Keener, *The IVP Bible Background Commentary* (see chap. 7, n. 15), comment on Eph. 6:10–20.
8. Dr. Gerry Breshears points out that these are all taken from Isaiah and are characteristics of Messiah. To put on armor means to put on Christ and Christlikeness (cf. Eph. 4:2).
9. Thomas Brooks, *Precious Remedies Against Satan's Devices*, Kindle ed. (GLH Publishers, GLH publishing.com, 2011).
10. Dr. Gerry Breshears points out that there are actually two ideas here: *stand* and *resist*. Believers are commanded to stand firm on biblical truths and to resist the devil (Eph. 6:13; James 4:7; 1 Peter 5:9). The word *resist* means to engage in active opposition (Acts 13:8; Gal. 2:11; 2 Tim. 3:8), including rebuke spoken directly to the demon in the authority of Jesus, the exalted Lord (Zech. 3:2; Matt. 4:4, 7, 10; Jude 9).
11. Ligonier Ministries, the teaching fellowship of R. C. Sproul. All rights reserved. www.ligionier.org.

ACKNOWLEDGMENTS

I want to thank the people from Mars Hill Church who provided the amazing testimonies that are woven throughout this book. I also want to sincerely thank Jake Johnson (thejakers.com) for being so helpful in the editing and shaping of this book. And I want to thank the leaders of our church for being so supportive of everything we do, especially the creative and media teams, lead pastors, and executive elders, Dave Bruskas and Sutton Turner. Lastly, thank you, Grace and the Fabulous Five (Ashley, Zac, Calvin, Alexie, and Gideon), for being pure joy to me.

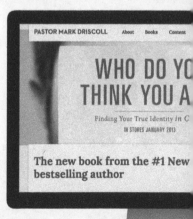

ABOUT THE AUTHOR

Mark Driscoll of Mars Hill Church, Seattle, Washington, is one of the world's most downloaded and quoted pastors. Mars Hill has been recognized as the twenty-eighth largest, third fastest-growing, and second most innovative church in America by *Outreach* magazine. His audience—fans and critics alike—spans the theological and cultural left and right. He was also named one of the twenty-five most influential preachers in the past twenty-five years by *Preaching* magazine. He received a BA in Speech Communications from the Edward R. Murrow School of Communication, Washington State University, and he holds a master's degree in exegetical theology from Western Seminary in Portland, Oregon. He is the author of more than twelve books, including *Real Marriage: The Truth About Sex, Friendship and Life Together.* With a skillful mix of bold presentation, clear biblical teaching, and compassion for those who are hurting the most—in particular, women who are victims of sexual and physical abuse and assault—Driscoll has taken biblical Christianity into cultural corners previously unexplored by evangelicals. Having spoken alongside notable contemporary theologians such as John Piper and Tim Keller, he has also discussed biblical sexuality as a guest on *Loveline* with Dr. Drew, *The View*, *Fox & Friends*, and *Piers Morgan Tonight*; was featured on *Nightline*; and preached for Rick Warren at Saddleback Community Church. Mark and his wife, Grace, have five children.

INDEX

as identity vs. apart, 70
Jew and Gentile reconciled, 87–90
and joint heirs with Christ, 173–174
reconciled to God, 90–93
independence, idols of, 10
inheritance, adoption with, 175–176
Ishmael, 88
Islam, 76
Israel, walls, 83–84
items, as idols, 7–8

J
James (brother of Jesus), 88
Jerome, 18
Jesus
adoption through, 173–174
anger of, 234n4
as glory of God, 119
God as Father, 49, 112
as High Priest, 108
Holy Spirit and, 181
as Jew, 85
as last Adam, 16–17
life apart from, 151
as Lord, 146
love of, 116, 189–192
love of church, 189, 190–192
as mediator, 111
ministry of, 122
prayers of, 59
righteousness from, 143
Satan and, 72, 226
as savior, 74
as Son of God, 38–39
suffering of, 104–105
victory on cross, 227
as vine, 24–25
Jews, as God's people, 84–85
John (apostle), 22–23
Josephus, 84
journaling, 53
Judaism, 76
justice, from God, 164–165
justification, 39, 88, 142–144
justified, 140–141

K
Keller, Tim, 228n2
Kierkegaard, Soren, *Sickness Unto Death*, 228n2
King, Martin Luther, Jr., "Letter from a Birmingham Jail," 92–93

kneeling for prayer, 112
knowledge, 125–126
Knox, John, 18, 223
komizo, 205

L
leadership, 133
legalism, 154
"Letter from a Birmingham Jail" (King), 92–93
Lewis, C.S., 44, 149, 217
life, new, 151
Lightner, Candace, 161
Live Under Lights and Wires (McCracken), 69
Livingston, David, 16
Lloyd-Jones, Martyn, 112
longings, as idols, 10–11
Lord, Jesus as, 146
love, 184–197
of God, 117–118, 144, 178
cross of Christ and, 188
of Jesus, 116, 187–192
longing for, 186–187
new capacity for, 148
love hunger, 192
Luther, Martin, 18, 77–78, 143, 174
on Paul, 19

M
MADD (Mothers Against Drunk Driving), 161
malice, 158
marriage, friendship in, 195–197
Marshall, George, 198–200
Marshall Plan, 199
Martin, James, 31–32
maturity in Christ, 117
vs. giftedness, 124
Maxwell, John, *The 360° Leader*, 198–200
McCracken, Sandra, *Live Under Lights and Wires*, 69
mediator, Jesus as, 111
Memento (film), 1–2
mercy, 133–134
Miletus, 57
mind, new, 147–148
ministry, 122
miracles, 127–128
errors regarding, 233n3
Moore, Russell, 172, 175
Moralistic Therapeutic Deism, 182
Moses, 85
Mothers Against Drunk Driving (MADD), 161
Muslims, conversion to Christianity, 94–95

redemption group, 178
reflecting God's goodness, 3
Reformed tradition of Christian faith, 34
regeneration, 39, 142, 144–146
relationship addiction, 192
relationships, 91–92
    with God, 120, 147, 154–155
    prayer and, 112–114
    single adults, 194
religion, 76, 149
remorse, of saints, 36–37
repentance, 142
revealing, prayer as, 119–120
revenge, 164
reward, 198–211
    from God, 203–208
        to those in authority, 209–210
        for those under authority, 208–209
righteous anger, vs. unrighteous, 160–163
righteousness, 143
    as weapon against Satan, 222
Roman Empire, infant mortality in, 170
Roosevelt, Franklin, 199
rudeness, 55

S
sacredness, 6
sainthood, history, 31
saints, 28–41
    Bible edition of being, 32–41
    Catholic edition of being, 30–32
    humility of, 39–41
    power of, 37–39
    remorse of, 36–37
    sin by, 33
    or sinners, 30
salvation
    past, present, and future work of, 69
    as weapon against Satan, 223
sanctification, 39, 152
    from Jesus, 191
Sapphira, 220
Sartre, Jean-Paul, *The Flies*, 33–34
Satan, 37, 146
    attack on Jesus, 226
    as enemy of God, 216
    fight by, 218–220
    freedom from captivity to, 225–227
    goal of, 222
    influence on Christian, 219–220
    Jesus and, 72
    perspectives on, 217

saved from, 72
    war with, 214–215, 220–221
saved, 66–78
    by God, 68–70
    God's reasons for, 75
    impact of, 75–77
    from Satan, 72
    from what?, 70–74
saving grace, 51–52
savior, Jesus as, 191
Schreiner, Thomas, 45
science, 216
scripture, as weapon against Satan, 223–224
sealed, blessing of being, 52
secret occult rituals, in Ephesus, 44
self-actualization, 41
self-esteem, 41
self-righteousness, 141, 155
serving, vs. performing, 61–62
Sickness Unto Death (Kierkegaard), 228n2
Simeon, 75
simplicity, 111
sin, 5, 152, 188, 228n2
    Jesus taking on our, 190
    by saints, 33
    Satan and, 215
    saved from, 71
sinful spiritual competition, 60
single adults, relationships, 194
sinners
    identity as, 139
    ourselves as, 70
    or saints, 30
slander, 158
slavery, 50
    authority of masters, 209
    Ephesians and, 200–211
    in New Testament, 201–203
    Paul' instructions, 208
    in U.S., 200–201
small group, 110
Smith, Christian
    Soul Searching: The religious and spiritual lives of American teenagers, 182
    Souls in Transition: the religious and spiritual lives of emerging adults, 182
Snodgrass, Klyne, 18
social prestige, 7
Solomon, prayer of, 85
sons and daughters of God, behavior and, 178–183
sons of disobedience, 73

Soul Searching: The religious and spiritual lives of American teenagers (Smith), 182
South Africa, 83
speech, bitterness vs. forgiveness in, 167
Spencer Perkins Center for Reconciliation and Youth Development, 81
Spirit-empowered gifts, 124–136
  administration, 130–131
  apostleship, 128–129
  basics, 124–125
  discernment, 128
  encouragement, 132
  evangelism, 131
  faith, 126
  giving, 132–133
  healing, 126–127
  helps and service, 130
  hospitality, 134
  knowledge, 125–126
  leadership, 133
  lists, 123
  mercy, 133–134
  miracles, 127–128
  pastoring/counseling, 131–132
  prophecy, 135–136
  teaching, 129–130
  tongues, 134–135
  wisdom, 125
spiritual battle, 215
spiritual separation, 84–86
Sproul, R.C., 156
Spurgeon, Charles Haddon, 18, 27, 36
  on God's adoption, 49–50
status, 7
Stephen, 155
strength from God, for fighting Satan, 220–221
Stump, Patrick, 54
submission, Paul on, 193
success, celebrating others, 60–61
suffering, 79–83, 95–101
  God in, 46–47
  as idols, 11–14
  impact on belief, 101–102
  of Jesus, 104–105
  of Paul, 95–96, 103
supernatural, 216

T
Taoism, 76
Taylor, Hudson, 16
teaching, 129–130

temptation, 38, 152, 222
testimonial affliction, 99
testimony, biography as, 15
thankful prayers, 53
thankfulness, 57
  vs. bitterness, 61
The 360° Leader (Maxwell), 198–200
tongues, 134–135
  rules for, 233n5
Tozer, A. W., 16
tribe, 9
Trinity, 5
  blessings from, 46
true prophets, 233n6
trust, forgiveness and, 166
truth, 1
  as weapon against Satan, 222

U
union with Christ, 18
unrighteous anger, vs. righteous, 160–163
The Usual Suspects, 217

V
Veblen, Thorstein, 7
vicarious affliction, 99
victim affliction, 98
victory, 212–227
vine, Jesus as, 24–25

W
walls, dividing groups of people, 83–86
war with Satan, 214–215
  weapons for, 221–224
Wedding Supper of the Lamb, 189
Welch, Ed, 210
Wesley, John, 16, 18
Westminster Catechism, 120
Wilberforce, William, 16
wisdom, 125
wives and husbands, 192–197
Word of God, 34
workmanship of God, 56, 76, 143
worldly living, saved from, 71–72
worm theology, 33
worshippers, creation as, 5–7
wrath of God, 156

Y
yearning, prayer as, 116–118
young adults, research on views, 182

RESURGENCE

Over two million leaders served every year

Our mission is to serve leaders, and to help equip you for your God-given mission. How can we serve you?

Each year, millions of leaders trust Resurgence for:

Timely articles: As the highest visited Christian leadership blog, we feature articles from prominent Evangelical leaders addressing the challenges of ministry in a post-Christian society.

Books: Re:lit has published dozens of books to equip leaders on theology and practical ministry.

Events: Resurgence conferences bring together some of the world's top speakers and preachers to transform hearts and minds for ministry action.

Teaching: Podcast and vodcasts feature select talks and lectures from Resurgence events.

Training: Re:train is a master's-level theology center with some of the best professors in the world, as well as practical training for day-to-day ministry from some of the most well-known and respected pastors today.

For more information about Resurgence, visit theResurgence.com

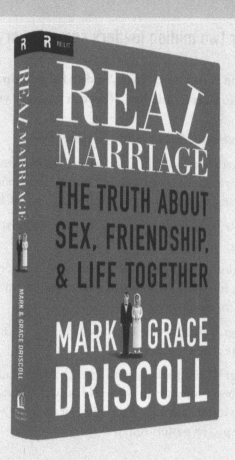